P9-CRG-593

ALCUIN, FRIEND OF CHARLEMAGNE

By ELEANOR SHIPLEY DUCKETT

THE GATEWAY TO THE MIDDLE AGES

ANGLO-SAXON SAINTS AND SCHOLARS

ALCUIN, FRIEND OF CHARLEMAGNE: HIS WORLD AND HIS WORK

ALCUIN, FRIEND OF CHARLEMAGNE

His World and His Work

BY

ELEANOR SHIPLEY DUCKETT

PH.D., D.LIT., L.H.D.

ARCHON BOOKS

HAMDEN, CONNECTICUT

1965

Reprinted With Permission 1965
With An Additional Bibliography

Library of Congress Catalog Card Number: 65-19596
Printed in The United States of America

PREFACE

Error at different times has told of Alcuin various stories: that he was abbot of St. Augustine's Monastery in Canterbury; that he taught the liberal sciences at Cambridge; that he founded the University of Paris; that he was Archbishop of York. He is still a very shadowy figure to many readers, and apology is scarcely needed for a book that bears his name. The text of this one is intended for the student of history sacred and secular during the eighth century in Anglo-Saxon England and the Frankish realm. It is centred in the life of Alcuin, and I have tried to give as clear a picture as I could of his character, of his many interests, and of his importance to his world and to ours. For the specialist I have appended footnotes and bibliography, should he wish to verify or to dispute the faith that is in me, or to wander down one of the many bypaths that beckon so persuasively to the researcher in the problems of this time. The bibliography records my indebtedness to experts in the history and literature of the period, in the liturgy and theology of the Church. Among the names recognized by all I should like to mention here those of Wilhelm Levison, master of this century in England and on the continent, of Arthur Kelinclausz, who fulfilled a life of distinguished scholarship in giving us his *Alcuin,* of Etienne Gilson, who dedicated to Alcuin in 1944 his *La Philosophie au Moyen Age,* and of J. C. B. Gaskoin, whose learned and well-known book was published in 1904. The most distinguished name at the present day in matters concerning Alcuin—literary, philosophical, philological, historical, and especially concerning his relationship with Charlemagne—is that of Luitpold Wallach, whose research and published studies, deep and penetrating, have constantly in recent years thrown light on many problems of Alcuin's life and work.

E. S. D.

Northampton, Massachusetts
June 1965

CONTENTS

CONTENTS

Chapter I

ALCUIN IN YORK

CHAPTER I

ALCUIN IN YORK

I

IN THE year 735 Bede "the Venerable" died at his monastery of Jarrow, and with him there passed from it that light of Anglo-Saxon learning which had burned steadily for two generations of men. The world on which he had looked out from his cell during his last years had held for him both content and sorrow. Content there had been in the ever-growing history of the Faith among Englishmen, in those many wise and brave thinkings and doings that had borne witness ever since the Romans had walked his land, in the kings and queens, nobles and commons, bishops and priests, monks, nuns and layfolk that throughout the good and evil days of history had served and were still serving God with joy in the isle of Britain. Especially in his own North country it was good to know that Ceolwulf who sat upon the throne of Northumbria was a king eager for the following of holy religion by himself and his subjects, a zealous supporter of his bishop Egbert, his cousin in family kinship, elected to the see of York in 732.[1] To this Ceolwulf, because he always gladly heard of the leaders of Church and State in his country's annals, Bede had submitted his *Church History of the English People* and had afterward placed Ceolwulf's name at the head of its Preface; to the same king, under the guidance of Egbert, men of good-

[1] *A-SC ann.* 734. *Baed. Cont.* places his election in 732.

will were looking for a rule of justice and piety in the years to come.[2]

Yet much foreboding for the land he loved so well was mingled with Bede's happiness; and in November, 734, six months before he died, he wrote his last counsels and warnings in a long letter to this newly-consecrated bishop of York, once his pupil, now his intimate friend, with whom he had talked of these same things the year before in a most rare journey to the outer world from his cell at Jarrow.[3] Storms were lowering on the political horizon and he had recognized them frankly: "Both the beginning and the progress of the reign of Ceolwulf have overflowed with so many and so great surgings of evil that not yet can we know what to write of them nor what end each of them shall find." [4]

History had already recorded certain of these troubles. In 731 King Ceolwulf had been seized, contemptuously shorn as a monk, then replaced upon his throne.[5] His devotion to his Church was stronger than his power to hold under control the chieftains who constantly schemed for their own ends on the wild moors and mountains of the North.[6] More grievous, however, were those tragedies which were bounded by no one time or place, so wide-reaching and so engrained in English life that Bede feared alike the ravaging of his country by barbarians from without and the dying away of religion by neglect from within. The flowering of this foul harvest sprang from two major roots, he declared. First, there were far too few bishops, and therefore the lonely dwellers in hills and

[2] *HE* Preface; *Epist. ad Ecgbertum* (*HE* I, 405ff.), c. 9.

[3] *Epist.* c. 1; *Alc. Vita*: *SS* xv,1,186: *Bedae doctissimi discipulus.* But cf. Leach, 53ff.

[4] *HE* V, c. 23.

[5] *Baed. Cont. ann.* 731.

[6] Stenton, 91 (Reference in these notes, unless otherwise indicated, is made to pages).

dales were starving for lack of spiritual support, untaught, untouched by sacramental grace, even of baptism, during many years; even in places more accessible, earnest-minded layfolk were bidden approach the altar only thrice a year, through the sloth and greed of their appointed pastors. The fewer the bishops, the wider the diocese on which each should batten; and, however hungry their flocks, many Fathers in God were quick to exact their toll of tribute from every parish in their sees. On the other hand, the faithful, for the joy of their souls in this life or after death, had bestowed so much of English land for the founding of monasteries that scarcely a castle was left to defend English borders from the invading Picts and Scots; while within very many of these "houses of God" monastic doors concealed homes of lust and luxury, free from discipline, to which crowded all who gladly shook off for comfort and idleness the burden of an honest life in the world.

Therefore, Bede exhorted, let Egbert now turn zealously to the work of bringing Northumbria into better order, and let him impel his king to the same endeavour. Let another bishop be consecrated, and let his seat be placed in a monastic centre; moreover, let Egbert himself pray the Holy See to grant his bishopric the dignity of metropolitan, so that once again an archbishop should wear in his cathedral of York the pallium which Pope Honorius long ago had granted to Paulinus. So might God give it of His grace that the spreading corruption of the last thirty years be cleansed from the land and His sheep be once again fed in sane and wholesome pastures.[7]

The warning fell on good ground. Egbert was no mean disciple of his master, and in 735, the year of Bede's death, he obtained the pallium and saw York raised anew to an archiepiscopal seat.[8] But his royal partner, Ceolwulf, longed to fol-

[7] *Epist. ad Ecgbert.* cc. 10, 17; *HE* I, c. 29; II, c. 17.
[8] *A-SC ann.* 735.

low those many other Anglo-Saxon kings and queens who had found peace within the cloister. Saint Cuthbert had always been his hero; in 737 he, too, departed to a cell in Lindisfarne, and his crown passed to his cousin Eadbert, the brother of Archbishop Egbert himself.[9]

It seemed now that Bede's hope might be realized, that fellowship between the brothers, prelate and king, might indeed be fruitful for renewed life in the North. Eadbert was a strong ruler, who held his thanes to due allegiance. In vain some of them rose to replace him by Offa, a son of Aldfrid, once King of Northumbria. Offa fled for refuge to Lindisfarne, was dragged nearly dead of hunger from its church by his pursuers, and Cynewulf, its bishop, was thrown into prison at the royal city of Bamburgh. Barbarians from the North were met on their own ground. In 750 Eadbert wrested Kyle in Ayrshire from the British of Strathclyde; six years later he marched, in alliance with Aengus, King of the Picts, to subdue their chief city at Dumbarton, Alcluith in ancient name.[10] In matters pertaining to the Church he aided his brother with energy and goodwill. We have a letter written in 757 or 758 by Pope Paul the first to both Egbert and Eadbert, commanding the king to restore to a certain Abbot Forthred three monasteries in Northumbria which Eadbert had bestowed upon one of his secular nobles. The indignant abbot, who had himself received these three houses of God as a gift from some Lady Abbess, had hastened to lay his complaint before the Holy See at Rome, and the Pope was exceedingly grieved to hear of such impious action. Yet the deep reverence in which Eadbert held the monastic life, and the name of Egbert in the address of the Papal letter, perhaps point rather to a desire on the

[9] Earle and Plummer II, 41; Sym. Dun. II, 32, 375f.; I, 47, 201; *Baed. Cont. ann.* 737.

[10] Sym. Dun. I, 47f.; II, 39ff.; *Baed. Cont. ann.* 750; Alcuin, *Versus de Sanctis*, ll. 1274f.

king's part to follow the counsel of Bede for the strengthening and protection of his Northern land than in any way to do violence to his Church.[11]

Egbert had been brought up from childhood in a monastery, by the wish of his father, Eata. He had made a pilgrimage to Rome as a young man and had been ordained deacon there.[12] From 735 onward, as Archbishop of York, he did all that lay in him to raise his people of the North from ignorance and vice. He did not succeed, so far as we know, in providing the bishops whom Bede had craved for them. Unity failed him, for he could not throw his influence across the barriers which Northumbria offered, cut into impregnable sections by physical and political forces. But he worked hard and well to administer those parts of his flock which he could reach. We possess under his name a *Dialogue,* generally held to be a genuine work of his, written for the instruction of his clergy in the various problems of Church discipline.[13] He strove to arrest the degraded, the corrupt, the deserters and unlicensed wanderers among his own clergy, to bring to public penance the idolators clad in priestly habit, the utterers of false witness and perjury, the thieves and the murderers, the "vessels of iniquities," source of scandal to the simple folk to whom they ministered the sacraments. He impressed upon all his people the requirement of regular giving of alms, and of abstinence, not only in Lent and other well-known times of prescription, but at the Ember Fasts of spring, summer, autumn and winter. He drew a veil of holiness around the altar, declaring that, "thanks be to God, it has been the custom in the English Church since the days of Pope Vitalian and of Theodore, Archbishop of Canterbury, and held, too, as matter of law,

[11] H.S. III, 394f.; Stenton, 160, note 3; cf. Mann I, ii, 340.

[12] Sym. Dun. I, 49.

[13] For works connected with the name of Egbert see Oakley, 78ff.; McNeill and Gamer, 237ff.; H.S. III, 403ff.

that not only clerics in monasteries, but also laymen with their wives and families should come to their confessors during the twelve days of preparation before Christmas, that with tears and giving of alms they may cleanse themselves from the fellowship of fleshly lust and more purely partake of the Communion of the Lord at the time of His Birth." [14]

Similar endeavour for the purifying of the English Church encouraged him on the part of his brother Metropolitan of the southern province. Here Cuthbert, once abbot of Lyminge, Kent, then consecrated bishop of Hereford and four years later elected Archbishop of Canterbury,[15] was struggling with the same evils that harried the North. So prevalent, indeed, were crime and oppression that Zacharias, Pope from 741 to 752, had written two letters of rebuke from Rome: Let the English mend their ways, he had warned, or they will find themselves outside the pale of the Catholic Church.[16] Further exhortation had come across the sea from the English mission in Germany, where Boniface, now over seventy, was Archbishop of Mainz, still passionately alive to all that was happening in his motherland. In 747 he wrote to Cuthbert in order to lay before him the measures which a General Synod of Frankish bishops had lately taken under his presidency for the uprooting of grievous crimes from their own people. These concerned the English, also, for the letter went on: "I frankly tell you, dear friend, the feeling of all the servants of God here among us who are most versed in Scripture and in the fear of God, that it would be good for the advance of honour and

[14] See the *Dialogue of Egbert,* H.S. III, 403ff.; Oakley, 79, 81; Watkins, 636f., 654f.; *DCB* s.v. Egbert (Raine). *The Pontifical of Egbert* (ed. Greenwell, *PSS* XXVII, 1853) is now thought to deal with Frankish ritual and to be of a considerably later date: Levison, 118.

[15] Kemble I, 104; Birch I, 231; Flor. Worc. I, 54; Sym. Dun. ed. Hodgson Hinde, 13; *Baed. Cont. ann.* 740.

[16] H.S. III, 360.

modesty in your Church and the decrease of foul living if your bishops and leaders would forbid your women, married and Religious alike, their constant journeying to and from Rome.[17] Most of them are lost, only a few remain unharmed. Of a truth few cities can be found in Lombardy or Frankland or Gaul in which there is not some harlot or prostitute of English race. It is a scandal and disgrace to your whole Church."

Equally forcible remarks follow concerning vices prevalent in England at the time: seizure of monasteries and convents by secular violence, luxury and ostentation in dress of monks and nuns, drunkenness seen commonly, not only among humble parishioners but among the very bishops themselves at their tables of good cheer. This last vice, Boniface mourns, "is an evil peculiar to the heathen and all English people; neither Franks nor Gauls nor Lombards nor Romans nor Greeks practise it. Let us restrain it, if we can, by decree of our Synods and the power of Holy Scripture; at the very least, by refusing and forbidding it, lest we take upon our own souls the blood of those lost in sin." [18]

Cuthbert was already moving toward action. In September of this same year he called together the bishops of his province at Clovesho, a place now unknown; King Ethelbald of Mercia also attended, with his chief nobles. The decrees passed at this assembly touched exactly those matters which were the daily concern of Egbert in the North. Let bishops refrain from

[17] Cf. the verses of Theodulf of Orléans: *PLAC* I, 557:

Non tantum isse iuvat Romam, bene vivere quantum,
Vel Romae, vel ubi vita agitur hominis.
Non via, credo, pedum, sed morum ducit ad astra,
Quis quid ubique gerit, spectat ab arce Deus;

and Zettinger, "Die Berichte über Rompilger aus dem Frankenreiche," *Römische Quartalschrift,* Suppl.heft XI, 1900, 100ff.

[18] Boniface, *Epp.* ed. Tangl, 1916, No. 78 (169f.), dated 747; H.S. III, 381f.; William of Malmesbury, *De Gest. Reg.* I, 82; Levison, 86, note 1, and 92. The latter part of these reproaches, however, rests only on the recipient's recording: Tangl, 170.

worldly business and distractions, recall to their priests the duties laid down by the Church in her writings and Synods. Let them visit every year the parishes of their dioceses to meet in person the high and the low, men and women, to teach and to admonish—above all, to forbid pagan and idolatrous rites and practices of every kind. Let abbots and abbesses, under the supervision of their bishops, see to it that all their religious keep strictly the monastic Rule of their community, observing the seven canonical Hours according to the use of Rome, interceding for kings and all Christian people, studying learned books with diligence. Let the allotted psalms be said with all reverence and seriousness; even those monks and nuns who know no Latin can assist by offering their wholehearted intention as they repeat the words prescribed. Monasteries shall not be houses of feasting and drunkenness, of makers of frivolous music, verse, and jesting, of those who prink themselves in worldly fashions and extravagant display. Religious shall not wander from house to house nor live outside cloister in the homes of friends in the world. Discipline shall be strictly meted out to so-called "monasteries" held by lay "abbots." Let priests enter upon their Ordering after strict examination; let them keep faithfully to the usage and custom of the Church of Rome, neither elaborating their Offices with illicit additions nor declaiming them as a tragic actor upon a worldly stage. Let them understand, at least in their own tongue, the meaning and purpose of the words they utter as they administer the sacraments and intercede before the Lord for their people's salvation. Moreover, let them keep from causing scandal to their flocks by gross sins of fleshly lust, by coarse and evil talk; a priest's life is a round of prayer, study, self-discipline, and ministry. Sunday is no day for gadding abroad on worldly business; Rogation Days are not set apart for sports and horse-racing, but for fasting and reverent procession of Cross and relics of the saints through the fields that the Lord shall bless. Finally, let them exhort their people to come more frequently to the altar for Communion; to remember that fasting is a duty in itself, and cannot be replaced by giving of alms, and that no number of vicarious offerings of self-denial and charity on the part of his obliging friends can relieve a sinner of his duty to fulfil in his own person the penance laid upon him by his priest.[19]

Egbert, also, received his own counselling from Boniface in Germany. Two letters can still be read, addressed to this "most dear and reverend brother." "When your gifts and books arrived," Boniface writes, "I lifted up my hands and gave great thanks to Almighty God, Who has given it me in my long exile from home to find a friend like you, a very comfort from Heaven to help me in things of this earth and things of the spirit, in prayer and unity of fellowship." He then tells of a letter he has sent to King Ethelbald of Mercia, who, he charges, has caused open scandal among his people by despoiling churches of their property and privileges, and, worse, by his lust and rape unspeakable in convents, brought upon nuns and virgins consecrated to God. No wonder that the heathen declare of the English that they scorn lawful wedlock and are living in foul riot of adultery! If Egbert marks such tares as these budding among his own people, will he not cut them away, root and branch, with the scythe of the authority given him of God? Presents accompany this admonition: a cloak, and a towel for drying the feet of the servants of God after their ceremonial washing by the Archbishop. In return, Boniface would gladly receive some of the writings of Bede, "that candle whom the Lord has given as a light to your Province." [20]

[19] H.S. III, 360ff.; W. of Malmes. *De Gest. Pont.* 9ff.; Birch I, 249ff. On vicarious penance see McNeill and Gamer, 48.

[20] Boniface, *Epp.* Nos. 75 and 73, both dated 746–747.

Another time he himself calls for advice on a problem familiar to Egbert—what to do concerning a priest who has fallen into wicked ways? "If I remove him from office, as the canons prescribe, then, because we have so few to minister, babies will die unbaptized and many of my people live as pagans without the sacraments. Please help me, and great shall be your reward in Heaven. I am sending you two little casks of wine, because we love each other; do enjoy them with your brethren." [21]

The bond between the Churches of England and of Germany held firm in this eighth century. In nothing was it shown more clearly than in their fellowships of prayer, both for the living and the dead.[22]

Even nearer to the thought of Egbert than his great diocese was his Cathedral Church of York. Here under his rule the Hours of Night and of Day were regularly observed; Mass was celebrated on Sundays, holy days, and days of special need or occasion; the texts of the Service-books used at York were carefully compared by Egbert himself with those he saw when he visited Rome.[23] He enriched its altars with precious metals and jewels, enlarged the body of its clergy, and cared for the music of its choir after the manner of Aedde and of Aeona under Wilfrid the first in this same Church, of John the Chanter under Benedict Biscop at Wearmouth, of Maban under Acca among the clergy of Hexham.[24]

And very specially he was concerned to carry on the tradition of learning which he had known under his master, Bede,[25] a tradition already founded in York by its former

[21] *Ibid.* No. 91, dated 747x754.

[22] *Ibid.* pages 57, 181f., 259, 288f.; cf. Levison, 101ff.

[23] *Dial. of Egbert*: H.S. III, 412.

[24] Alcuin, *Versus de Sanctis,* ll. 1262ff.; Eddius Stephanus, *Life of Wilfrid,* ed. Bertram Colgrave, 1927, c. 14; *HE* IV, cc. 2, 18; V, c. 20.

[25] *Alcuini Vita,* 186, c. 4.

bishops, Bosa, John of Beverley, and Wilfrid, the second. These three men had been strictly trained in Irish discipline of books under Abbess Hild of Streanaeshalch, the later Whitby, and had then followed their search after truth in the wider ways of Rome. What they had learned of both they had imparted to the younger men and boys who served in their Cathedral, and Egbert in his time could build upon a foundation already well and firmly laid.[26]

Under him this somewhat informal body of teachers and pupils began its development into a School which was to become the most famous centre of learning in England, and which attracted first the young sons of Northumbrian thanes, then students from other parts of England and from countries across the sea. In its early years its education had been concerned almost entirely with matters of religion; but Egbert widened it to include the study of the liberal arts, of secular literature and secular science, such as Bede had sought and told and recorded at Jarrow for the better understanding of the doctrine and the ritual of the Church.[27]

The aim and the manner of life of the Cathedral clergy and School at York under Egbert and his successors have given rise to varied argument.[28] From an impartial view of the evidence, however, one may safely imagine there a community living under definite rule of prayer, discipline, and study, yet not bound by the threefold vow of stability, of conversion of life, of obedience, which was now heard more and more often in monasteries of the North, as the Benedictine Profession

[26] Roger, 313ff.
[27] *Alc. Vita*, c. 4.
[28] See A. Hamilton Thompson, ed. *York Minster Hist. Tracts: The Building of York Minster*; ed. *Bede*, 89; *Vict. Hist. York* III, 5; *English Monasteries*, 19f.; *Archaeological Journal* LXXIV, 1917, 140f.; Raine, *DCB* II, 218; Stubbs, *ibid.* I, 74; Raine, *York*, 1893, 165, 171; Leach, 57f.; Hauck, II, 130, note 4; page 26 *infra*, note 70. The School belonged to the city of York, as well as to the cathedral: Leach, 58.

gained wider ground; meeting regularly for Mass and the monastic Offices, for meals in a common refectory, and for common conference, yet free to own each his property and to dwell in his own house, did he so desire; obedient to a common code expressed in detailed provisions, under the authority of the Archbishop in general and of the "vice-dominus" or "abbas" in particular,[29] yet possessed of freedom to move and act independently in matters outside its reach. From such corporate society and its broader associations Wilfrid, the first, from time to time had sought monastic retreat in his cloister at Ripon, John in his enclosure amid the woods at Beverley. Desire for this "canonical" life, so like in many details to that of the monk that there is often difficulty in interpreting the exact significance of "monastery" and its derivative "minster," yet entirely distinct in its fundamental essence, spread far and wide in this century. It was encouraged and formulated on the continent of Europe by the zealous work of Saint Chrodegang, bishop and, subsequently, Archbishop, of Metz from 742 until 766, who compiled for his clergy a Rule which drew much of its content from the provision laid down in the sixth century by Saint Benedict himself.[30]

2

It was during this "golden age" of Egbert and Eadbert, as long afterward he thought of it, that Alcuin grew up at York from child to man, in its Cathedral School.[31] He was brought there as a little boy early in Egbert's time of office.

[29] *Versus de Sanctis,* l. 1217; Du Cange, s.v. *vicedominus,* 315.

[30] ed. W. Schmitz, 1889; cf. A. Werminghoff, *NA* XXVII, 1902, 646ff.; de Clercq, 146ff.; Nottarp, *Die Bistumserrichtung in Deutschland im achten Jahrh.,* 1920, 178.

[31] Stenton, 92. The name was originally Alchvine (consonantal u; latinized to Alchuinus): *PLAC* I, 283, 351; Manitius, 275; Traube, *Karol. Dicht.* 47, note 1. Alcuin and his friends liked the name Albinus: *Epp.* IV, 350: *Albinus habeo nomen inter notos et filios sanctae Dei ecclesiae.*

We do not know exactly either the date or the place of his birth, but the place was near York, if not the city itself, and the year somewhere between 730 and 735. His family was of noble line, and related to that of Saint Willibrord; the monastery of Saint Andrew, which Wilgils, Willibrord's father, had founded upon the headland overlooking the mouth of the Humber, came by right of legal possession into the patronage and ownership of Alcuin, and played a very real part in his life.[32]

Among the sons of nobles of the surrounding country who were now coming in increasing number to learn in this School under its Archbishop, Alcuin progressed quickly and well. His biographer has left us a happy picture of Egbert. Twice a day the Father would retire to his oratory to pour forth his soul in secret prayer, kneeling on the ground, his hands outstretched as the arms of the Cross: before he broke his fast, and again in the evening, before the Cathedral family gathered for Compline. After this, the last Office of the day, all his sons knelt one by one to receive his blessing; not one of them ever ventured to go to bed without this final rite. For them constantly he offered the Holy Sacrifice, praying lest they fall unawares into the snare of sin. He trained their unaccustomed lips in the words of prayer, after the manner, we may think, of the *Book of Cerne* and of the devotion to our Lord and our Lady left from this century by the anchorite Alchfrid.[33] But Egbert was almost as keen for the instruction of minds as of souls. Nearly every morning found him sitting upon the couch in his cell, ready to discuss and explain mysteries of Holy Scripture to any and all who were eager to hear; and so many came that he was busy until midday, often until well on in the

[32] Alcuin, *Vita S. Willibrordi,* c. 1; Epp. IV, 178f.: *genti nostrae;* Dümmler, *NA* XVIII, 1892, 54.

[33] Levison, 295ff.; Kuypers, ed. *The Book of Cerne*; Bishop, 192ff., and, in Kuypers, 283.

afternoon. There, while he criticized, they rehearsed arguments on sacred doctrines, that in days to come they might find answer ready to hand for the Faith that was in them. Always, except during Lent, he shared supper with his household in the refectory, when the only voice that broke the evening silence was that of the monk set apart as Reader for the week.

Egbert loved all his boys, but Alcuin, it seems, held from the first a special place in his heart.[34] Already as a child Alcuin felt that fear of evil, a tiny shadow on his mind's horizon, which was to beset him in later years and trouble his old age. Lessons were his joy—in the Bible, in the Lives of men of Christian history, in the Psalms and Lections of the calendar. He often went to hear the brethren reciting the Hours in the Church at the appointed times of day; now and then, on some special occasion, he was allowed to be present at a Night Office. It was wonderful. But so were other things, as well. Was it really wrong, as some people had said in books, to love too much the poetry written by heathen men who did not know God and the Saints? How could it be wrong when the poetry sounded so beautiful as his teacher read it aloud, as it told of those who suffered and were sad, just like many in his own land?

> *Iam gravis aequabat luctus et mutua Mavors*
> *Funera, caedebant pariter pariterque ruebant*
> *Victores victique; neque his fuga nota, neque illis.*
> *Di Iovis in tectis iram miserantur inanem*
> *Amborum, et tantos mortalibus esse labores. . . .*

A story has come down to us which points, perhaps, to some such struggle in a child's conscience. He was eleven years old, it records, when one night he happened to share

[34] *Alc. Vita*, 186.

the cell of a humble brother who was nervous at sleeping alone. His master had given permission when this simple man begged for company. Before he went to sleep, the boy, like Saint Jerome long before him, had been thinking over that mediaeval problem of spiritual ethics, the dangerous attraction of pagan literature. The brother, no longer alone and homesick, snored in peace—in so deep peace that the bell bidding him rise for Night Vigil troubled him not a whit. Alcuin, however, was awake; and from below he heard to his dismay the brethren chanting the opening psalm. His companion would be dreadfully late, and he was just hurrying over to the other bed to rouse him when suddenly he saw a crowd of foul and hideous shapes bending over the sleeper. "Why sleep and snore you here alone, friend," they hissed, "while your brethren keep watch?" The slothful brother was soundly beaten; the child, terrified at this sight and fearful of yielding to the Devil in indulgence as well as in sloth, vowed then and there never to hold Virgil dearer than the psalms of holy Church.[35]

Now and again he went with one or another of the Cathedral household on some errand through the streets of York, and thus he learned to know the city. Something of its history, too, he was taught from the pages of Orosius and of Bede. Here, on the bank of the river Ouse, the Romans had maintained a strong fortress for the protecting of Britain against the Picts and Scots of Caledonia; hither in the third century the Roman emperor Severus had come to crush these same enemies; here he had reigned in state; here he had worshipped his heathen gods, and here he had died. Here in the fourth century the Caesar Constantius had seen Britain under his power; here he, too, had met death; here his son, Constantine, had begun that reign full of import for Christianity. In this city, already old, merchants had gathered, bringing their wares by

[35] *Ibid.* 185. But, for Alcuin's "inconsistency," see Long, 377ff.

land and water into a market of wealth and prosperity; hither sailors had navigated their ships from the Ocean by the riverway of the Ouse. To this city the Angles had come early in the sixth century to settle and to rule in conquest.[36]

But of this conquest had been born joy, and the child Alcuin knew well that at the centre of what had once been the great Roman camp, Edwin, King of the Northumbrians, had been baptized on Easter Eve, 627, by Bishop Paulinus in a little wooden church which he had quickly raised for this very purpose and had dedicated to Saint Peter. Here he had purposed to build a splendid church of stone, but death had intervened, and it was left to his successor, the good King Oswald, to bring the work to completion. Here Wilfrid in 670 had laboured to restore this cathedral of his see from slow decay to its rightful beauty; and here Cuthbert, drawn so reluctantly by conscience from his island retreat, had been consecrated its bishop on Easter Day, 685.[37]

Outside the city, far and wide, lay long forests, broken here and there by waste and fen, pools of water and impassable bogs. In the Forest of Galtres, stretching from the gates of York north and northwest between the Ouse and the Foss, the Saxon kings hunted the wolf and the wild boar; beyond this the traveller toward the monastery of Whitby made his way across the moors and woodlands of Pickering. The old Roman roads, lined with their ancient tombs, still led to towns: Tadcaster, Malton, Aldborough, Catterick, among those nearest to York. But in many places the wilderness of the brakes and marshes was broken only by the strongholds of the Saxon nobles, who drew as best they could their living from the unharvested acres of their enormous estates and found their live-

[36] *HE* I, cc. 5, 8, 12; Stenton, 74ff.; R. Hodgkin, 148ff.; Collingwood and Myres, *Roman Britain and the English Settlements,* 1936, 418f.

[37] *HE* II, c. 14; IV, c. 28; Eddius, ed. Colgrave, c. 16.

liest joy in war against their neighbours, man and beast. To a lord of great tracts of lands it seemed but a short step to a crown; the kings of Northumbria in this eighth century sat precariously upon their royal seats.[38] Now and then the brethren of the Church in York journeyed for conference to Ripon, to Lastingham, to Whitby, more frequently to Jarrow, and doubtless enjoyed their meeting all the more for the difficulty and danger it entailed.[39]

We know little about actual happenings during Alcuin's boyhood. But one of these probably left its remembrance in his mind—the burning, it would seem, of the cathedral and clergy-house at York on Sunday, April 23, 741, when he was about nine years old. Ancient annals tell that the year was marked by a great drought, and this may have had its share in the disaster. The buildings, then, must have stood marred and blackened throughout Alcuin's younger days.[40]

As he grew up, another teacher became of even greater moment to him than Egbert. This was Aelbert,[41] of noble blood through kinship with Archbishop Egbert, who had taught Aelbert among his students in York, had ordained him deacon and priest, and made him *Defensor Cleri,* or warden of the privileges, rights, revenues and possessions belonging to the diocese and its cathedral. His special bent, however, lay toward books and teaching; and now Egbert increasingly gave over to

[38] R. Hodgkin, 407ff.

[39] Cf. J. W. Fawcett and R. B. Hepple, *Notes and Queries,* 1936, CLXX, 441; CLXXI, 13, 82f. Dümmler, however, dates *Epp.* IV, No. 284 (274J.), between 793 and Alcuin's death.

[40] *A-SC ann.* 741; Earle and Plummer II, 42; Sym. Dun. II, 38; Roger of Hoveden, *Chronica* I, *RS* LI, 6; *Baed. Cont. ann.* 741. It has been doubted whether the "monasterium" of Symeon of Durham was the Cathedral. But delay in rebuilding is not surprising; cf. Raine, *HCY* I, 394; F. Harrison, *York Minster,* 1927, 3ff.

[41] He is also known as Ethelbert (Æthelberht): *DCB* (Raine), and as Coena: *ibid.* (Hole).

him charge of the education of the boys and young men of the School in which Aelbert himself had been trained.[42]

Under Aelbert the same instruction was given in the doctrine and history of the Church, in the writings of Apostles and Fathers, in interpretation, moral, theological, symbolic and allegorical. In these lessons, Alcuin writes, the master "opened out the mysteries of Holy Scripture and gave us to look into the abyss of law ancient and unfulfilled." [43] Much thought was also given to apologetics; Alcuin remembered long afterward that "my master told me to rise with all that was in me to the defence of the Catholic Faith if anywhere I should hear of the springing up of strange sects, opposed to Apostolic doctrines." [44] Secular studies advanced apace, for the better learning of these spiritual truths. Latin language and grammar of prose and verse were thoroughly analysed, and the students wrote their own compositions in both forms, elaborating their sentences by reference to the rules of rhetoric.[45] Mathematics gave them some arithmetic and astronomy for the understanding of the Church's year, especially of the varying dates of Easter; under the tracing of "various figures" we may perhaps see some study of geometry. Natural science led them further to consider eclipses of the sun and moon, tides, earthquakes, the laws that govern the life of men, beasts, and birds, in the pages of Pliny, of Isidore, of Bede. In a learned discussion by letter on the zodiac and calculations of astronomical time Alcuin writes: "My master very often used to say to me, 'They were the wisest of men who discerned these arts in Nature. It is a great disgrace for us to let them die out in our time.' " [46] Some familiarity with canon law was required of those who

[42] *Versus de Sanctis,* ll. 1426ff. [43] *Ibid.* 1447f.
[44] *Epp.* IV, 332. [45] Raby, *SLP* I, 178.
[46] *Versus de Sanctis,* ll. 1439ff.; *Epp.* IV, 239. For Alcuin's conception of the liberal arts as the work of God in Nature, see Gilson, *La Philosophie au Moyen Age,* 192.

looked forward to the priesthood, and probably some form of music—at least, the Gregorian chant.[47] All, of course, were trained to recite the various Latin Offices with accuracy and reverence; some must have spent many hours in the scriptorium, poring over and trying to imitate scripts of both the Anglo-Saxon and the Irish types.[48]

Such time as Aelbert could spare from church and classroom he devoted to the Cathedral Library, his own particular charge and delight. Its number of books increased rapidly under his constant search, and Alcuin has left us some account of these in "the first catalogue of an English library," apologizing for his many omissions, due to exigencies of space and metre.[49] This Library held, of course, some writings of the four great Fathers of the Western Church and something of the Greek Fathers, very probably for the most part in Latin translation. Alcuin undoubtedly learned Greek at York, after the manner practised by Archbishop Theodore at Canterbury and by Bede at Jarrow; but judging from the evidence of his writings, he borrowed his Greek from his learned sources when he used it.[50] General information was drawn for the students at York from Aelbert's manuscripts of Pliny, of Gregory the Great, of Cassiodorus, of Bede, and of Isidore, although this last name is absent from Alcuin's summary. Cicero gave rhetoric; Aldhelm's tortuous periods were there, and grammarians in number. Boethius represented both himself and such knowledge as he afforded of Aristotle.[51] Christian poets abounded, such as

[47] Roger, 315f.

[48] Cf. Lowe, *CLA* II, xiv, and Nos. 125, 132, 138, 147f., 152, 194, 213.

[49] *Versus de Sanctis,* ll. 1535ff.; Manitius, 276f.; Roger, 317f. Laistner points out the defects of Alcuin's list: *Bede,* ed. A. H. Thompson, 237.

[50] Laistner, *Thought and Letters,* 192; G. R. Stephens, *The Knowledge of Greek in England in the Middle Ages,* 1933, 34ff.

[51] Laistner: *Bede,* ed. Thompson, 262. Cf. *PLAC* I, 295 (LXXIII); page 114, note 108, *infra*.

had been known to Aldhelm or to Bede: Juvencus, Sedulius, Paulinus of Nola, Arator, Fortunatus, possibly Avitus.[52] Poets of pagan Rome read in the School included Virgil, Lucan, and Statius. In later days Alcuin quoted from Terence, Horace, and Ovid, but how far his knowledge came from quotations in secondary sources rather than from their own writings is a matter of question.[53]

The eagerness of Aelbert to secure more books for his students and deeper knowledge for himself as teacher sent him off from time to time on journeys to the continent of Europe. On at least one of these expeditions he took Alcuin with him, to Italy and to Frankland.[54] Among the memories of this pilgrimage were the sight of Rome and a few days' stay in Pavia, capital city of the Lombard kings, where Alcuin "listened to a certain Jew, Lul by name, arguing in public with Master Peter," a learned scholar of Pisa. Among the Franks he visited the monks of Murbach, to whom he wrote when he was an old man: "Once I came with my master to your community and saw and loved its excellent way of life—so much that I longed to be there as one of you." [55]

Through journeys such as these the renown of the School at York and of its master grew high; again and again Aelbert was invited by kings in other parts of England and on the continent to found another such house of study for their people. He continued, however, to spend his energy on the numbers attracted to York by his learning, his skill in discussion, and his ready friendship.[56] Of the fellow-students of Alcuin under Aelbert we know one or two names: of Eanbald, whom Alcuin looked back upon all his life as "father and brother and most

[52] *Versus de Sanctis,* l. 1551, *emend.* Froben. On Avitus cf. Ogilvy, *MAA* 1936, 21.

[53] He knew at first hand Virgil, Ovid, and Christian poets: Raby, *SLP* I, 179f.

[54] *Versus,* ll. 1453ff.; *PLAC* I, 206f.; *Epp.* IV, 285; cf. 225, 290.

[55] *Epp.* IV, 429.

[56] *Versus,* ll. 1449ff., 1459ff.

faithful friend,"[57] and of Seneca, a youth somewhat older than himself, with whom he often talked over the problems that beset their serious adolescent minds. This led to a thrilling incident, well remembered long afterward in Alcuin's mature years. One night Seneca had a vision. He was praying in the Lady Chapel, when suddenly a dazzling light filled the place and he saw a man arrayed in white, who held out before his terrified eyes an open book and read from it these words: "Now you know, but soon you shall see greater things." The visitant then disappeared. Some months passed, and one day Seneca was seized with sickness, so great that soon he lay, to all seeming, dead in Alcuin's arms. After a short while, however, he recovered consciousness and told of a second vision. Some one—he knew not whom—had taken him to a fair Paradise where many folk, known and unknown, walked in joy, especially those who had worshipped in the Church of York. They had wanted to keep him there, but his guide had called him back to his body on earth, saying: "In the rising of the sun you shall regain health, but another of your brethren shall die today and here you have seen his seat prepared."

All happened as had been told, though young Seneca himself did not long survive this second experience. In a third vision another brother, "an honest and truthful man," saw a Shining One descend from on high to embrace and carry away Seneca's soul. Many years later Alcuin wrote from Frankland to the brethren of his old home in York: "Keep me in mind, dearest of fathers and brothers. For I shall be yours, in death as in life. And it may be that God in His compassion will grant that you, who nurtured my childhood, will also bury my old age. But if another grave be assigned my body, yet I think that God will listen to the prayers of men like you and give me with you somewhere some haven of peace for my soul. For—as our young Seneca declares he saw—we believe that

[57] *Epp.* IV, 162.

the souls of our brotherhood must be gathered together in one and the same place of joy." [58]

As Alcuin entered manhood, he was gradually promoted from student to teacher under Aelbert in the School. During these years of its ordered peace the secular world outside was following a stormy course. In 754, when he was in his early twenties, news had come of the murder of Boniface in Germany. Shortly before, Boniface had consecrated the English Lul as his assistant bishop in Mainz, and now Lul succeeded him as Chief Pastor there.[59] In 757 King Ethelbald of Mercia, whom Boniface and other bishops in Germany had rebuked for notorious evil living, was killed treacherously by his own bodyguard in Seckington, Warwickshire. He had tried to make amends by freeing Church lands from taxes, but was revealed to a holy man as suffering torments at the hands of demons after his death.[60] Nevertheless, he had been great in rule, and all the kings of England south of the Humber had owned his supremacy.[61] He had even invaded Northumbria and ravaged its fields—in 740, when Eadbert was away from home, having crossed the border to fight against the Picts.[62] Ethelbald's kingdom was now seized by Beornred of untraced descent, described in one chronicle as his assassin, and in another as the usurper of his crown.[63] In any case, Beornred was as quickly driven out by Offa, of the Mercian royal line, who was to reign over Mercia until 796, and to claim, with the style *rex Anglorum,* supreme rank among English kings.[64]

[58] *Versus,* ll. 1601ff.; *Epp.* IV, 86.

[59] Levison, ed. *Vitae S. Bonifatii,* 1905, 45 and note 2.

[60] Boniface, *Epp.* 146ff., 249; Kemble I, 119f.; Birch I, 254ff.; H.S. III, 350ff.; *Baed. Cont. ann.* 757; Sym. Dun. II, 41; Plummer, ed. Bede II, 342; *A-SC* (E) *ann.* 755, at end.

[61] *HE* V, 23.

[62] *Baed. Cont. ann.* 740.

[63] Will. Malmes. *De Gest. Reg.* I, 79; Flor. Worc. I, 56.

[64] Stenton, 210f. and *EHR* XXXIII, 1918, 446ff.; cf. Jerrold, *Introd. to the Hist. of England to 1204,* 1949, 278f.

Change, also unwelcomed, came to pass in Northumbria. The victory of Eadbert over the British at Alcluith in 756 was followed directly by an overwhelming attack at their hands, in which almost all his army was destroyed on the march to "Nova Civitas," probably Newburgh on the Firth of Tay.[65] The disaster had a lasting effect upon the king. Moreover, the example of Ceolwulf was calling, and two years later Eadbert, too, resigned his crown, to devote the rest of his days to prayer and meditation within the precincts of his brother's Cathedral at York. In spite of this recent reverse he left his kingdom in secure standing and in happy relations with other rulers. King Pepin of the Franks, we are told, was his friend; his brother kings in England—but in vain—begged him to stay with them for their aid and comfort.[66]

And well they might, for within a year Oswulf, his son and successor, was killed, like Ethelbald of Mercia, by men who served in his own house, and popular support from the retainers of great estates raised to the throne in 759 Ethelwald Moll, a Northumbrian chieftain. His reign was marked by repeated onslaughts of Nature. First, in the second year, an epidemic of dysentery carried off many victims from the North. After this, the "mickle winter" of 763–764 held the land in the grip of frost, ice and drifting snow, remembered for many a year to come. Trees withered away throughout the countryside, and vegetables in the gardens; even the sea cast up its creatures dead upon the shore. This was followed by sudden outbreaks of fire which raged in York and other cities of England, ruining both castles and monasteries alike.

Another happening gave interest to the Cathedral of York, when in November, 762, Ethelwald took in marriage at Cat-

[65] Sym. Dun. ed. Hodgson Hinde, 20; J. B. Johnston, *Place-Names of Scotland,* 1934, 262.

[66] Sym. Dun. I, 48f.; *Baed. Cont. ann.* 758.

terick the Lady Ethelthrith. Alcuin was to remember her in letters after her husband was dead.[67]

The welcome that had greeted Ethelwald as king lasted only a few years. In 765 he found himself deserted, and was forced to yield his rule to Alchred, who claimed descent from Ida, ancestor of the royal house of Bernicia.[68] Alchred had not yet ended his second year of control when Archbishop Egbert died, on November 19, 766, leaving the diocese in charge of Aelbert. A day in the following spring, April 24, 767, saw Aelbert consecrated to the see of York, where the Pope allowed him, too, office as Archbishop. From this time onward, Alcuin, under his superintendence, assumed more and more of the general charge of its School.[69]

3

It was at this time, it seems, when he was about thirty-five years old, that he was ordained deacon. He never received the priesthood. Although the evidence is not conclusive, it is wiser to believe that he continued throughout his life to live as he had been taught in York, and that he never became a professed monk, whether of the Benedictine or of other Rule.[70] Moreover, to complete the negative side of the picture, he was never the student and researcher, in the higher sense of the

[67] Sym. Dun. II, 41f.; Earle and Plummer II, 49; *Baed. Cont. ann.* 759.

[68] Sym. Dun. II, 43: *regnum amisit*; Will. Malmes. *De Gest. Reg.* I, 74: *insidiis Alcredi occubuit.*

[69] Sym. Dun., *ibid.*; *Baed. Cont. ann.* 766; *A-SC ann.* 766.

[70] For Alcuin as monk see Mabillon, *Acta SS.OSB* IV, i, 163ff.; *Alcuini Opera,* ed. Froben I, xixf.; Hauck II (note 28 *supra*); Delius, *Theol. Stud. und Kritiken* CIII, 1931, 465ff.; Werner, 95. Against this see Pückert, 248ff.; Kleinclausz, *Alcuin,* 169, note 145 (who, however, regards the "monastery" of York as one of "monks": 24 and 155); Möller-Hahn, *RPTK* I, 369; Monnier, *Alcuin,* 16f. With regard to Alcuin as deacon, it must be remembered that in early mediaeval days the diaconate held in itself high importance and responsibility of administration.

words, that Bede had been before him. Within his religion two intense forces played upon him: the need to teach, to help, to inspire, and the need to make and keep friendships, wherever he went. Behind both these motives lies personal attachment, and to one who has read his Letters it may well seem that in his desire to fulfil what he believed to be his own vocation, he shrank from taking upon himself responsibilities, however excellent in themselves, which might hinder his free progress along his allotted path.

He could and did exercise authority among the great of his time in England and on the continent, in State and in Church. He spoke boldly amid the constant crises of his century, dealing rebuke and counsel to king and archbishop, noble and commoner, wherever he judged there was evil or weakness in word or in act. Of course he enjoyed immensely his standing in his world, religious, intellectual, social, the throngs who called him "Father," the confidence of kings and queens, of prelates and statesmen, of monks and soldiers, of ordinary men and women, in the words he so readily offered them. But behind all can be felt in him now and again a hint of an inner uncertainty, of a lack of confidence in himself and his standing, which rarely allowed him to rest tranquil and secure, which gives a touch of truth in his case to the conventional expressions of humility so natural to the writers of mediaeval days.

One of the first cares of Aelbert as Chief Pastor of the diocese and Province of York was the rebuilding of his Cathedral. This work he placed in charge of his former students, Eanbald and Alcuin. When all was finished, the church stood supported by lofty, massive pillars and arches; windows and ceiling recalled the beauty of Ripon and of Jarrow. In galleries high above the aisles, like those at Hexham, and also on the ground floor were side-chapels, with as many as thirty altars, richly arrayed. At the place where King Edwin had received baptism, a hundred and forty years before, Aelbert raised an altar of silver and gold, shining with jewels; it was blessed in the name of Saint Paul, "teacher of the world, whom Aelbert, also a teacher, loved exceedingly." Above this altar he hung lamps, arranged in symmetrical order, and raised high near it "the standard of the Cross," also covered with precious metals. Another altar of like dignity he dedicated in honour of the Holy Cross and various martyrs; on it he set an ampulla of pure gold, from which the priest of the Mass should pour wine into the chalice.[71]

No more fitting teacher and administrator than his former pupil could have been found by Archbishop Aelbert for the School of York. A few names stand out from the multitude that looked back upon Alcuin there as father and guide in their young years of study. There was a younger Eanbald, who was called by him affectionately "Simeon," and was in his thought, sometimes with anxiety, to the hour Alcuin died.[72] Another Anglo-Saxon, Sigulf, received the nickname of "Vetulus." He was well trained under the direction of his uncle, a priest of Northumbria named Autbert, who not only took young Sigulf from their native England to Frankland, but also to Rome, to study Roman rites and ritual, and to Metz, "for the sake of its song," as a pupil in the famous School of Church music established there by Bishop Chrodegang. In Metz the two travellers suffered much hardship; at length, after his uncle had died, Sigulf returned to York, was made *custos* of its Cathedral,[73] and became one of Alcuin's most intimate friends. Two other

[71] *Versus de Sanctis*, ll. 1489ff.; Clapham, *Eng. Roman. Archit. before the Conquest*, 1930, 47, 73; Benson, *York from its origin to the end of the eleventh century*, 1911, 31f.

[72] *Epp.* IV, 167, 170, 347; Sym. Dun. II, 58; pages 296ff. *infra.*

[73] *Alcuini Vita*, 184, 189. As *custos* he probably had charge of the sacred property. Hauck, however, explains: "Seelsorgepriester an der Metropolitankirche": II, 151.

natives of England whose names appear in Alcuin's letters, Calvinus and Credulus, may also have been his students in York.[74]

Others came from different nationality. The Irish Joseph was to work and to write in Frankland after he had learned to do both in York; Joseph's Irish teacher, Colcu, seems for a while to have lived and taught there.[75] Especially dear to Alcuin was Liudger, who came from Frisia. His family knew and loved Saint Boniface and Saint Willibrord, and his parents had sent him to learn from Gregory, abbot of Saint Martin's in Utrecht and leader in the Frisian Church. There Liudger was professed as monk. Then one day there arrived at Saint Martin's a young Englishman, Alubert, eager to help in its work of converting the ignorant. Abbot Gregory was delighted. Utrecht and its mission and monastery needed badly a bishop. Gregory himself did not aspire to this office. After some time of probation, therefore, he called Alubert to be his bishop, and Alubert, accompanied by Liudger and another older monk, named Sigibod, crossed the Channel and travelled to York to ask consecration at Aelbert's hands.[76]

In 767 this was given him, and he was appointed "bishop of the Old Saxons." [77] Moreover, Sigibod was ordained as priest, Liudger as deacon, and all three remained a year in York to learn from Alcuin. Then, to Abbot Gregory's joy, they returned to Utrecht, and Alubert threw himself zealously into his episcopal mission. Liudger, however, yearned for the Library and his teacher in England; soon he was begging to be allowed to return. After much persuasion this was granted, and

[74] *Epp.* IV, 346, 379; *PLAC* I, 266.

[75] *Epp.* IV, 32, 34. That this Colcu was head of Clonmacnoise (*DCB* s.v. Colga (1); cf. Gaskoin, 55, and Waddell, *Wand. Schol.* 33) is held uncertain by Kenney, 534, note 104.

[76] Altfrid, *Vita S. Liudgeri*: *SS* II, 406f.; Liudger, *Vita Gregorii abb. Traiect.*: *SS* XV, i, 75.

[77] Sym. Dun. II, 43.

he spent a longer stay, of three years and six months, in complete content among Alcuin's scholars. But unkind necessity intervened. Hostilities broke out between men of Yorkshire and raiders from the continent; the son of a noble family was killed by a Frisian trader, and all Frisian settlers fled from Northumbria in terror of vengeance. Liudger was promptly despatched back to Utrecht in charge of a deacon, Pyttel, who was told to make sure he did go there, instead of slipping away alone to carry on his beloved studies in some other part of England. Fortunately Liudger was well educated by this time and brought with him an abundance of books. Abbot Gregory was only too glad to have his aid. His escort, Pyttel, relieved of his uneasy task, went happily on pilgrimage to Rome before returning to his duties in York.[78]

For a while the history of Northumbria progressed peacefully for Alcuin and his School. Much interest was aroused in 767 by the death of a hermit, Echa or Etha, who had lived his lonely life of devotion at Crayke, twelve miles north of York, near Easingwold, and was famous for power of prophecy.[79] The next year another recluse died—King Eadbert, in his retreat at Aelbert's Cathedral. He was buried beside his brother Egbert in one of its "porches" or chapels.[80] About the same time King Alchred married Osgearn, known also as Osgeofu; a letter is still extant from this royal pair to Lul, bishop of Mainz, written to ask the prayers of the Church in Germany for themselves and their friends, of whom they enclose a list. They send also gifts—twelve woollen cloaks and a gold ring.[81]

[78] Altfrid, *SS* II, 407f.

[79] *Versus,* ll. 1387ff.; Sym. Dun. II, 43. Cf. Alcuin's narrative of the anchorite Balthere who fought demons in his retreat at Tyninghame in East Lothian: *Versus,* ll. 1318ff.; Sym. Dun. I, 48; *DCB* I, 240f. (Stubbs).

[80] Sym. Dun. II, 44; I, 49.

[81] *Epp.* III, 410; H.S. III, 434.

Letters, too, went across the water as token of sympathy between Lul and Aelbert. Lul writes from the midst of "affronts and tribulations" in Germany to beg his fellow-bishop in York to remember the tie of friendship between them: "Daily the Church here suffers blows, oppression, weariness; for the princes of our time bring about new ways, new laws, after their own desires." He sends to Aelbert a pall of pure silk of the very best quality; would the Archbishop send him for the solace of his pilgrim's exile some of the writings of Bede? It is, indeed, a great thing to ask; but, then, in true affection nothing is grievous. And would the Church in York be mindful of Lul's brethren and friends in Germany who have departed this life? A list of their names is enclosed. Another time he asks for books on natural science, and Aelbert answers: "You asked me about the tides of the sea and their action on the soil—nothing can be ascertained about this, and all is uncertain. The books on cosmography have not yet come to hand. . . ."[82]

Another link with the mission on the continent was forged when about 770 King Alchred and Archbishop Aelbert called their bishops and abbots, together with secular leaders of the State, to a Council to bless and approve one, Willehad, departing to carry on the ministry of Willibrord among the Frisians. The event was of particular interest to Alcuin, for Willehad, like himself, was related to Willibrord's family, and, indeed, a cousin of his own. The young candidate for work overseas had received an excellent education in Northumbria and had already been ordained priest. His life abroad was to be marked by many adventures, leading in turn to a bishop's stool and a Feast in the calendar of Saints.[83]

[82] *Epp.* III, 413f., 412f.

[83] Anskar, *Vita S. Willehadi*: *SS* II, 380 (see also ed. Langebek, *Script. rer. Dan. med. aev.* I, 342ff.); H.S. III, 433. Hauck (II, 362) suggests that he was trained under Egbert.

In 774 the calm was suddenly broken. During Eastertide, which he was keeping in York, Alchred was forced by his household and nobles to flee for his life, first to Bamburgh, and afterward to Kenneth, King of the Picts. The victorious rebels then placed the crown of Northumbria upon the head of Ethelred, son of Ethelwald Moll. But his power was constantly threatened, and he held it only by acts of violence. In the second year of his reign one of his chieftains, Eadwulf, was treacherously taken by him and put to death; three years later three more of his nobles, Ealdwulf, Cynewulf, and Ecga, were also betrayed and killed by his express orders, through his constant fear of revolution. Revolt did quickly follow. In 779 this king, also, was driven into "the sad ways" of exile, and Elfwald, son of Oswulf and grandson of Eadbert, received his throne.[84]

For a while the land once more had rest from turmoil. Elfwald has come down in history as "a just and righteous" king. But the troubles of Northumbria had taken their toll of stress in Archbishop Aelbert's mind; no wonder that often he had told his students to beware of further sorrows surely to come.[85] It would be good, he had thought more and more, to end his days in cloistered peace, as King Eadbert had done, within his own Cathedral precincts. His successors were ready at his hand, his own sons in the Lord, prepared for high responsibility under him in his own School. At last the thought had ripened into decision. In 778 he had resigned his Cathedral and his see of York, to which the elder Eanbald was elected as his successor; to Alcuin, now in the later forties, he had given full charge of its School and Library.[86]

[84] Sym. Dun. II, 45ff.

[85] *Epp.* IV, 171.

[86] *Versus,* ll. 1520ff., 1562ff. Cf. Sym. Dun. II, 47; Earle and Plummer II, 52; Raine, *DCB* II, 218; *HCY* II, 336; Dümmler, *NA* XVIII, 55; *PLAC* I, 204; Gaskoin, 56. Aelbert himself had received the pallium from Pope Hadrian I in 773; Sym. Dun. II, 45.

The years following were perhaps the most eventful of Alcuin's life. Their significance reached its height when he was sent by King Elfwald to ask from the Pope the granting of the pallium, in official confirmation of the metropolitan dignity for York and for his friend, its Archbishop Eanbald. The petition was readily granted. On his way back, shortly before Easter, 781, he fell in with Charles, King of the Franks, at Parma. It was not their first meeting, for at some earlier time—we cannot tell when or why—Aelbert had sent Alcuin to Frankland on a mission to Charles,[87] and the thought of this youth from York had stayed with the King, awaiting future need.

Now, in 781, this King was full of energetic purpose for his family and his nation. Alcuin's scholarly repute was known far and wide. What better man could Charles call to head the School attached to his Court in his royal house, at Aachen or wherever it might stay? Or to develop all those plans of education for his people, now simmering in his mind?

But Alcuin had held himself devoted to England and to York. His arguments to this end only sharpened the King's desire, and he persisted, until Alcuin was almost persuaded that, whereas in York the harvest was far advanced, in Frankland but few sowers were to be found, and these lacked for their hands the grain of learning, of experience and of encouragement. Charles, too, was a man and ruler after Alcuin's own heart. His aim as King of the Franks was the conversion of the barbarians and heathen under his dominion to the Catholic Faith, and the use of secular knowledge for this end. He had already despatched Willehad to teach and to baptize the Saxons living between the Weser and the Elbe. Now a master was needed to organize and promote at headquarters the training of missionaries and scholars who were to go forth in streams to

[87] *Alc. Vita: SS* XV, i, 190, c. 9. Cf. page 71 *infra* and note 75.

call into the Church all whom Charles, the Christian monarch, should increasingly gather under his sway. Such was the royal dream; with Alcuin as fellow-worker, surely it would become reality.[88]

The vision appealed also to Northumbria; Eanbald and Elfwald could not refuse. Nor in the end could Alcuin himself. After long and anxious debate his long life in York drew near its end, and he found himself making ready to follow Willehad across the Channel to new life and work in a foreign land. The decision had doubtless been made easier for him by the death of his beloved master, Aelbert, two years and two months after his retiring from office. Ten days before he died he came out from his cell to join with Eanbald in dedicating "to nurturing Wisdom" the cathedral he had loved and lived in so long, now finished in all its glory.[89]

Many of the hours that still remained to Alcuin in England he spent in trying to describe his feeling for this man from whom he had inherited the principle which dominated all his life; that learning, however delightful in itself, is the handmaid of even a nobler art, of teaching—*disce ut doceas.* Under him he had watched the gradual growth of the best library in the Europe of his time. In him he had seen an ideal of a life of simplicity, hard work, and devotion. All of this he summed up in the lines of his *Epitaph for Aelbert,* a poem of fourteen elegiacs:

Euborica doctor celebri praeclarus in urbe,
Qui semper sophiae magnus amator erat.[90]

It was probably also in these last days at York that he wrote two other compositions in verse. One looks back upon his past life in England, and is called *Verses on the Saints of the Church*

[88] H. Bastgen, *HJ* XXXII, 1911, 811. [89] *Versus,* ll. 1517ff.
[90] *PLAC* I, 206; cf. *Versus,* ll. 1562ff.

of York. It is a long poem of 1657 hexameter lines telling of the great men of York's history in Church and State. Most of its content is drawn from Bede; and its interest and value lie only in the last part, which is concerned with the men and events Alcuin himself had known.[91] The other poem looks forward to the future. Its eighty-one lines, also in hexameters, are written to remember and to greet in affectionate play men who had become his friends during his recent stay on the continent.[92] It is, in fact, a little letter which traces again the journey of its writer. In Utrecht it salutes Alberic, nephew of Abbot Gregory of St. Martin's Monastery, now abbot himself, and also bishop of Utrecht. He seems to be enjoying life, Alcuin hints, calling him "lord of many cows," well supplied with butter and honey by his Prior, Haddo.[93] Other bishops each receive remembrance as the letter goes on its way: Riculf of Cologne, Lul of Mainz, Bassinus of Speyer. Two places call for special notice. Along the Moselle greeting travels from Alcuin to the monastery founded near Trier by Willibrord, Echternach, dear retreat of Boniface. There the Anglo-Saxon Beornred—"Samuel," as Alcuin chose to call him—was now abbot, cousin both to Willibrord and to Alcuin himself, possibly at one time Alcuin's student in York.[94] Most important of all, the letter renders due reverence to Charles at his Court at Aachen, and, only in less measure, to the teachers already gathered there by the King, especially the Italians: Peter, that learned scholar of Pisa, and Paulinus, soon to be Patriarch of Aquileia.[95] Rado, also, Chancellor of Charles, must have his share of gay salutation. If, however, any of these learned men try

[91] *PLAC* I, 162, 169ff.; Jaffé, *Mon Alc.*, 80ff.; Raine, *HCY* I, 349ff.
[92] *PLAC* I, 220ff.; Levison, 165; Gaskoin, 55f.
[93] Hauck II, 177, and 48, note 4.
[94] *Epp.* IV, 133; *PLAC* I, 228, 239; *SS* XIII, 738, 740; Dümmler, *NA* XVIII, 56.
[95] Manitius, 452ff., 368ff.

to snap at Alcuin with the tooth of envy—and here, perhaps, is a thought of Alcuin's future days among them—Charles, Alcuin already knows, will give ready protection to this new member of his Palace School.[96] Lastly, the verses seek out Abbot Fulrad in his famous house of St. Denis near Paris. Fulrad, too, was well-known. As chief of clerics at Pepin's court he had put the great question to Pope Zacharias in 750: "What hinders Pepin, who is king in power, from becoming king in name?" To him Boniface had written in his last days to beg his care for the English missionaries in Frankland. Fulrad was Archchaplain for Charles himself and surely a man most meet for honour.

In this way the last months slipped by, and the time came for farewell to York. Not yet, however, in permanence. Alcuin left the door still open for his return, if life under Charles should not prove to be his destiny. It was now in or about the year 782, and he was about fifty years old.

[96] *PLAC* I, 222, ll. 40f.; Gaskoin, 56. For Rado see Sickel, *Acta Karol.* I, 78ff.

Chapter II

CONTINENTAL BACKGROUND

717–782

CHAPTER II

CONTINENTAL BACKGROUND, 717–782

I

THE HISTORY of the eighth century on the continent of Europe is marked by four developments of primary importance: the iconoclastic strife and its influence upon the alienation of East from West, of the Constantinople of the Emperors from the Rome of the Popes; the final passing from the Byzantine Empire of that dominion over Italy won in the sixth century by the generals of Justinian and exercised since that time in constantly decreasing measure by Imperial Exarchs, or Governors; the growth of temporal power and sovereignty in the hands of the Popes of Rome; the gradual binding into even firmer alliance of the Papal State and the kings of the Franks. Each of these developments was to play its part in shaping the thought and action of Alcuin under Charles the Great. It will be well, therefore, to consider briefly their progress previous to the year of his arrival at the Frankish Court.

The Emperor reigning in the East at Constantinople when Alcuin was a child in the Cathedral School of York was Leo the third, commonly called "the Isaurian," but very possibly of Syrian birth.[1] Unfortunately for the unprejudiced historian our information concerning him and his son and successor comes very largely from authorities who could see little good in him and none in his son. Such were two Byzantine historians: Theophanes, "the Confessor," abbot, Saint of both the Greek and Roman calendars, active in administration under Leo's

[1] Vasiliev I, 333ff.

son in this eighth century;[2] and Nicephorus,[3] also Saint of both East and West, and Patriarch of Constantinople, 806–815. Other writers were equally hostile, men who wrote to condemn Imperial iconoclasm and to glorify the martyrs of its rage.

Modern scholarship, however, has seen something to relieve this prevailing blackness.[4] Leo was, above all, as man and ruler, a worker of reform, following his own conscience and beliefs to the end, bitter as it might be, and justifying the means by this end. He therefore threw himself wholeheartedly into administration. Whether the three official books on law as established in various Imperial departments of government—the Rural Code, the Military Code, the Maritime Code—actually belong to Leo's reign is a disputed question. But undoubtedly he did reorganize legal workings in his Empire, and most students of this time attribute to his activity both these codes and the careful re-editing of the laws of Justinian issued under the name of *Ecloga,* "the Selection." His aim in this, he states, was to bring legislation throughout his dominions more into accord with Christian and humane principles. Through the taxes and levying of census needed to finance his administration he earned for himself a comparison with Pharaoh in his treatment of the Egyptians;[5] yet undoubtedly he left Constantinople functioning far more efficiently than under the long disorder of previous Emperors. Moreover, he defended this same capital city well and ably from the Arabs in the critical

[2] See bibliography, s.v. Theophanes. [3] *Ibid.* s.v. Nicephorus.

[4] See, especially, Louis Bréhier (Fliche-Martin V, 431ff., and *Le Monde byzantin* I, 1947, 75ff.); Bury, *Hist. lat. Rom. Empire* I–II, 1889; *CMH* IV (Diehl, Brooks, Collinet); *DACL* s.v. *Images* (Leclercq); *DTC* s.v. *Iconoclasme* (Emereau); C. H. Diehl, *Hist. of the Byz. Empire,* trans. Ives, 1925; Diehl and G. Marçais (Glotz, *Hist. du Moyen Age* III, 1936, 249ff.); J. L. LaMonte, *The World of the Middle Ages,* 1949, 122ff.; G. Ostrogorsky, *Gesch. des byz. Staates,* 1940, 103ff.

[5] Theophanes, 410; Collinet, *CMH* IV, 708ff.

siege which marked the beginning of his rule, and continued sturdily throughout his reign to resist Saracen attacks in different parts of his Empire.[6]

So much should briefly be noted before we read the horrid tale of his iconoclastic onslaught. And even here we must pause a moment to remember that the cult of images in the East had so greatly deepened by this time that people in their multitudes were bowing before icons and statues numberless; that of these multitudes a formidable part scarcely thought to distinguish between the saint and the earthly likeness; that visits of veneration and worship formed a necessary act of faith to countless Christian hearts and minds; and that monks, both cloistered and roaming, whose name was legion and whose power over pilgrims was unmeasured, depended very largely for the existence of themselves and their shrines upon the offerings of the devout.

Within these elements, in these stormy, unsettled days, lay potential revolution. This aspect of the matter Leo so constantly bore in mind that his religious persecutions were often linked with fear of political manoeuvre. If we add to this the thought that he had been brought up in Asia Minor among people of fierce Monophysite or Paulician traditions, that both he and his son were eager for the conversion of their subjects from widespread error, as they judged it, and firmly believed that theology and matters of Church law and doctrine lay *ex officio* within the province of the Emperor, that they were both of extremely practical temperament and abhorred extravagance in any form, we shall understand something in regard to the soil from which their persecutions sprang—persecutions, it may finally be said, aimed rather at the mockery than at the destruction of their victims.

[6] Theophanes, 395ff., 405f.; Nicephorus, 52ff.; Brooks, *CMH* IV, 119ff.

Leo had come to the throne in 717, and it was not until 726, nine years later, that he broke out openly into campaign against the veneration of sacred statues and pictures. Our historians tell that in the summer of this year a dark, ominous vapour as from a fiery furnace had seethed up from the depths of the Aegean Sea between the isles of Thera and Therasia; that after some days its smoke had turned to flame and had rained pumice-stones over ocean and shore as far as Macedonia and Lesbos and the coast of Asia Minor. The Emperor had seen in this awful manifestation a mark of Divine wrath.[7] He, therefore, "had stirred up the shameless war against the holy and august images, having Beser, the denier of God, to spur him on with equal folly." Beser had once been a Christian slave in Syria, but had become a convert to Arab doctrines and, according to Theophanes, had won Leo's favour through his fierce enthusiasm for image-breaking. The Emperor's action bore instant fruit. Immediately, from among the people of Constantinople, always ready for violent argument on matters of religion, many rose in riot; their leaders even beat to death officials who were taking down the image of Christ above the door of the Chalke, the great entrance to the Imperial Palace. Punishment followed quickly, in fines and banishment and mutilation, according to the barbarous manner of the time; even the schools of learning were closed, lest scholars might be found aiding and abetting the people. But popular resentment soon spread to Greece and the isles of the Cyclades, where in rebellion men shouted "Down with Leo" and proclaimed one, Cosmas, as Emperor. In April, 727, they arrived with a fleet to capture Constantinople itself, but were beaten off by flame-throwers from Leo's arsenal, and the survivors soon yielded.[8]

[7] Theophanes, 404f.; Nicephorus, 57; Ostrogorsky, *Gesch.* 108.
[8] Theophanes, 405; Nicephorus, 57f.

Meanwhile officialdom itself within the Empire did not lack courage for rebuke. John of Damascus, high in the administrative government of Syria, was hurling his reasoned arguments against the Imperial wickedness: "It were good that I kept silence toward men and spoke only to confess my sins to God. But how keep silence when the Church of God is tossed in the storms of evil spirits? Even against the Emperor will I speak, to quell his seductive power. . . . Should a man enter a house and behold upon its walls the story of Moses and Pharaoh in picture, and should he ask, 'Who are these who walked through the sea as if on dry land?' Would you not answer, 'The children of Israel'? 'Who is he who struck the source with a rod?' Shall he not be told, 'Moses'? And likewise, if any one shall paint the picture of Christ Crucified, and shall be asked, 'Who is this?'—shall he not answer, 'Christ the Lord, made flesh for us men'? Even so, Lord, all things that are Thine we adore, and, as we fear to touch red-hot iron, not for the nature of iron, but for the fire that holds it, so do we adore Thy Body, not for the nature of flesh, but for the Godhead united with Thy Humanity. We adore Thy Passion. Yet who ever saw death adored? Who has ever deemed tortures worthy of worship? Yet we adore the death of God in the flesh—we adore all things, O Lord, that are Thine—ministers, friends, above all, Thy Divine Mother. And so we beseech the people of God, the holy race, that they cling more nearly to the uses of the Church. For, truly, the forsaking of traditions, once begun, little by little destroys the whole fabric, as stones that are one by one drawn from a building. God grant that we abide, steadfast and unmoved, founded upon that rock which is Christ." [9]

Before long the Emperor came into open conflict with

[9] *Oratio apologetica prior: PG* XCIV, coll. 1232f., 1281, 1284. See *RPTK* IX, 286ff., *Johannes von Damaskus* (Kattenbusch).

Germanus, Patriarch of Constantinople, aided in secret by the treachery of Anastasius, the Patriarch's *syncellus,* an official who combined the duties of private secretary and chaplain. Leo had tried conciliating measures at first, and Germanus, we read, had hoped for peace in his time. "The destruction of the holy images," he is said to have told the Emperor, "will take place, men declare, but not under your reign." And when Leo asked him, in whose reign? "In the reign of Conon," he answered. "But my name, as given in baptism, *is* Conon," replied the Emperor. Thereafter Germanus knew the worst. In January, 730, Leo called an assembly in Constantinople to denounce this cult of images, and summoned the Patriarch to attend. Germanus promptly resigned his office, declaring: "If I am Jonah, then throw me into the sea. For no change dare I make in the doctrine of the Church, save in obedience to an Ecumenical Council of the same." Then he retired to live in retreat for the rest of his life upon his family estate, and Anastasius, an eager iconoclast, was appointed Patriarch in his place.[10]

If Leo the third, however, smote the devout of his Empire with whips, his son, who succeeded him as Constantine the fifth upon his death in 741, undoubtedly lashed them with scorpions. In turn, the fury evoked from the orthodox by his warfare against their piety knew no bounds of language. Foul nicknames were hinted against this "most godless son, heir of evil, forerunner of Antichrist, dwelling from childhood in all pursuits that destroy the soul." [11]

Yet he, too, was brave and able. He put down with a firm hand the insurrection that in 741–742 attacked his throne and city. He conquered again and again the Arabs and Bulgars who rose from defeat to ravage his Empire. In 747 he led his

[10] Theophanes, 406ff.; Nicephorus, 58; Bréhier, V, 454, note 3.
[11] Theophanes, 399f., 412f.

people with skill and energy through the horrors of epidemic plague within Constantinople and Greece. He left the Imperial finances in order and the Imperial treasury in ample funds, even if he earned the description of a "new Midas, who heaped away gold, stripped bare the farmers, and drove men by taxation to sell cheap the appurtenances of God." [12]

For a long time he was busy with the barbarian invaders who called him away from Constantinople, and contented his conscience by "preparing the way for future action." At last, however, having made successful progress against the Egyptians and the Saracens, having secured the loyalty of his soldiers and settled his rule upon a lasting basis, he felt free to turn his mind to religion. Soon he assembled a synod of three hundred and thirty-eight bishops from various parts of his Empire in the Palace of Hieria on the Asiatic side of the Bosphorus.[13] It met in 754,[14] and sat from February until August. No representative of Rome, or Alexandria, or Antioch, or Jerusalem was present, and no Patriarch of Constantinople during the first months of its session, as Anastasius had lately died, "body and soul, in piteous sickness." Finally the Emperor declared one Constantine, bishop of Sylaeum, as Patriarch, after the assembly had moved across the water to Blachernae, suburb of Constantinople. On the 29th of August the fruit of this long conference was revealed to the public. In the Name of the Holy Trinity, on the authority of Holy Scripture and of the Fathers of the Church, the assembled bishops condemned absolutely every image of every sort, with degradation for any in sacred order and excommunication for any monk or lay person who should dare to make, venerate, or place such image in church or house, or even secretly possess

[12] Theophanes, 417ff., 422ff., 443; Nicephorus, 59ff., 62ff.
[13] Theophanes, 427f.; Nicephorus, 65f.
[14] Ostrogorsky, *Gesch.* 117; Bréhier, V, 468.

the same. The law of the State, moreover, was to be brought into action against transgressors with as firm a hand as the penalty decreed by the Church.[15]

War with the Bulgars now again turned the Emperor's attention elsewhere, and for some time retribution moved slowly. But ten years later, when victory had repeatedly brought relief, the tide of persecution rose high, and Constantine "raged in fury against every one who feared God." Ribald insult and torture, maiming and violent death, were the destiny of the faithful, and of these martyrs there were many, even if there were found some, "seduced by deceit or flattery, enticed by bribes or offers of distinguished office, who renounced their holy profession and habit and appeared in long hair instead of shaven, who became familiar with women and lived with them." [16] Conspicuous among the enduring was Saint Stephen the Younger, abbot of the monastery on the Mount of Saint Auxentius in Bithynia, who was first cast into exile for two years on the island of Proconnesus in the Sea of Marmora, then dragged by ropes through the streets of Constantinople, then torn to pieces by the excited mob, now veering to the Emperor's cause.[17] Suspicion of disloyalty soon forced the Patriarch Constantine himself to mount the ambo of Saint Sophia and swear upon the wood of the Holy Cross that he was not of those who worshipped paintings. Nonetheless, rumours continued to reach the Emperor's ears from secret sources; the unhappy prelate was dethroned, banished, brought back to the city, beaten until he could not walk, enthroned in mockery in Saint Sophia, while an Imperial Secretary read aloud a long list of his misdeeds and struck him a blow on the face at every detail. Meanwhile Nicetas, a

[15] The decisions of this Council are known from the records of the Seventh Ecumenical Council in 787, which refuted them: Mansi XIII, 203–364; Hefele-Leclercq III, 2, 693ff.

[16] Theophanes, 436; Nicephorus, 71f.

[17] *Vita: PG* C, coll. 1145, 1176f.; Theophanes, 436f.

eunuch, who had been appointed Patriarch in defiance of canon law, sat and looked on. The next day the ex-Patriarch, riding on an ass with his face toward its tail, and more dead than alive, was publicly exposed to the insults of the people in the Hippodrome. Finally his head was cut off and stuck high upon the pillar of the Milion and his mutilated body thrown into the graveyard of criminals and suicides.[18]

The lowly suffered with the great throughout the Empire. Monks were compelled to walk amid the jeering crowds of Constantinople, holding each a nun by the hand. In Asia Minor an Imperial governor, "imitating his teacher," gathered the monks and nuns in his district into a public square and bade them choose between marriage on the spot, or blindness and exile. Many chose the latter fate. To this zealous official the Emperor wrote in congratulation: "I have found a man after my own heart." No wonder that many hastened to do likewise.[19]

In 775 Constantine died, leaving his son to rule as Leo the fourth. "For a short time he seemed to be pious, reverent toward the Mother of God and toward monks." He allowed high office in the Church to men of religious vocation, and gained goodwill from the people at large by generous gifts from that Imperial treasury so amply filled by his father. Always of frail health, he reigned only until 780, and toward the end he, too, "laid bare his hidden wickedness" in action against the sacred pictures and those who reverenced them.[20] At his death he left a woman, his wife, upon the throne, as co-ruler with their son, Constantine the sixth.

And now the Imperial hatred of images turns suddenly to reverence. The Empress, Irene, had come from Athens, brought up among the Greeks, a people who loved paintings

[18] Theophanes, 437ff., 441f.; Nicephorus, 75.

[19] Theophanes, 437, 445f.; Nicephorus, 74. It must always be remembered, however, that these narratives come to us from the opposition.

[20] Theophanes, 449, 453.

and statues of the saints and bitterly resented the iconoclastic scourging. She had received, moreover, an excellent education, and her loyalty to her faith and Church was exceeded only by her hungry craving for personal power and dominance.[21] Future news from Constantinople, as Alcuin drew to the end of his life in York, promised to be of unusual interest.

2

For a very long time before this eighth century the rift had been widening between Rome, old and new: the Rome of the Popes in the west and the Constantinople of the Emperors and Patriarchs in the east. In the fifth century the Monophysite heresy and the *Henoticon* of the Emperor Zeno had sown bitter seed of dissension between them. In the sixth century the struggle concerning the "Three Chapters" under the Emperor Justinian and the humiliation of Pope Vigilius had drawn them wide apart. The assuming of the title of "Universal Bishop" by the Patriarch of Constantinople had led to long and strenuous remonstrances from Pope Gregory the Great. During the seventh century theological differences in the Monothelete strife had brought insult and a death in exile to Pope Martin the fifth, and the canons of the Council *in Trullo* had threatened, though in vain, a like fate for Sergius the first.

On the political side forces were also active in alienation. When the Emperor Leo the third began his reign in 717, the encroachments of the Lombards had left to him as ruler of Italy dominion over the "Exarchate" of Ravenna, with the duchy of Perusia, the Aemilia, and the Pentapolis,[22] in the

[21] Diehl, *Byz. Portraits,* trans. Bell, 1927, 79ff.

[22] For the Pentapolis see Diehl, *Etudes sur l'administration byz. dans l'Exarchat de Ravenne* (*568–751*), 1888, 61; Bury, *Later Rom. Emp.* II, 146, note 4; for the Aemilia, Diehl, *ibid.,* 57; T. Hodgkin VII, 223.

region bordering the northeastern shore; over Venice and Istria and neighbouring towns; over the duchies of Naples and of Calabria in the south. Over Rome and its duchy he exercised nominal power, although in practice this lay under the control of the Pope. Indeed, the Papal jurisdiction in Italy had been steadily increasing since the days of the first Pope Gregory, through the necessity of daily grappling with problems rising from Lombard aggression and from the administration of vast lands and revenues of the Church. Even the Lombards were now devout Catholics, and as such came under the spiritual authority of the see of Rome. The responsibility of the Popes was by far greater on account of lack of aid from Constantinople; the Emperors in the East were hard beset by the ever-recurring inroads of barbarians, and Italy had to think for herself.

The Lombard kingdom held the north and northwest, with Pavia as capital; it included the regions called Austria, Neustria, and Tuscia [23] to the north of the duchy of Rome. In the centre and south the great duchies of Spoletium and Beneventum were of independent Lombard origin, and struggled mightily and long with varying success to maintain their liberty.

Pope Gregory the second, who had ruled the Holy See since 715, was possessed of prudence and sagacity. He was most deeply concerned in the conversion of barbarians, especially under Boniface in Germany. In Italy he was prepared to acknowledge the suzerainty of Constantinople and the justice of tribute in the form of taxes, paid to the Imperial treasury by Italy as part of the Empire controlled from the East. But he was equally ready to defend his land from tyranny, and when Leo, driven by need of money for the financing of his military campaigns, assessed his Italian subjects in heavy sur-

[23] T. Hodgkin VI, 393, note 1.

tax, the Pope promptly forbade its payment.[24] This resistance on his part was naturally reinforced by the news of the action against images followed by Leo from 726 onward.[25]

The veneration of sacred pictures and statues had never caused in Italy the difficulty encountered in the East. The people of the West, in their more uniform faith and discipline, were not prone to become excited, man against man, in theological controversy as were those dwelling on the shores of the Bosphorus. Moreover, deeply as they reverenced their holy symbols, their practical character and temperament did not understand the natural familiarity of the East with extreme manifestations of obeisance toward persons and things. The feeling in the West had been well expressed in letters of Pope Gregory the Great to Serenus, bishop of Marseilles: "I have heard, my brother, that lately, on seeing certain persons adoring images in your churches, you broke these images and threw them away. Certainly I praise your zeal that nothing made by hand be adored. But you should not have broken those images. Pictures are placed in our churches in order that people who cannot read may learn from gazing upon the walls what they cannot get from books. It is your business to keep such images for the instruction of the ignorant, and to keep your people from sinful adoration of the same. . . . It is one thing to adore a picture, and another to learn from it what should rightly be adored." [26]

Revolt, thus encouraged by the head of the Church, spread throughout the Imperial dominion in Italy. Not only did Pope Gregory the second write in severe censure to Leo, but the people rose in quick wrath, first against undue taxation, then

[24] *Lib. Pont.* I, 403. Cf. 412, note 27, and Bury II, 441, note 1; T. G. Jalland, *The Church and the Papacy,* 1944, 368f.

[25] Theophanes, 404.

[26] Gregory, *Epp.* II, ed. Hartmann, 195, 269ff.

against the offence to their religion. Basil, duke of the territory of Rome, was driven out and compelled to become a monk. Feeling was intensified when rumours spread that the life of the Pope was in danger from Imperial agents. The towns of the Pentapolis and of the region of Venice united in resistance; much of Imperial Italy passed to the rule of the Lombard king, Liutprand; officials of the Emperor were banished or killed, including Paul, Exarch of Ravenna. The threat of Leo, conveyed by an Imperial messenger, that he would depose the Pope unless submission were forthcoming, only evoked further rebuke from Gregory. It was, however, due to the Pope's influence over secular politics that the proposal to elect an emperor in Italy and lead him to replace Leo at Constantinople was quelled. Resentful Italians were now throwing themselves and their towns into the hands of the Lombards; but to Gregory's mind, of the two evils, government from Constantinople was to be preferred to an Italy under Lombard rule.[27]

The expelling of Germanus from the Patriarchate of Constantinople and the appointment in his place of Anastasius, supporter of iconoclasm, led to even more energetic condemnation from Rome. Anastasius was no brother bishop of the Church, wrote the Pope in his anger, and, unless he yielded to Catholic ruling, was to be deposed forthwith.[28]

Nor did resistance from Italy grow less energetic under the third Gregory, who succeeded to the Papal See in 731. Before the year ended, he held in Saint Peter's a synod of ninety-three bishops, with priests and other clerics, secular nobles, and representatives of the people. Here he solemnly declared excommunication from the Church as the penalty for

[27] *Lib. Pont.* I, 404ff.; Paul. Diac. *Hist. Lang.* VI, c. 49. For the letters of Gregory II see G. B. Ladner, *MSPI* II, 1940, 130, note 16; Ostrogorsky, *Gesch.* 99 and note 5; Starr, *Byzantium* XV (Amer. Series I), 1941, 488f.; Caspar, *ZKG* LII, 1933, 29ff.

[28] *Lib. Pont.* I, 409.

all who should depose or destroy, insult or profane, the sacred likenesses of our Lord, His Holy Mother, or His saints.[29] In retaliation Leo not only arrested and kept in prison messenger after messenger bearing to him the Pope's reprimands, but in his rage assembled and despatched a Greek fleet to reduce to obedience this obstinate rebel, as he held him. When this, too, failed, and the fleet was wrecked in the Adriatic, the Imperial "enemy of God" imposed fresh taxes on southern Italy and Sicily. Moreover, he transferred the churches of these regions from the keeping of Rome to that of the Patriarch of Constantinople, and the revenues of Papal patrimonies in the south of Italy to his Imperial treasury. This, together with the enormous influx of Greek refugees from the persecutions of Leo and his son, Constantine the fifth, made the south once again into a "Greater Greece," to the loss of Papal influence and holding.[30]

A lull followed under the next Pope, Zacharias. He was remarkably able in dealing with international problems, and during his rule in Rome the Emperor Constantine the fifth was busy in beating down barbarian invasions of Imperial lands. In the time of Zacharias' successor, Stephen the second, elected in 752, matters came to a twofold climax. The Lombard King was now Aistulf. He was making ready to invade Papal territory. Immediate aid was necessary, and the government at Constantinople offered none. Stephen sent his envoys to Constantine with desperate appeal: "Come," he wrote, "and deliver this city of Rome and all your Italy from the jaws of the son of iniquity." Litany chanted in procession, fervent prayer of priests and people, ashes on their heads, cried to the Lord for succour. At length Rome could wait no more. Stephen turned in the opposite direction for the help that did

[29] *Ibid.* 416.
[30] *Ibid.* 416f.; Bury II, 446f.; Mann I, ii, 206f.

not arrive from the East, and Italy, save in the south, was lost to the Byzantine Empire.[31]

Soon ratification of election of the Popes of Rome was no longer sought from Constantinople. Letters still passed from Popes, admonishing and condemning the Emperor Constantine, but quickly Rome began to fear an enemy in its Imperial Lord of so many years. In 757 the Holy See was driven to beg for protection against the Greeks, "that the Church of God may be freed from their pestilential malice." A year or two later Pope Paul the first was full of apprehension that the Imperial army would arrive to seize Ravenna and Rome, that the Imperial fleet would dash from Sicily against Otranto. About 760 he wrote: "Three hundred ships are hurrying from Constantinople toward us, with a Greek squadron from Sicily. What they mean to do and why they are sent, we do not know." About 764 he declared that "the Emperor is very angry and plotting against us, because we have in no way kept silent from admonishing him in regard to sacred images and the keeping of the Faith, true and entire." [32]

It was to Pepin, King of the Franks, that these dire happenings were told. That the various attempts from the Imperial East upon Italian shores failed was due to Frankish decision and power. In 769 Pope Stephen the third, in the Council held at the beginning of his rule in the Lateran at Rome, again solemnly upheld the veneration of holy images; in 781 Pope Hadrian the first ceased to date his official acts by the regnal years of the Emperor in the East.[33] The last tie

[31] *Lib. Pont.* I, 442, 444. It was in the time of Pope Stephen that the Emperor Constantine V and the Council of 754 condemned sacred images.

[32] *Epp.* III, *Codex Carol.* Nos. 11, 15, 17, 20, 30, 32, 36, 38: pages 506, 512, 515, 521, 536, 539, 546, 551, ed. Gundlach.

[33] J. W. 289.

which had bound the Popes of Rome to Imperial dominion from Constantinople had broken apart; henceforth they looked westward for the secular strength which should uphold their spiritual decrees.

3

The spiritual bond between the Church of Rome and the Frankish Empire had steadily been growing firmer during the years of Alcuin's youth in England. In the first place, the devotion of Saint Boniface to the Holy See, his scrupulous referring of all problems to the Popes of his time—Gregory the second, Gregory the third, and Zacharias—had deepened the power of Rome in Frankland, Catholic since the days of its founder, Clovis.[34] The Frankish monarchs, it is true, always deemed it their right to lead the administration of Church matters within their lands, to sit as King in Church councils, and to issue under their sovereignty laws regarding Church as well as State. But they never questioned the place of the Pope as head of the Church Catholic, and in all the vexed history of Frankish conflict his right, in theory, was always maintained. Moreover, the Franks were the "eldest sons" of the Church, and their career of conquest from Clovis to Charles the Great was allowed by Rome as a crusade for the winning of pagan barbarians to the fold of Christianity. Secondly, the final answer of Pope Zacharias to the envoys of Pepin the Short had confirmed by the blessing of the Church what had long been true in practice, and in 751, when Alcuin was somewhere between seventeen and twenty-one, had changed Pepin, Mayor and ruler of Frankland, to its ruler in royalty. Henceforth the Church could, and did, look to the Frankish kings as

[34] J. P. Whitney, "The earlier growth of Papal Jurisdiction," *Camb. Hist. Journal* IV, 1932, 23f.; Moss, 201, 210; Hauck I, 552ff.

dedicated by the oil of anointing at Boniface's hands for the work of supporting and defending her rights and possessions.[35]

The hour was at hand. This same year Aistulf, King of the Lombards since 749, crowned a long advance of Lombard conquest by the capture of Ravenna.[36] All northern Italy, except the regions of Venetia and Istria on the Adriatic Sea, now lay within his grasp. Zacharias died in March, 752. The Exarch who had been appointed to govern for Constantinople, Eutychius by name, was powerless, and the next Pope, Stephen the second,[37] saw himself charged with the responsibility of defending the duchy of Rome, destined to be the next prize of Aistulf's advance. Mission after mission from the Holy See to the Lombard King failed of lasting effect; he demanded tribute, he broke pact, he "raged furiously as a lion, threatening all with death." [38]

At last Stephen took the decisive step and sent a secret appeal to Pepin.[39] Some thirteen years before, in 740, Pope Gregory the third, beset by menace from the Lombard King Liutprand, had also asked aid of the Franks, and Charles Martel had replied with reverent words, splendid gifts, but no soldiers and no promises.[40] To Pepin, however, anointed son of the Church, fresh from scourging the heathen Saxons of the north in this very summer, the vision of himself rushing to the aid of the Holy See was good; it was even brighter when he thought of victory over the Lombards. He readily sent that

[35] *ARF ann.* 749f.; *Clausula de unctione Pipini: SRM* I, 465; *Fredeg. Cont.: SRM* II, 182; Arquillière, *L'Eglise au M.A.*, 83f.; Pirenne, *Hist. of Europe*, 78f.

[36] Muratori, *Antiq. Ital. Med. Aevi* V, 1741, col. 689A: *Ravennae, ann.* 751; *Il Regesto di Farfa* II, ed. Balzani, 1879, 33, doc. 18.

[37] Sometimes known as Stephen III.

[38] *Lib. Pont.* I, 441f.

[39] *Ibid.* 444; *Codex Carol.: Epp.* III, 488ff.

[40] *Epp.* III, 476ff.

eminent prelate, Chrodegang of Metz, with a certain Duke Autchar, to conduct the Pope, as Stephen had asked, into Frankland to the royal Court. On October 14, 753, the three set out from Rome, with a few priests and officers of the army, followed by a crowd that wept and wailed as they saw their Chief Pastor depart on his toilsome way.[41]

It led through Pavia, and there Stephen met the Lombard King. Aistulf remained, as before, obdurate in regard to his restoration of Ravenna and his withdrawal from the duchy of Rome; yet he could not make up his mind to refuse passage to the head of the Church of which he was a follower, to the invited guest, moreover, of the all-powerful Frankish lord. Again and again he tried to divert the Pope from his purpose; he "gnashed his teeth" in fury; he held the unhappy passenger detained for weeks. At last on November 15, after one final but unsuccessful effort of the angry Lombard to hold him back, Stephen was free to continue his journey. He crossed the Alps and arrived, worn out by travel and its complications, at the monastery of Saint Maurice in Valais, Switzerland. From there, after a few days of rest, he went forward to meet Pepin near the castle of the Austrasian kings in Ponthion, Champagne.

At this point we find our first mention of Alcuin's future hero, his friend, patron, Lord and Emperor, Charles the Great. For Pepin sent this son of his, now a boy of about eleven years, to accompany the august visitor on the last stage of his march. The King, with his wife, Queen Bertrada, and his younger son, Carloman, met the Pope about three miles from the royal seat. It was the Feast of the Epiphany, January 6, 754. Pepin bowed low before the Chief Pastor and walked humbly by his side to bring him into his Court with psalms of thanksgiving. There Stephen and his priests, with sackcloth on their

[41] *Lib. Pont.* I, 445; Hauck II, 18ff.

shoulders and ashes on their heads, implored the aid of their Frankish host for the succouring of the Church which was his as it was theirs. Without hesitation Pepin gave his word to defend this Church from Lombard aggression.

The promise was fulfilled. Three times in the course of the year Pepin sent letters to Aistulf in Italy, praying the instant return of captured cities and lands, and three times he was refused. Carloman, his brother, since 747 a monk, first upon Mount Soracte at Rome, and now in Monte Cassino, left his cell and travelled to Frankland to uphold, strangely enough, the Lombard cause, "by persuasion of the Devil," as the Papal biographer put it. He was firmly led to a Frankish monastery, where he died not long afterward; his sons were also shorn of their hair and placed behind monastic doors. In the spring or summer, at the Abbey of St. Denis, Stephen with his own hands solemnly anointed Pepin and his Queen and two sons as the royal and reigning house of the Franks; he also honoured Pepin and these boys, Charles and Carloman, by the illustrious title of "Patrician of the Romans." If record tell us truly here, he declared that no one save of this lineage should henceforward be appointed King of the Frankish people. In conference of the King with the Pope and with leaders of the Frankish council and army at Quierzy-sur-Oise, it was determined that war should follow, did negotiations fail.[42]

Further deliberation, in 755, now made the path clear, and Pepin set out with his army for Italy. Quickly the Lombard Aistulf attacked in hot confidence of victory, was thrown back, and fled to Pavia, his capital; the Franks followed, laden

[42] *Lib. Pont.* I, 447ff.; *ARF ann.* 754; *Chron. Moiss.: SS* I, 292f.; *SRM* I, 465; Lavisse, 273; Halphen, *Charlemagne,* 28ff.; Lot, 327f.; Seppelt, 123; Kern, *Kingship and Law in the M.A.,* trans. Chrimes, 1948, 40ff.; *Storia di Roma* IX (Bertolini), 529ff.

with spoil, to encamp beneath his walls. But the siege was short. Aistulf yielded, promising with oath and written treaty to surrender Ravenna and other cities he had captured. The Pope returned to Rome in joy, and Pepin marched home content.[43]

The Pope's joy is of note in the pages of history. To his mind the moment had come amid the causes and circumstances of Divine Providence when the Holy See should exercise not only spiritual rule over the Catholic Church throughout its length and breadth, but temporal rule over the lands formerly administered by the representative of the Emperor in Constantinople. This representative was now but a figure-head. It was, therefore, in Stephen's view, only right and meet that Pepin, who had wrested from the Lombard king his unlawful conquests, should solemnly, as defender of the Faith to which he was sworn and dedicated, deliver these to that Papal keeping and care from which Papal judgment held that they had been dishonestly torn. It was in these times, we may think, that the "donation of Constantine," ascribed to the misty past as offered to Pope Sylvester, was introduced to tradition.

Bestowal, it would seem, Pepin had already made. Records tell that at the Conference of Quierzy in 754 the Frankish King, in the presence of his nobles and of the Pope's retinue, had declared and promised that the Lombard should render these lands to Stephen, in perpetual holding for him and his successors. It may well be that at this time the Pope had caught a vision of the Holy See, not only Lord of the duchy of Rome, which had long been under Papal administration, but over adjacent towns, over Ravenna, over the cities of the Pentapolis, over Venice and Istria in the north; even, in the centre and approaching the south, over the broad territories of

[43] *Lib. Pont.* I, 450f.; *ARF ann.* 755; *Ann. S. Amand. ann.* 755; *Fredeg. Cont.: SRM* II, 184; *Chron. Moiss.* 293.

Spoletium and Beneventum which various dukes had held in recurring surge of conflict these many years.[44]

The outcome of these years 753–755 was also of highest importance to the Kings of the Franks. The national character of the rule in Frankland, as it had been founded by Pepin's Mayor predecessors, was now in process of development into an infinitely wider sphere of influence, as attractive to Pepin's political ambition as it was demanding in its responsibility, and of significance to the future history of both Church and State in Western Europe.[45]

Hardly had the Pope returned to Rome when it became clear that Aistulf, freed from immediate menace, had no intention of keeping his word. There followed a series of anguished letters from Stephen to his "most excellent son and spiritual fellow-father" Pepin, King and Patrician of the Romans. "For the sake of your eternal soul," he wrote, "as you shall answer at the Day of Judgment for your acts on earth, in gratitude for the mercy granted you in your victories by our Lord God, and in solemn memory of that day on which we anointed you as King before Heaven, see to it that justice be done to the Church of blessed Peter, according to the deed of gift which your generosity has made. For once again the Enemy of the human race has invaded that treacherous Lombard heart, and his sworn oath seems but a thing of nought. Not one rod of land has he returned to the Sacred See! Nay more! from that day on which we parted from one another, most excellent son, he has continued to vex and to hold in contempt the holy Church of God. All Christians look to your strong arm for the rendering of justice. Be heedful of your pledged word, held

[44] *Lib. Pont.* I, 498; T. Hodgkin VII, 199ff.; *CMH* II, 585f., 588f. (Burr). Cf. Levison, *Aus rhein. und fränk. Frühzeit,* 383ff.; Gebhardt, *Handbuch,* 154f.

[45] Hauck II, 71.

even now in written record as witness to your deed. Better were it not to promise than to promise and not to fulfil."

Another letter, addressed to all the Franks, told of far more dire happenings. On January 1, 756, the whole Lombard army pitched camp before the gates of Rome, Aistulf at its head. "And often," went on the Pope in his distress, "he has sent word to the Roman people: 'Open to me the Salarian Gate and hand over your Bishop, lest I overthrow your walls and slay all with one sword. . . .' The Lombards have destroyed all things far and wide outside the City; they have burned the churches and hurled the sacred images into the fire; they have carried off the very Host from the altars and devoured It in their mouths, sated with carnal meat. Monks and nuns they have defiled; men, women, and little children they have wounded and slain. Five and fifty days have we borne the siege of affliction. Help us, for we perish; into your hands, after God, have we commended the lives of all who dwell about Rome." [46]

These wicked deeds, we are told, "resounded in the ears of the King of the Franks," and he made ready a second expedition against the Lombards. While he was on the march to Italy, envoys from the Emperor Constantine the fifth arrived from Constantinople at Rome, travelling to him in Frankland. They refused to believe the Pope's triumphant assurance that the Frankish King was already on his way; hurrying to Marseilles by the sea route, for the Lombards held the land, they discovered it was true. One of them, George, the Imperial Secretary, slipped off quietly to overtake Pepin near Pavia, where he begged the King with promise of rich tribute to hand over Ravenna and other cities of the former Exarchate to his master, Constantine. But Pepin would have none of

[46] *Epp.* III, 494ff., Nos. 8ff.; *Lib. Pont.* I, 451f.; Arquillière, *L'Eglise au M.A.*, 87ff.

this, declaring that no favour of man, no treasure of money, could turn him from loyalty to the See of Peter in rendering to it these cities, as rightly due.

So in this year, 756, Pepin laid siege to Aistulf's capital, Pavia, and soon once more the Lombard King was sueing for terms of peace. All the possessions demanded of him by the Frankish conqueror he again promised to yield to the Pope, and this time Pepin sent his well-trusted friend, Fulrad, Abbot of St. Denis, up and down Italy to see that all was done in correct order. The conquests of Aistulf, now surrendered to the Papacy, make an imposing list in the Papal *Life of Stephen*; they stretched along the east coast from Comacchio to Senigallia, and inland from the Adriatic to the Apennines. Then Abbot Fulrad carried the keys of this wide territory, once governed by the Imperial East, to the shrine of Saint Peter in Rome and laid them, with a document attesting this gift of King Pepin, to abide in permanence as witness to the spiritual and temporal dominion of the Popes.[47]

The gratitude of Stephen knew no bounds in his letters to the Frankish King. "Blessed be God, for He hath visited and redeemed His people!" was his cry, as he wrote again and again to thank the deliverer of his See and of his people: "For the tyrant, the follower of the devil, the devourer of Christian blood, the destroyer of the Churches of God, has been smitten by Divine might and thrust down to the pit of Hell." [48]

The words come from the last letter of Stephen in our record. He died early in 757, a few months after he had heard of the death of Aistulf, this Lombard tyrant and destroyer, in December, 756, through a fall from his horse in the hunting-

[47] *Lib. Pont.* I, 452ff.; *ARF ann.* 756. "Er" (Stephen II) "ist der Begründer und erste Herrscher des Kirchenstaates": Seppelt, 131; Caspar, *ZKG* LIV, 1935, 139.

[48] *Epp.* III, 505f., No. 11.

field.[49] In these few months, however, Stephen had had time to influence the Lombard succession. Desiderius, Duke of Lombard Tuscany, had summoned his army to secure for himself its throne, and was declared its rightful owner by his duchy. Then Ratchis, brother of Aistulf and formerly King himself of the Lombards from 744 to 749, who had yielded his crown to Aistulf that he might become monk with Carloman in Monte Cassino, decided, like Carloman, to leave his cell for political contention. He could not brook a Lombard King whom he considered unworthy in origin; the Lord God, he decided, was calling him, as one born of the royal Lombard House, to assume its throne. He therefore gathered around him Lombard nobles who shared his views, descended upon Pavia, and actually held the city as king for three months, until March, 757.[50]

Desiderius in his wrath hastened to the Pope, promising to ensure the return of Lombard territory still claimed as subject to the Holy See. Possibly, now that return of lands conquered by Aistulf had been duly promised, Fulrad, the Papal counsellor, thought it fitting to request, further, those seized by Aistulf's predecessor, King Liutprand. Stephen, hopeful of Desiderius' will to keep his word, wrote a strong letter to this King Ratchis, who had forsaken his cloister without leave. The monk-king judged it well to return to monastic life, and the Pope then quickly sent to Pepin a prayer for his goodwill toward Desiderius, should this new leader in very deed abide by his promise of full restitution to the Church of God in Rome. Henceforth Desiderius was King of Lombard Italy.[51]

Paul the first, brother of the late Pope, now ruled the Holy See for ten years. His letters to Pepin are full of references to Desiderius. Now he laments the perfidy and arrogance of the

[49] *Fredeg. Cont.: SRM* II, 186.
[50] *SRLI* 503.
[51] *Lib. Pont.* I, 454f.; *Epp.* III, 506.

Lombard king, his treacherous negotiations with Imperial Constantinople; now he rejoices that "our most excellent son," the ruler of the Lombards, in peace and great humility, has come to Rome on pilgrimage and is willing to restore at least part of his ill-gotten gains; now again he bursts out that Desiderius will not be true to his pledge, that he is raiding the harvests of the Pentapolis, with Spoletium and Beneventum, and has even set up a Duke Arichis of his own confirming in Beneventum. Again and again the Pope asks for aid in urgent words. He thanks Pepin fervently for all his loyalty in the past, delights in the gift of the white blanket in which Pepin's baby daughter, Gisela, was wrapped as she came from the baptismal font, sends presents to the king from the treasures of the Papacy: a sword richly jewelled, a ring set with a jacinth, a cloak adorned with peacocks' feathers; books—"an Antiphonal, a Responsory, a treatise on grammar by Aristotle and by Dionysius the Areopagite, works on orthography, on geometry; a clock to use by night." [52] About the same time a notable gift arrived for Pepin from the Emperor Constantine the fifth, of an organ—an event marked by the Frankish annals for its importance to Frankish ritual and music.[53]

But Pepin was too busy with affairs at home to have leisure for further battling against Lombard oppression in Italy. In 758 he worked great slaughter among the Saxons and once more reduced them for the time to submission. The next year he captured Narbonne and drove the Saracens back beyond the Pyrenees. In 760 he began, as a natural consequence, the first of those campaigns against Duke Waifar of Aquitaine which were to occupy Frankish men and might until Waifar lay dead, struck down by his own followers in 768, and Aqui-

[52] *Cod. Carol.*, Nos. 12, 14–22, 24, 27, 31, ed. Gundlach; for the books see *ibid.*, page 529.

[53] *ARF, Ann. Petav., Fuld., ann.* 757.

taine was made part of Frankland by Pepin's victorious settlement. It was the Frankish king's last triumph. At Saintes on the river Charente, where from his seat as conqueror he had looked down in his pride upon the captive mother, sister, and nieces of Waifar, he was seized by sickness. He hastened to Tours, to pray for recovery at the tomb of Saint Martin. But the Lord willed otherwise. On September 24 he died at St. Denis, and a few days afterward his two sons, Charles and Carloman, were proclaimed kings of the Franks.[54] Alcuin was now about thirty-six years old, and Charles some ten years younger.

The last two years of Pepin's life had seen struggle, tumult and tragedy in Rome. Upon the death of Pope Paul the first, a band of insurgents, led by Toto, Duke of Nepi, a small town near Rome, declared by military force Toto's brother Constantine, a layman, elected Pope, and compelled by the same means his tonsuring, his ordination to the various grades of the sacred ministry, and, finally, his solemn settlement upon the Papal throne in July, 767.[55]

Constantine remained in possession of the Holy See for more than a year. We have two letters written by him as Pope to King Pepin. "As a ship tossed by tempestuous waves," he writes from his precarious seat, "so am I, unhappy and useless, beaten by storms of trouble, by the shouts and wails of the people who cry aloud, from great to small alike, everlastingly their own griefs and angry hurts." [56] Not until Rome had seen armed invasion, intervention by the Lombards, the announcing of yet another "Pope," Philip by name, did peace again descend upon the City, and a general assembly of the Roman

[54] *ARF ann.* 758–768; *Chron. Moiss. ann.* 759; *Fredeg. Cont.* 186ff.; *Ann. Mett. ann.* 768.

[55] *Lib. Pont.* I, 468f.

[56] *Cod. Carol.,* Nos. 98f.: *Epp.* III, 649ff.

clergy and people, gathered by Christopher, chief of the Papal Chancery,[57] declare the priest Stephen duly and lawfully chosen bishop of the See of Rome.[58]

Fearful retribution came upon the offenders in the late disorders: death, maiming, torture. Constantine, after enduring mockery in public, was stripped of Papal insignia at a synod in the Lateran, subsequently seized and blinded, then brought before another assembly of bishops, held under the presidency of this Pope, Stephen the third, in April, 769.

To this synod came twelve learned prelates from Frankland, called there by a letter written by the Pope to Pepin, but delivered to Pepin's sons, his successors. The unhappy Constantine, abjectly declaring his guilt, was driven out with blows from the Lateran; all the clergy and people present cried in chorus *Kyrie eleison,* in that they, too, had sinned in receiving Holy Communion from his hands. The bishops, priests, and deacons of his false ordaining were required to submit to valid Ordering from Stephen.[59]

Yet more clouds gathered on the horizon. In the next year, 770, Queen Bertrada, widow of Pepin, journeyed across the Alps to Italy.[60] Alliance between the Lombards and the Franks was the motive of this bold step, a step hastened by past events. In 763, in the very middle of the war against Aquitaine, Tassilo, Duke of Bavaria and nephew of Pepin, had thrown off his allegiance to his uncle, and shortly afterward had married Liutperga, a daughter of Desiderius. Naturally, this combination of Lombard and Bavarian power was formidable to

[57] *primicerius notariorum:* R. L. Poole, *Lectures on the Papal Chancery,* 1915, 13ff.
[58] *Lib. Pont.* I, 469ff.
[59] *Ibid.* 472f.; Mansi XII, 718ff.
[60] *ARF ann.* 770.

Frankish eyes. An olive branch must be proffered, and King Carloman, whom his mother visited on her way, approved her design. It was threefold. The Queen, once face to face with Desiderius, was to propose that another of his daughters should become the bride of her elder son, King Charles; that a son of Desiderius, Adelchis, should marry her daughter, Gisela, sister of Charles and Carloman, now a little girl twelve years old; that the Lombard king should make his peace with the Papal See by restoring, at last, cities still claimed under its present Pope Stephen.

Stephen had already found occasion of sorrow in regard to the royal family of Frankland, through the quarrelling of the two brothers at the outset of their joint reign. Hardly had he despatched a letter to tell them of his joy in their reconciliation when the news of these marriage proposals fell on his astonished ears. His indignation was intense. "This, if it be true, is the work of the devil," he wrote; "no wedding bond but fellowship of most evil sort. For, excellent sons and mighty kings, what folly is it that your well-famed race of the Franks, illustrious above all other peoples, should be tainted by that treacherous—God forbid! and foul race of the Lombards, that has no accounting among the peoples of the earth! No! But this thought of yours is not even possible. You both are already united in lawful marriage to wives of Frankish blood. And, in regard to your sister Gisela, did not your father Pepin in awe of the Apostolic See refuse consent to the Emperor Constantine, seeking her in wedlock for his son? I beseech you by the living God, Judge of quick and dead, that you do not these things." [61]

The marriage of Gisela did not take place, but it was too late to prevent that of Charles. He had, indeed, loved for a

[61] Constantine V, for his son, Leo IV; *Cod. Carol.,* Nos. 44f.: *Epp.* III, 558ff.; Abel-Simson I, 80ff.

while a Lady Himiltrud, and she had borne him a son, Pepin the Hunchback. The Pope's assertion, however, that this was true matrimony is contradicted by other records which name her his mistress.[62] Wife or not, she was now put away by Charles. When Queen Bertrada returned from Italy she brought with her a daughter of Desiderius—her name is unknown [63]—and the wedding was duly solemnized. It lasted but a year, and then the Lombard princess travelled back, rejected and repudiated by her husband, to her father Desiderius in Pavia.

The reasons for this act of Charles are also hidden from us; perhaps the girl did not suit the energetic and ambitious character of her husband; very probably political motives lay behind it.[64] The Pope was silent on the matter. As for Desiderius, naturally from this time—771 or early in 772—any and every mention of the Franks sounded abominable in his ears.[65]

Pope Stephen, in truth, had other troubles to lay before sympathizing eyes, those of Queen Bertrada. His latter days were pathetic, full of confusion and turmoil wrought by opposing factions of Papal officers. Against Christopher and his son Sergius, both ranking members of the Chancery, there had risen in active strategy the Papal chamberlain, Paulus Afiarta, in league with the Lombards. The records still extant concerning the Pope himself reflect this chaos. His biographer tells

[62] Cf. *Epp.* III, 561; Paul Diac. *De Episc. Mett.: SS* II, 265; Einhard, *Vita Karol.* c. 20.

[63] For "Desiderata," noun or adjective, see S. Hellmann, *NA* XXXIV, 1909, 208f.; Paschasius Radbert (*SS* II, 525); cf. Abel-Simson I, 80, note 5; B.M.L. 64, No. 139a; *Storia di Roma* IX, 648 ("Ermengarda"; cf. Manzoni's tragedy, *Adelchi*).

[64] Cf. Einhard, *Vita Karol.* c. 18; Delaruelle, *RH* CLXX, 1932, 213ff.; Lintzel, *HZ* CXL, 1929, 18ff.; *Storia di Roma* IX, 669.

[65] T. Hodgkin VII, 326f. The exact date is not known: Halphen, *Eginhard,* 55, note 6; *Charlemagne,* 103; Glotz I, 440, note 11 *bis;* Lintzel, *ibid.*

of Desiderius marching to the gates of Rome, imprisoning Papal officials within the barred gates of Saint Peter's; of Paulus Afiarta, in concert with the Lombard king, seizing Christopher and Sergius to gouge out their eyes. Stephen, on his part, wrote inconsistently to Bertrada a strange and quite different tale, of the treachery of Christopher and Sergius, those "most wicked men, who attacked us in the Lateran, plotting our death; scarcely were we saved from peril by Desiderius, our most excellent son, present in Rome to render full justice of dues to Saint Peter's Church." [66]

In December of this same year, 771, Carloman died, and Charles, at about the age of thirty, assumed full and sole sovereignty over the Franks and their lands. Carloman's widow sharpened the enmity between Charles and Desiderius by hastening with her children to Italy, to the shelter of the Lombard court.[67]

Two more events remain to be noted here. King Charles married a Suabian girl of high rank, named Hildegard; and, early in 772, Pope Stephen the third passed from this distracted earth, lamenting at the end the perfidy of Desiderius. Then Hadrian the first, friend for many years of Alcuin and of King Charles, succeeded to his rule and to his legacy of Lombard vacillation. Once again letters bearing the seal of the Pope travelled from Rome to Frankland with an appeal for aid in obtaining restitution of cities and land, promised so long ago and still held firmly in that dishonest Lombard grasp; but once again the mind of the Frankish king was set on other things.

In 769, at the beginning of his reign, he had crushed a revolt in Aquitania and put the last touches to the victory

[66] *Lib. Pont.* I, 478ff.; cf. 484f., 487; *Epp.* III, 566f.; Halphen, *RH* CLXXXII, 1938, 238ff.; Amann, 48f.; *Storia di Roma* IX, 662.

[67] *ARF ann.* 771; Einhard, *Vita Karol.* c. 3.

won by his father, Pepin. This present year of 772 saw a new and fiercer war against the Saxons; it was to last, with short intervals of truce, for thirty-two summers, until the death of Alcuin in 804.[68] Now finally, Charles determined, the heathen people dwelling in the northeast, between the Rhine and the Elbe, should be conquered by his sword and brought by his might into the fold of the Church. In this spirit he now marched forward on his crusade, fortified by a great assembling of his nobles, spiritual and secular, in Worms. Speedily he captured the fortress of Eresburg, destroyed the famous Irminsul, one of several pagan shrines fashioned from the trunk of a tree to resemble a pillar, "upholding all things created," focus of Saxon life and prosperity,[69] and laid his ravaging hand on Saxon country as far as the Weser. The old annals tell of miracles attending his progress: that when dearth of water vexed his army encamped near the tree-idol, a torrent suddenly leaped from the ground to supply their need.[70]

Yet the voice from Rome cried on, ever more insistent. As Charles, having held conference on the Weser with the heathen Saxons and received twelve hostages in token of submission, was awaiting the coming of spring at Diedenhofen, near Metz, envoys arrived with alarming news.

Pope Hadrian had begun his leadership of the Church in 772 with firm determination. The bodies of the Papal officers, Christopher and Sergius, not only blinded but dead through the partisan strife now ending, were given reverent burial. Paulus Afiarta, confessing his guilt, was sentenced to imprisonment. It is of some interest to read that Hadrian sent him off

[68] See Halphen, *Etudes critiques,* 146–218; *Charlemagne,* 66ff.

[69] *ARF ann.* 772; Rudolf of Fulda: *SS* II, 676; Chantepie de la Saussaye, *Religion of the Teutons,* trans. Vos, 1902, 124f.; Haug, *Germania* II, 1918, 68ff.; Löwe, *Deutsches Archiv f. Gesch. d. Mittelalt.* V, 1941, 1ff.

[70] *ARF ann.* 772.

to endure this punishment under the Emperor of the East, still, in this year, Constantine the fifth; the authority of the Byzantine capital, as we have seen, was recognized, at least nominally, in Rome until 781. But, against the Pope's express will, the unhappy Paulus as he travelled eastward was arrested and put to death at Ravenna.[71]

To the end he had been in league with the Lombards. As a guest at the Lombard court he had boasted to Desiderius: "I will bring the Pope to your presence, even if I have to tie a rope around his feet." And Hadrian, of course, immediately after his consecration, had met with distrust and scorn the envoys sent to him from the Lombard court: "How can I believe in the good faith of your king?" he had retorted to their offers of friendship; "Did not the late Pope Stephen tell me of his dishonesty?" [72]

The Lombard king was quick to retaliate. Promptly he assembled his soldiers and seized city after city in the Pentapolis and the neighbourhood of Rome, killed leading citizens, carried off booty and burned the land. Envoys constantly travelled to and fro between him and the Pope. But to no avail, especially when the Lombard tried to induce Hadrian to anoint as king with holy oil the sons of Carloman, "that he might separate the Pope from the affection and friendship of King Charles." Hadrian made defiant answer to the messengers: "Certainly I will come to confer with your king, and quickly, too, on matters pertaining to the welfare of the people of God; provided always that he shall have already restored the cities of which he has robbed the Holy See. Unless he does this, let him not trouble himself; he will never see my face." [73]

In 773 Desiderius, like Aistulf before him, drew near to attack the city of Rome, and Hadrian, like Gregory long be-

[71] *Lib. Pont.* I, 486f., 489ff.
[72] *Ibid.* 489, 487.
[73] *Ibid.* 491ff.

fore, bade his people stand ready in the Name of God and of Saint Peter. The doors of the great Church were barred fast. "Never shall he enter," declared the Pope, "unless he tear them down, to the loss of his own soul." With these words he hurled the menace of excommunication upon the king, now but fifty miles distant. That king, despite his robberies, insults and obstinacy, was a Catholic, as his fathers had been before him; he dared not imperil his salvation. He heard, hesitated, and at last withdrew, "in confusion and deep awe, from the city of Viterbo to his own land." [74]

Here the name of Alcuin himself is suggested in our story. For Charles, when he had listened at Diedenhofen to the messengers from the Pope, sent off his own envoys to Rome to find out whether another report, that Desiderius had now made full restitution to the Papal See, could really be true. The envoys were George, bishop of Ostia and of Amiens, Wulfhard, abbot of Saint Martin's monastery at Tours, and one described as "Albuinus, deliciosus ipsius regis." As Alcuin commonly calls himself Albinus, it is possible that he may have been a member of this mission: a suggestion of interest, but by no means proved.[75] Its support lies in Alcuin's previous acquaintanceship with Charles, formed by that early visit to Frankland.

The envoys assured the king on their return that nothing had been restored, and nothing would be. Once again Charles sent messengers, this time even promising much money, much weight of gold and silver, as an inducement. At least, so we read. Even so, "neither by petitions nor by presents could he turn that most fierce heart." Action, he decided, was therefore in order for the material aiding of the Papal power; as

[74] *Ibid.* 493f.

[75] See Levison, 154, note 3; *Lib. Pont.* I, 494; M. Papetti, *Sophia* III, 1935, 216ff.

his father had done, so would he, and even more splendidly.[76] War was applauded at a Frankish assembly held at Geneva in the spring of 773; then Charles divided his army, part marching over Mont Cenis under his command, part, under his uncle, Bernhard, brother of Pepin, crossing through the Great St. Bernard Pass. At the frontier of Italy both divisions reunited, and, after encountering various perilous adventures and defeating Desiderius in a first encounter, the Frankish king reached Pavia, the Lombard capital, in safety and settled down to reduce it by blockade.[77]

It was now the beginning of October. During the next six months Charles returned to Frankland to bring his Queen Hildegard and her baby son to share his stay in Italy; he captured Verona, where Adelchis, son of Desiderius, had taken refuge in the company of Gerberga, widow of King Carloman; he received the surrender of this lady and her sons; he allowed Adelchis to escape in flight.

Then again it was spring, of 774, and, as the end of Lent drew near, Charles felt a longing to spend his Easter in Rome. The story of his arrival is told by the biographer of Hadrian. On Holy Saturday, the Pope, thrilled in his innermost heart by the news that this King of the Franks was indeed approaching, sent out the leading State officials to meet him thirty miles from Rome, carrying high the Papal Standard. A mile from its gates its whole army of soldiers, and boys from its various schools, greeted him with waving of branches of palm and olive, with cheers and shouts, with the ceremonial Crosses of the Church of Rome, always carried in procession to welcome with due honour the arrival of the Exarch or a noble of Patrician rank. Then, the narrative goes on, Charles, King of the Franks and Patrician of the Romans, in reverence of the Holy

[76] *Lib. Pont.* I, 494f., 516, note 27.
[77] *ARF ann.* 773; Einhard, *Vita Karoli,* c. 6.

Cross dismounted from his horse to walk humbly on foot to the steps of Saint Peter's, each one of which he kissed as he ascended to meet Pope Hadrian, standing to receive him in front of the great doors. There, in sight of the multitude of priests, soldiers, and citizens, they exchanged the kiss of peace, then hand in hand entered the Church to the music of the ancient psalm, *Benedictus qui venit.*

When the rites of Easter had been duly celebrated and high feasting had been held in the Lateran, Pope and King settled down for serious talk on matters of State. On this day, Wednesday in Easter week, April 6, 774, words of lasting import were spoken, written, sealed and signed, if our records tell the truth. In them Charles solemnly promised that all lands, cities, and territories which his father Pepin had donated to the Church of Rome should be in fullness and in reality the permanent possession of the Papal See. The deed of ownership, confirmed by the oath of bishops, abbots, dukes and counts attending, was placed by the hands of Charles himself, first upon the altar of Saint Peter, then within his shrine.

So far the narrative is still held correct in the light of later history. But certainly the extent of these lands, as described by the Papal biographer of Hadrian, runs far beyond the limits of actual rendering. Neither Hadrian himself nor his successors laid claim to all that is set forth in this *Life of Hadrian* as then promised by Charles. For it included the island of Corsica; Venetia and Istria; the Exarchate of Ravenna, as established of old; the duchies of Spoletium and Beneventum: in other words, "all Italy, with the exception of Piedmont, Lombardy, the immediate neighbourhood of Naples, and Calabria." Either, then, we see in these details an interpolation of a later date; or we may believe that Charles merely had it in mind to restore to the Papacy such property as actually had belonged to it within the wide limits here described; or we may think that the Pope in after days was content, in act if not in word, to accept far less than Charles in the exalted mood of that Easter pilgrimage had desired to give.[78]

Charles now returned to Pavia, where in June its defenders yielded to his siege. As a result Lombardy surrendered to his power. Desiderius, its king, and his wife were sent as captives to Frankland; the son of Desiderius, Adelchis, fled to Constantinople, and Charles, Patrician of the Romans, defender of the Papal lands and now sovereign over the Catholic but rapacious Lombards, was free to return to his war against the heathens of Saxony. His well-known moderation of temper toward those he had conquered—conquered in permanence—was content to send Desiderius to the abbey of Corbie in Picardy, where the defeated king spent the rest of his life.[79]

Now once again invasion upon his neighbours felt the directing hand of the Frankish victor. During his absence in Italy, the Saxons, enraged by the destruction of their sacred Irminsul, had tried to avenge this by marching upon Fritzlar, the monastery founded by Saint Boniface on the river Edder. It was saved from their fire by a miracle, according to the Frankish annals, when two of the heavenly host protected the church and terrified the enemy into flight.[80] Ravaging and plundering Saxon land occupied the days of the summer that followed. But in 775, after another assembly, at Düren, between Aachen and Cologne, Charles advanced once more to the river Weser and from there to the Ocker, where many submitted to his power—successes tempered somewhat by reverse and slaughter, wrought upon the soldiers he had left to guard the Weser

[78] T. Hodgkin, *Charles the Great*, 99ff.; *Italy* VII, 377ff., 387ff.; *CMH* II, 599f. (Seeliger).

[79] *ARF, Ann. Fuld., Petav. ann.* 774. Liége as place of exile is preferred in Glotz I, 442, following *Ann. Lobien.: SS* XIII, 229.

[80] *ARF ann.* 773.

by a sudden rush of Saxons at "Lidbach," usually identified with Lübbecke, between Minden and Osnabrück. Before he returned home, retribution was meted out by the king to these insurgents in Westphalia, western division of Saxony.[81]

At home again, he hoped for relaxation, but news of continued trouble across the Alps came to break his peace. Hadrian, left to control an Italy still simmering with strife, had made busy use of his pen since Charles had departed. He had vented his anger against the disloyalty of Leo, Archbishop of Ravenna; he had rejoiced that Saint Peter was giving the King victory over the pagan Saxons; he had reminded him of a promise to return to Italy in 775.[82] Nevertheless Charles did not appear. Toward the end of that year, however, the Pope wrote of matters which seemed to demand action, even in the midst of a war already in full tide. Hildeprand, Duke of Spoletium, Arichis, Duke of Beneventum, Hrodgaud, Duke of Friuli, and Raginald, Duke of Clusium—so the letter warned—were conspiring with an army of Greeks under the leadership of Adelchis to invade Rome, to despoil Saint Peter's, even—God forbid! to take Hadrian himself prisoner and set up again a Lombard king in defiance of Charles. An appeal for help followed: "Forsake us not, delay not to aid us, lest all peoples of the world cry aloud, 'What has befallen that confidence of the Romans which, next to God, they placed in the king and the kingdom of the Franks?' "[83]

At last, further tidings of alarm, that Hrodgaud had indeed risen in rebellion, against his sworn loyalty, sent Charles early in 776 again hurrying to the rescue. In Italy he captured Friuli

[81] Cf. Kurze, ed. *ARF ann.* 775; Halphen, *Etudes,* 150f.; Abel-Simson I, 229ff. For the renown of Charles at this time cf. the letter written to him by Cathwulf: *Epp.* IV, 502ff.; Rüngeler, 35f.

[82] *Cod. Carol.,* Nos. 49–57: *Epp.* III, 568ff.; Hodgkin, *Italy* VIII, 24ff.

[83] *Epp.* III, 582f., partly in the words of Pope Stephen II to Pepin.

and Treviso, with other cities leagued in the revolt, placed Frankish officers in command, and was back once more in Frankland for the onset of his summer warring against the Saxons. Both now and in the years to come the Pope was greatly disappointed that Charles could find no time to visit the Holy City.[84]

Meanwhile the crusade against the heathen proceeded apace. Word arrived that Saxon soldiers had recaptured the fortress of Eresburg, had driven out its Frankish soldiers, and destroyed its walls. Immediately Charles started in hot pursuit, followed the fleeing Saxon army to the river Lippe, held a military assembly at its source, Lippspringe, rebuilt Eresburg, raised on the banks of the Lippe another fortified castle, named in his honour Karlesburg, and under its shadow rejoiced in the baptism he levied as condition of peace upon an "innumerable multitude" of Saxons, with their wives and children. In deep satisfaction the king returned to keep his Christmas at Herstal.[85]

The year 777 saw another event of import for the future. Now, this time to Paderborn in their country, the Saxons came in their thousands for the rendering of sworn allegiance to this Christian king, and, as token of the same, the receiving of baptismal water upon their heathen brows.[86] One of them, however, was noticeably absent. He was Widukind, a chieftain of Westphalia, whose independent, pagan heart could brook no domination from without, secular or spiritual. Nine years, from 777 until 785, he was to fight Charles and the Frankish army and to become the inspiration and rallying-point of all this Saxon war.

[84] Hodgkin VIII, 40f.

[85] *ARF, Ann. Mosell. ann.* 776; Halphen, *Etudes,* 152ff.

[86] Cf. Hauck II, 375f., 385f., criticized by Halphen, *Etudes,* 155, note 4; *CMH* II, 611 (Seeliger); *De Conversione Saxonum Carmen: PLAC* I, 380f.

But this was for the future. At the moment, "conscious of many deeds wrought against the king and fearing his wrath, he had fled to Sigfrid, King of the Danes," [87] and Charles unwisely, in his brief relaxation of content in conquest, yielded to a sudden temptation. Among the multitude assembled at Paderborn were three Arab chieftains from Islam Spain, who had come to ask his aid against their bitter enemy, the renowned warrior Abd-er-Rahman, Caliph of Cordova and Emir of Spain.[88] The prospect of quelling this war-lord was alluring, and early in 778 Charles crossed the Pyrenees for a lightning campaign.

Disappointment, and worse, awaited him. After some preliminary success he had advanced as far as Saragossa, when an unexpectedly firm resistance broke down his hopes.[89] At Autun word arrived that Widukind was at home again and in the absence of Charles was leading the Saxons to open revolt. Return was imperative. In the march back through the mountains the Frankish rear-guard was attacked by ambush of the Basques, whose fierce fighting spirit was always ready to leap upon invaders. Many of the Franks were killed and much spoil was carried off. The place was famous in later saga and song as Roncevalles, where on this tragic day Hruodland—Roland—Warden of the Breton March, was slain. Remembrance of it was doubly bitter to Charles because the quick scattering of the mountain Basques made revenge impossible.[90]

During all this activity he had never been forgotten by the Pope. Letter after letter had conveyed Hadrian's anxious fears, his delight and congratulations, his assurance of constant supplications on the part of all priests, monks, and lay folk of Rome. "Even as the people of Pharaoh were drowned

[87] *ARF* ("Einhardi") *ann.* 777.
[88] Dozy, *Spanish Islam,* trans. Stokes, 1913, 204ff.
[89] Buckler, *Monographs, MAA,* No. 2, 1931, 12.
[90] *ARF* ("Einhardi") *ann.* 778; Einhard, *Vita Karol.* c. 9.

in the Red Sea," was the burden of their prayer, "for that they believed not in God, so by aid of Saint Peter may the Lord deliver these unmentionable Saxons into your hands for the glory of His Church." "But," the Pope asked, "*why* did you not come to us for this Easter of 778? And do not forget the donation made to the Holy See by the pious Emperor Constantine in the days of Pope Sylvester; as then, so now may the Church of God and Saint Peter rejoice in the glory of a new Constantine." [91]

Charles had need of encouragement. On his return to Saxony he found that his lately baptized Saxon neighbours had reached the Rhine and pillaged far along its banks, burning churches and monasteries. Some success was won against them by the troops which he again sent in pursuit. In general, however, the war continued its course for the next two years without spectacular victory. The king made good his advance in the region of the Weser and the Ocker, receiving his enemies little by little not only into subjection but also into the Christian religion, sending bishops and abbots to evangelize the Saxon peoples as he spread over them gradually the power of conquest.[92]

In 780 he decided that affairs at home allowed another visit to Italy for inspection and spiritual refreshment. At Pavia, now his own, he kept Christmas with his Queen Hildegard, his children, and his Court, in the old Palace of the Lombard kings. The middle of March, 781, found him in Parma, where, as we have seen, he asked Alcuin to cross the Channel for the educating of his clergy and people in Frankland. Once again Easter was celebrated with Hadrian in Rome. This time the feast was marked by the baptism of his

[91] *Cod. Carol.,* Nos. 59–62; *CMH* II, 802, 805.

[92] *ARF, Ann. Lauresh., Mosell. ann.* 779, 780; Halphen, *Etudes,* 155ff. (critical).

son by the Pope in the name of Pepin, by the anointing of this child, also at Hadrian's hands, as King of Italy, and of another little son, Louis, as King of Aquitaine.

One more incident marked this Easter visit. Envoys arrived in Rome from the Empress Irene, ruler of the East at Constantinople jointly with her son, Constantine the sixth. They came to propose marriage between this son and the Princess Rotrud, daughter of Charles and Hildegard. The young Emperor was but eleven years old and Rotrud only nine. But the betrothal was formally arranged, and a Greek official, Elissaeus by name, was sent to the royal household in Frankland to instruct the child "in Greek language and literature and the customs of the Empire of the Romans." [93] In this same year Pope Hadrian, as we have also noted, no longer held it needful to date his acts by the years of the ruler of this Empire in the East.[94] He was looking for secular support to the rising "Emperor of the Romans" in the West.

[93] Theophanes, 455; *Ann. Lauresh.*, *Mosell. ann.* 781; Einhard, *Vita Karol.* c. 19.

[94] Page 53 *supra*.

Chapter III

THE FRANKISH COURT AND SCHOOL

CHAPTER III

THE FRANKISH COURT AND SCHOOL

I

MUCH OF what we have briefly described was already, we may be sure, known to Alcuin when he reached the Court of Charles at Aachen or was soon told him by the various members of its lively company. The hesitation he had naturally felt in leaving, even for an indefinite time, the land that had taught and nourished him for fifty years, the home of scholars and saints, the centre of intellectual life in his present world, was doubtless stayed in his mind by the thought, which never left him, of "that most holy man, gifted with the spirit of prophecy, who revealed to me in my own country that the Lord was calling me to the service of King Charles." And apparently he did not travel alone; we are told that Pyttel, now a priest, was with him.[1]

Alcuin came, it is true, to bring to Frankland the light of English learning in things sacred and secular; yet, as he knew well, not to kindle, but to fan into livelier flame a fire that had never been extinguished on the continent of Europe.[2] There the Irish of the sixth, seventh, and eighth centuries had laid their foundations far and wide: in the monasteries of Columban—Luxeuil and Bobbio—and in a multitude of other religious houses that owned his influence, such as Faremoutiers, Jouarre, Rebais; in the cloister of St. Gall, the work of Columban's fellow-traveller, Gallus; in the passion for scholarship

[1] *Epp.* IV, 332; H. Hahn, *Bonifaz und Lul,* 1883, 304; *Alc. Vita: SS* XV, i, 189; *Vita Liudgeri: SS* II, 408.

[2] Cf. Ueberweg-Geyer, *Grundriss* II, 160.

burning among those many wandering Irish students, of whom perhaps most renowned was that Virgil who worried so deeply the great Boniface and who ministered so long as bishop of Salzburg. There were the centres of monastic and scholarly devotion raised by Merovingian builders: of Chelles near Paris and of Corbie in Picardy, gifts of the Anglo-Saxon slave Balthild, who by her loveliness and her charm captured the heart of King Clovis the second and became his queen;[3] of Fleury—Saint Benoît-sur-Loire—founded by Pepin of Heristal and his wife, Plectrude; of St. Denis, fruit, with many other abbeys, of the piety of King Dagobert and his nobles.[4] In the region of the Somme during the eighth century relics of a "monk of a forest cell" whose name was Richarius were drawing around them a community near the ancient town of Centula in an abbey which was to bear his name and become famous as the school of St. Riquier.[5] The end of the seventh century had seen Willibrord receiving as gift of Abbess Irmina and of Pepin land and buildings for his monastery of Echternach in Luxemburg.[6] Communities had gathered in the eighth century for prayer and study under Pirmin at Reichenau on Lake Constance, under Chrodegang at Lorsch near Mainz,[7] and in many Anglo-Saxon monastic schools: under Boniface at Fritzlar in Hesse and at Fulda in Hesse-Nassau, under Wynnebald at Heidenheim near Ulm, under Burchard, its bishop, at Würzburg, that city where the Irish Kilian had sown his seed.

[3] *SRM* II, 476f., 489ff.; Levison, 10. For foundations promoted by Irish influence, see Levison, "Die Iren und die fränkische Kirche": *HZ* CIX, 1912, 1ff.

[4] *DACL* V, col. 1710; IV, coll. 595ff. (Leclercq).

[5] *Vita Richarii: SRM* VII, 438ff.; IV, 381ff.

[6] *Diplom. reg. Merow.* 93f., 173; cf. G. H. Verbist, *Saint Willibrord,* 1939, 147.

[7] Kenney I, 518f., 783f.; Levison, 78f.; *DCB* s.v. *Chrodegang* (Gregory Smith); *DACL* V, col. 2337 (de Lasteyrie).

Not only Anglo-Saxon men, but women, too, had been pioneers of learning in Frankland. In the time of Boniface his kinswoman Lioba had called her nuns to study in her convent of Tauberbischofsheim on the river Main; Thecla had done the same at Kitzingen; Hugeburc, once the "anonymous nun of Heidenheim," had written there her Latin *Lives* of the Englishmen Willibald, bishop of Eichstätt, and Wynnebald, abbot of Heidenheim's monastery near that town.[8]

The "Palace School" of the Frankish kings was not founded by Charles the Great. He had himself been taught by the scholars who were brought to Court for the education of the royal children. Such had been the custom under Charles Martel and under Pepin the Short.[9] Training, however, had been hitherto largely in manners and in Court procedure rather than in the liberal arts; Pepin had himself been instructed by the monks of St. Denis.[10] The books "on grammar by Aristotle and by Dionysius, the manuals of orthography and of geometry" which Pope Paul the first had sent to Pepin, were, no doubt, handed over for the use of the Court tutors. One would like to know to what end such books served.[11]

But now under Charles all was to be very different; and soon Alcuin, like all around him, found himself caught up into the magnetic current of this man's inspiration. "David, the King"—they called him in the "academy" or fellowship, which bound together all members of the royal family, King, Queen, sons, daughters, uncles or aunts or cousins, teachers,

[8] Levison, *Vitae S. Bonifatii,* 35, 44, 95, 138; *England and the Continent,* 43f., 294, 80f.; Eigil, *Vita Sturmi: SS* II, 367ff.; *Vitae Willbaldi et Wynnebaldi* (Hugeburc); *SS* XV, i, 80ff.; Rudolf of Fulda, *Vita Leobae: ibid.* 118ff.

[9] Ardo, *Vita Benedicti Anianensis: SS* XV, i, 201; Paschasius Radbert: *SS* II, 525.

[10] *CMH* V, 772f. (Deanesly); Hauck II, 126 and 3f.

[11] Page 63 *supra; Epp.* III, 529.

students, friends and visitors, who could and would contribute to the rising flow of mental activity that was to stir in the royal Palace. The name, "Palace School," is for the time of Charles excellently apt, for it mirrors in two words the aim and ambition of the King. Lord he would be of a mighty kingdom which should be devoted to the glory of God and of His Church, which should draw into subjection to himself as God's agent upon earth the peoples of Europe who still sat in heathen darkness around him. "Let there be light," God had said, and it was for him, Charles the King, the Anointed of God, to spread that light through the schools and churches and abbeys of his realm into the furthest corners of his ever-growing influence. War, to be sure, there must be, with its blood and pain and horror, year after year, till the final hour of conquest struck; but even war should minister to peace, and the conquered races should bow their heads in subjection to the earthly prince who opened to them the way of Christian life.

The genius of his father Pepin in matters military and politic had been inherited by Charles. But to this was added in the son a thirst for knowledge and a curiosity which impelled him to wrestle with things strange and obscure, to ask and search and learn. This was pure desire. Further, he craved within his mind the application of this knowledge. He had a passion for efficiency. The King must know of those things wherein he should speak with authority, whether they concerned State or Church. He held himself not only ruler of the Frankish kingdom, not only head of the Frankish Church—a Church which he held indissolubly united, as soul with body, with the Frankish nation—but also the inheritor from Pepin of the responsibility, and of the power behind this, which underlay the defence and support of the Catholic Church centred in Rome. It was Charles who issued edicts for the ruling of the Church in Frankland, who appointed, warned and advised its bishops and abbots, as he did his secular officials. It was Charles, also, who wrote to Leo the third upon his election to the Papal throne: "My duty it is by Divine aid to defend everywhere with armed might the Church of Christ from inroads of pagans and from ravaging of infidels without; from within to fortify it by the learning of the Catholic Faith. It is your part, holy Father, to support our fighting by hands raised to God as those of Moses, so that, through your intercession and the guidance and gift of God, Christian people may ever have victory over His enemies, and the Name of our Lord Jesus Christ be glorified throughout the world." [12]

If, then, the King must know whereof he should speak, so, in the mind of Charles, must all who worked in State and Church under him. Knowledge was to him necessary for all—of politics for the statesman, of strategy for the soldier, of theology for the clergy, for the training of those placed under them. Moreover, to learn was to him not only necessary but delightful. Why not, therefore, to others? Hence the necessity for the "Palace School"—the heart and wellspring of learning throughout the Frankish lands.

Writers of the time have vividly pictured, by prose and by verse, this King "David" in his many various businesses and interests. He worked constantly, from one council, from one battle-field, to another. In the fourteen years which Alcuin spent with the Court, the King kept Christmas at ten different places, and only four times at Aachen.[13] Naturally, the Court moved with him, and, although Alcuin did not accompany Charles on his military campaigns, life must have been rest-

[12] Hauck II, 126f.; *Epp.* IV, 137f.; A. von Martin, *Archiv f. Kulturgesch.* XIX, 1929, 311; Carlyle, *Hist. of Medieval Political Theory in the West* I, 1930, 263ff., and cf. Kantorowicz, 60. For the library assembled by Charles cf. Einhard, *De Karoli test.*: Halphen, *Eginhard*, 98: *de libris, quorum magnam in bibliotheca sua copiam congregavit.*

[13] *ARF passim.*

less, physically as well as mentally, for all whom the King delighted to have around him. Aachen, then, must not be thought of as an abiding home for the royal company during these fourteen years. Its Palace only began to attain its magnificence during the latter part of Alcuin's stay at Court. The great Minster, also, began to rise shortly before he left in 796, and he actually watched from Aachen only its early stages when, after about 787, Pope Hadrian gave Charles permission to take from the Palace at Ravenna marbles and mosaics for its adorning. Its design was Byzantine, after the model of the sixth-century Church of San Vitale at Ravenna.[14] Nor did the other Palaces on which Charles lavished his love of art and architecture reach their final splendour during these fourteen years: at Nijmwegen in Holland, and at Ingelheim, near Mainz, although the Court spent the Christmas of 787 at this latter house upon the Rhine.[15]

Wherever he was, the King was the centre of activity. Now he discussed either war with his generals or policy with his representatives in administration; now he criticized and revised a document of ecclesiastical importance offered for his inspection by his churchmen; [16] now he argued with his professors of learning questions of dialectic, of rhetoric, of astronomy, in which he was especially curious; now he exchanged poems with one or another of his "academy"; constantly he received messages of praise, congratulation and gratitude from

[14] *Cod. Carol.,* No. 81: *Epp.* III, 614; *Karol. Magnus et Leo Papa,* ll. 98ff.: *PLAC* I, 368f.; Clapham, *Romanesque Archit. in Western Europe,* 1936, 11, Plate 6a, Fig. 10; Kleinclausz, *Charlemagne,* 183ff.; *DHGE* s.v. *Aix-la-Chapelle,* coll. 1249, 1257f. (Boiteux); R. C. Reade, *Camb. Antiquar. Communications* V, 1886, 133ff. Cf. the delight of Alcuin, on returning to Aachen in 798, over the pillars of "the beautiful and marvellous Church which your wisdom has designed": *Epp.* IV, 244.

[15] For the paintings which afterward adorned the Palace and Church at Ingelheim see Ermold. Nigell. IV, 179ff.: *SS* II, 504f.

[16] Levison, 124, note 9; von den Steinen, *NA* XLIX, 1932, 220, 278.

the many, Pope and bishop, King and noble, who saw their present world dependent on his word. The scene passes quickly from grave to gay. He presides at the dinner-table in his great hall, serving generous portions to his crowded guests, giving and taking jest and riddle, delighting in merriment; he celebrates a victory with his family and friends, welcoming benignly the gifts of flowers, of fruits, of poem and song, which each one hastens to offer; he gives a party in the swimming-pool, fed by the mineral springs of Aachen, and stops amid the noise and splash of sport to discuss with Alcuin a complicated question of Biblical interest; he leads out his sons and daughters to hunt, as he loved to do, in the forest which lay beyond the gates of his Palace.[17]

We are grateful too, for the many details of his daily life which have come down to us. Every morning saw him at Mass in his Minster, every morning, evening, and night at the Hours of the Church; eagerly he sought for manuals of prayer for his own use, and joined in the responses of the daily Office. But he was no ascetic. Fasting he endured, but he declared it was bad for his health. He loved a feast, but his meal must be savoury roast venison, hot from the spit; boiled dishes he abhorred. And his active mind never ceased to desire stimulant. During dinner, when he was not arguing or sparring with his friends, he listened to music, or a reading from some book of history, sacred or secular. Augustine's *City of God* was a favourite; naturally, polemic against the pagan dwellers in this world's kingdom of the devil, and the *compelle intrare* of the Lord's doorkeepers, found quick sympathy in his thought. He was a true Frank. He dressed much the same as any one of his Frankish people, in simple linen tunic or leather

[17] Theodulf, *PLAC* I, No. XXV (796), 483ff., No. XXVII, 490ff.; Angilbert, *ibid.* 360ff.; Alcuin, *ibid.* 245f.; *Karol. Magnus et Leo Papa* (author unknown; cf. K. Heldmann, 19; P. Lehmann, *SBM* 1934, Heft 9, 9), *ibid.* 366ff.; *Epp.* IV, 420.

jerkin, covered with a cloak of blue, and always with the Frankish sword at his side. Only on feast days and at time of special audience did he assume royal state, in cloth of gold, sparkling with jewels. Twice, in Rome, he appeared in Roman dress at the Pope's asking. He made his secretaries copy the ancient poetry of the Franks which told the deeds and wars of the Merovingian kings; and he set his scholars to work at a grammar of the native language. Names of the twelve months of the year he changed from the Latin form then in use to others, fashioned from native words which told their characters in the German fashion. So also he renamed the winds of various quarters.[18]

His hospitality was unbounded, and he delighted to surround himself with men of all races. Goth sat side by side at his table with Frank, Saxon with Celt, each admiring or despising his neighbour, each adding his individual note to the general medley. Their host required only that they bear repute of sound learning, spiced with the salt of robust humour, and that they should be strong to argue and debate. Men such as these he sought after, conscious that the old missionary zeal for learning which the Irish, especially, had mixed with their spiritual devotion had waned in the latter days of the Merovingian kings. Frankland, he knew, needed new blood, and he called this to his Court from Italy, from Spain, from England, from Ireland, ever longing to give his realm that knowledge which he himself thought wholly needful. The story of the old "Monk of St. Gall" may not be true in fact, but it is true in spirit: "So the most glorious Charles, seeing the pursuit of letters flourish, indeed, throughout his whole kingdom, yet grieving that it did not reach the ripeness

[18] Einhard, *Vita Karol.* cc. 22ff.; Halphen, *Eginhard,* 83f., note 5. On the influence of Augustine upon the King's conception of rule see Wiedemann, 8ff.; Arquillière, *L'Augustinisme politique,* 1934, 111; Gilson-Böhner, *Gesch. der christ. Philosophie,* 1937, 243f.

of the Fathers of olden time, though he toiled with energy passing the measure of mortal man, at length lost patience and cried: 'Oh, if only I had twelve such clerics, so learned and perfectly versed in all wisdom as were Jerome and Augustine!' Whereupon the learned Alcuin, though in comparison with these he naturally held himself most ignorant, dared to answer the terrible Charles more boldly than any other would have dared, hiding from his face the indignation he felt within: 'The Creator of Heaven and earth Himself had but few such men, and you want *twelve* of them!' "[19]

In this family and fellowship, then, headed and inspired by the King, Alcuin soon found his place as teacher, counsellor, father and friend. He grew to know each member and loved each in a wholly individual way through his own special genius for friendship. To each he gave affectionately a name which came to be used generally in the Court, after the manner, he said, of our Lord, in His intimate friendships with Peter, whom he called "Simon," and with the children of Zebedee, "the sons of thunder."[20]

Among all, when Alcuin arrived in 782, none was more reverenced than the Queen-Mother, Bertrada. As we have seen, she was a lady of strong purpose. Only once did her son Charles oppose her, when he sent back to Italy the daughter of Desiderius whom she had willed him to marry. She died the next year, in July, 783, and was buried with great pomp and ceremony among the kings of Frankland at St. Denis.[21]

Shortly before, on the eve of Ascension Day in the same year, Charles had lost his Queen Hildegard, that girl of high Suabian rank who had succeeded the Lombard princess at the Court. She was only twelve years old when he married her,

[19] Monach. Sangall. (Notker Balbulus), ed. von Knonau, 8.

[20] *Epp.* IV, 386. For verses of Alcuin to Charles, "David," see *PLAC* I, 252, 254, 257ff., 296f.

[21] *ARF ann.* 783; Einhard, *Vita Karol.* c. 18.

and in the twelve years of their wedded life she bore him nine children. Alcuin must have seen in her a young woman of beauty and charm, if her epitaph by him reflects his inner mood. She travelled in Italy and Frankland with her husband; her name is found with his in the offering of gifts to the Church, and Pope Hadrian prayed for the soul of his spiritual "fellow-mother." [22]

Of her children Alcuin saw six grow up. Three others lived but a short while: Adeleid, born in Italy during the siege of Pavia, Hildegard, and a boy named Chlotar in memory of his Frankish ancestor. One or other of the Court poets wrote verses in memory of each.[23] Alcuin knew the remaining six as children in the Palace household. In after years he wrote to the eldest boy, Charles, as "my most dear son," asking the blessing of the Lord upon him as destined heir of his father, Charles, and bidding him beware of bribery in his government.[24] The next son, Pepin, we have seen baptized in Rome by Pope Hadrian at Eastertide, 781, anointed and crowned King of Italy. He remained during most of his boyhood in Italy, being brought up for the distinguished career in arms which awaited him under his father. Perhaps it was for this reason that Alcuin called him "Julius." [25] A special partiality seems to have linked Alcuin with the third boy, twin of the dead Chlotar, who did succeed to his father's empire as Louis "the Pious." He was shy and retiring, unlike his high-spirited brothers, and loved to consult Alcuin on matters of religion and conscience.[26] Soon after birth he, too, had been crowned with Pepin by Hadrian at Rome, as King of Aquitaine.[27]

[22] *PLAC* I, 58f., 95, 107; *Cod. Carol.* No. 79: *Epp.* III, 611; *SS* II, 266.

[23] *PLAC* I, 59f., 71ff.; Manitius, 258; Paul. Diac. *De Episc. Mett.: SS* II, 265, 267.

[24] *Epp.* IV, 315f.

[25] *PLAC* I, 237.

[26] *Alc. Vita,* 193; *Epp.* IV, 316.

[27] *ARF ann.* 781.

The three daughters of Charles and Hildegard enlivened the Court with much of their father's enjoyment of its varied occupations, were treated by him with indulgent affection, but, it would seem, strictly chaperoned against misfitting alliances in marriage.[28] Rotrud—"Columba," "the Dove of Peace," to Alcuin and her many friends—as we have seen, was formally betrothed to the boy Constantine, Emperor in the East; [29] but the marriage never took place.[30] She grew up a quiet and serious girl, not striking or handsome in appearance.[31] For many years she lived under her aunt Gisela, abbess of the "double" monastery of Chelles. Alcuin wrote letters of counsel and exhortation to them both there. There they gained by petition from this "dear teacher and father" his commentary on the Gospel of Saint John and sent him gifts in gratitude. There his reproaches reached them in his last years: Why have those so near to him in Christ, his spiritual sister and daughter, not written to him of late? Have words of greeting failed them, or have they nothing of interest for his ears? Surely distance on this earth should not cut off the joy of love, a flame that "neither deep waters nor the wide ocean can quench." [32]

The lively camaraderie of the royal Palace gave to two of these girls an escape from convention. It was not really strange, in the curiously blended life of Charles and his Court, so eager to enjoy the fruits of the world of tomorrow without losing those of today, that Rotrud bore in forbidden birth a son to Rorigon, Count of Maine. His name was Louis, and

[28] Halphen, *Eginhard,* 62, for criticism of the *Vita Karol.* c. 19; Theodulf, *Ad Carol. Regem: PLAC* I, 485; Raby, *SLP* I, 190.

[29] Page 79 *supra.*

[30] Page 138 *infra.*

[31] Angilbert: *PLAC* I, 361; cf. *Karolus Magnus et Leo Papa, ibid.* 371.

[32] *Epp.* IV, 322ff., 354ff., 359f., 371f. Such open expression of affection was, indeed, characteristic of letters among Anglo-Saxon friends.

he was abbot of St. Denis and high among Court officials in the time of Charles the Bald. The same was true of her sister, Bertha. She was the most attractive of the three, very like her father, who refused to allow her to marry the son of Offa, King of Mercia.[33] By her charm she won the heart of Angilbert, the constant companion and counsellor of Charles. Angilbert was not of royal blood; but Charles for long acquaintance's sake allowed their secret love and its fruit of two sons. Her lover, who wrote verses in his leisure moments, sang of her as "worthy of all songs," and looked forward in his lines to seeing again the pleasant garden where his little boys played at home among the flowers. "Are they well?" he wonders, "and are they growing fast? Tell them, poem of mine, to take care, to keep safe by God's mercy within their walls, from fire, and thief, and sickness that plucks, greedy to devour." [34] One of them was Nithard, the well-known historian, who writes briefly of his mother's union with this "memorable man, whose body was found whole and sound twenty-eight years after his death." [35] To Alcuin, like her sisters, this Bertha was his "dearest daughter," but, unlike them, she comes to us with no name of his bestowing.

The third daughter, Gisela, he renamed "Delia." [36] She had been baptized as a little child in 781 at Milan by its Archbishop Thomas.[37] Alcuin records that "Delia" was skilled in music; [38] and he writes to her in jest that he finds comfort for her neglect of him in the poetry of Virgil. Perhaps she

[33] Levison, 112.

[34] *PLAC* I, 361ff. Cf. *Karol. M. et Leo Papa, ibid.* 371, where, as Raby notes (*SLP* I, 201, note 2), the picture of Bertha argues against the authorship of Angilbert.

[35] Nithard, *Hist.* IV, 5, ed. Lauer, 1926, 138f.; *SS* XV, i, 180.

[36] This is the usual assumption. Dümmler remarks that "Delia" might be Bertha: *PLAC* I, 253, note 2; cf. 237.

[37] *ARF ann.* 781.

[38] *PLAC* I, 237.

will make amends by courtesy to his distinguished friend, Regenbert—unknown, but possibly the bishop of Limoges.[39]

Chief, however, of Alcuin's friends among women in Frankland was the elder Gisela, sister of Charles, the abbess of Chelles. From a very early age she had been a nun, but from time to time she was warmly welcomed by the King at Court.[40] Alcuin wrote to her as "Lucia," and frankly told her, as Boniface told Lioba, what her life meant to him: "I am so happy, high handmaid of God, in your letters, and so comforted by your friendship. From the day I counted you my friend there has hardly been a moment when I have not drawn upon your dear support, the protection of your prayers, as you promised I should. . . . Please do not mind if in my folly and presumption I write some words of counsel for your understanding ear; let your humility teach you to welcome the word of warning when it comes from one who loves." There follows a lengthy sermon, which doubtless the Reverend Mother kept to read and reread in her cell! [41] And, like Radegund to Fortunatus, she sent him at Aachen gifts from her Abbey: "And I, your brother, delighted so in the psalter and missal which you sent to me, and especially in the cloak—it came at exactly the right time." [42] She was a keen student of sacred books; and we hear from Alcuin during these same years that she was reading his copy of *Bede on the General Epistles*.

Not for long did Charles endure the loss of a wife. In the second year of Alcuin's stay at his Court he married at Worms, for the third time.[43] The lady, named Fastrada, came from the Eastern Franks, a daughter of Count Radolf of Aus-

[39] *Ibid.* 252f.; *Epp.* IV, 456f.
[40] Theodulf, *PLAC* I, 486, ll. 109ff.; Einhard, *Vita Karol.* c. 18.
[41] *Epp.* IV, 40ff., 357; *PLAC* I, 237: No. XII.
[42] *Epp.* IV, 127; cf. *PLAC* I, 253: No. XLI; 303: No. LXXXV, ii.
[43] If, as is probable, Himiltrud was not his wife.

trasia.[44] Tradition has left a dark picture of her character. Einhard, the biographer of Charles, declared that her own cruel temper turned the King so radically from his usual mild and kindly manner that he actually drove men to conspire against his reign. There were, it is true, two plots of major importance between the time of her marriage to Charles in 783 and her death eleven years later.

The first appeared across the Rhine among her own Eastern Franks, led by Count Hardrad. It threatened to become serious, but was soon quelled, and its instigators condemned to blindness or death.[45] The second was a far greater shock to the King. It was prompted by Pepin the Hunchback, that unhappy son of Charles' first union, with Himiltrud. His handsome face at Court ever bore the sullen shadow of misery for his misshapen body and his inferior place. He had no hope from his father of succeeding him; it is even possible that his eldest half-brother, who had been named Carloman at his birth, had been baptized by Hadrian with the name of Pepin to emphasize this fact.[46] Charles was spending the summer at Ratisbon in Bavaria, busy with the war against the Avars, when the news reached him that the Hunchback had risen in revolt with other Frankish nobles, because "they could not bear the cruelty of Queen Fastrada." His purpose, the old records declare, was to kill the King and all his brothers, "as Abimelech slew his seventy brothers upon one stone," and to seize the throne for himself. A Lombard exile's loyalty revealed the plot in time. Its leaders died upon the sword or the gallows, except this unwanted youth, whom his father could not put to death but sent to live as a tonsured monk in the cloister of Prüm, in Lorraine.[47]

[44] *ARF ann.* 783.

[45] *ARF* ("Einhardi") *ann.* 785; Einhard, *Vita Karol.* cc. 18, 20.

[46] Hodgkin, *Italy* VIII, 53. His rejection did not follow necessarily from illegitimate birth; cf. Fichtenau, 49.

[47] *ARF* ("Einhardi"), *Ann. Lauresh.* = *Chron. Moiss. ann.* 792.

But, whatever the Frankish people felt about their Queen Fastrada, her husband gave her due honour. A letter from him to her, written in 791, tells of the conquests of his son Pepin, the King of Italy, among the Avars.[48] "Greeting with my love," he writes. "Thank God, I am safe and sound." Then follows the story of the triumph of "our beloved son." "So we have held three days of solemn litany, beseeching the Lord for peace and health and victory and safe return. Our priests prescribed a fast during this time from wine and meat; but those who needed wine through sickness or advanced years were allowed it on payment of one solidus a day, if they could afford it—if not, of one denarius. Everyone was bidden to give alms according to his goodwill and means. Each priest, unless he was sick, said a special Mass; each one who knew his psalter well enough chanted fifty psalms; and they all walked barefoot in procession.

"Now I should like you to consult the clergy at home for the same ritual there. Only please do not, yourself, do more than your little strength allows. I worry because your letter has not yet reached me. Do please let me know constantly how you are, and anything else you will want to tell."

She died three years later and was buried by Charles with much magnificence in the Church of Saint Alban at Mainz.[49] One of the King's special friends, Theodulf, wrote for her tomb an epitaph, entirely conventional and reminiscent of Ovid.[50] Verses of the Court poets also tell of the two daughters she left her husband at her death. Theodrada is described as offering the King wine at a family festival in Aachen, sitting her snow-white horse as she goes out with him and her brothers and sisters to hunt in the royal forest, her hair shining brighter than gold. Fastrada's other daughter, Hiltrud, rides last in

[48] *Epp.* IV, 528f.; Jaffé, *Mon. Car.* 349ff.

[49] *ARF, Ann. Fuld., Guelferbytani, ann.* 794.

[50] *PLAC* I, 483. Its tone is remarkably chilly; cf. H. W. C. Davis, *Charlemagne,* 1899, 147.

the array, as the youngest girl.[51] They were only children at this time. Both, however, grew up to be abbesses—Theodrada at Argenteuil, near Paris, and Hiltrud at Faremoutiers, in the Brie district of France. Yet their lives, also, do not seem to have been entirely regular; for their half-brother Louis on succeeding to the throne made it his first business to bring them to due order.[52]

Before long Charles was again a husband. The new Queen, Liutgard, was of Alemannian origin, and, according to the verses of Theodulf, was gracious to all, courteous, generous, kind, delighting in books and in all the arts.[53] She was to become the friend of Alcuin, who admired her greatly, asked her aid and gave her his, in the few years of her life at Court.

2

Next to the royal family, who joined habitually as learners in the discussions at Court, Alcuin must have found his interest in meeting the men who taught them and their fellow-students in the Palace "School." [54] When he arrived, its instruction was in the hands of teachers from Italy, a natural first choice for Charles in following the tradition of the past. One of these teachers, the deacon Peter of Pisa, Alcuin had already heard debating in Pavia. His special subject was grammar, the correct and traditional usage of words as shown in Greek and Latin texts. The Greek was little enough, partly through lack of material. Peter wrote or, rather, compiled a textbook for the use of his pupils, made, as he tells, "for the love of his lord," no doubt Charles.[55] The King, however, sought him out

[51] *PLAC* I, 360, 372, 486; Einhard, *Vita Karol.* c. 18.

[52] Thegan, *Vita Hlud.: SS* II, 618.

[53] *PLAC* I, 485 (ll. 83ff.: *pulchra virago*), 522f.; cf. other witness: *ibid.* 360 (l. 56), 370f. (ll. 184ff.). On the date of his marriage see B.M.L. No. 327a; Abel-Simson II, 214f.

[54] Laistner, 150; Gilson, *La Philosophie au Moyen Age,* 189ff.

[55] *PLAC* I, 73; Hagen, *Anecd. Helvetica,* 159ff.

for gayer purposes as well, and Peter from time to time wrote poems under the royal name.[56] He had probably joined the Court after the Frankish conquest of the Lombards, but, when Alcuin saw him in Aachen, he was growing old and seems to have been held of little account.[57]

Also an Italian teacher of grammar in the Palace, but far more influential during Alcuin's years with Charles, was Paul the Deacon. He was a Lombard of good family of Friuli, who was educated, tradition says, at the Court of King Ratchis at Pavia, in Latin and some Greek learning, lived under monastic discipline, was ordained deacon, and guided the studies of the Princess Adelperga, daughter of Desiderius and wife of Duke Arichis of Beneventum. For her he enlarged, continued, and made suitably Christian the pagan *Roman History* of Eutropius.[58] His first experience of the cloister seems to have been in the monastery of Saint Peter of Civate, near Milan, where apparently he instructed novices in the Benedictine Rule.[59] At any rate, he is known as the author of the first extant commentary on this Rule, reproduced in substance by the priest Hildemar of Civate in the ninth century.[60] We find him next in the monastery of Monte Cassino, troubled by the fall of his Lombard land before King Charles. Then even more serious trouble came upon him through his brother, another Arichis, who had imprudently lent himself to a Lombard rising of 776 in Friuli. This compelled Paul in 782, just

[56] *PLAC* I, 48f., 50f.: Nos. XI, XIII, probably also XXXVIf.

[57] *Ibid.* 54: No. XV (l. 45); Einhard, *Vita Karol.* c. 25; *Epp.* IV, 285 (of Alcuin in 799; from the tense of *claruit* Peter seems to be no longer teaching at the Palace); Manitius, 452ff. On the verse of Peter and of Paul the Deacon see Raby, *SLP* I, 197ff.

[58] *Epp.* IV, 505f.

[59] Hauck II, 165; Manitius, 257ff.; Traube-Plenkers, *Abh. der kg. bayer. Akad. der Wiss., phil. hist. Kl.* XXV, 2, 1910, 42f.

[60] Schroll, Sister M. Alfred, *Bened. Monasticism as reflected in the Warnefrid-Hildemar Commentaries,* 1941, 22ff.

about the time of Alcuin's coming, to approach the King as a petitioner for this brother, now a wretched prisoner in Italy.

Paul was now a guest in the Frankish Court. Here, because of his reputation in letters and learning, he had been received with ready welcome, and he settled down for four years to teach and to write with Alcuin and Peter. But at first not with happiness. He had grown to love Benedictine life, especially at Monte Cassino, and a Palace seemed no home at all. He writes on January 10, 783, from "the bank of the Moselle, clear, bright as glass," to Theodemar, his "Father Abbot": "I could not possibly tell you, letters are too short, how I long for you and the brethren, almost every minute. When I think of that calm, quiet life—of the Divine Offices, the Work of God, of all your kindness to me, of all that army of Christ that labours in sacred paths of learning, of those examples of virtue, each with its own particular light, of our happy talks on the glories of our home in Heaven—I simply sit down here, sick with despair, and the tears *will* come, do what I can. They are Catholics here, it is true, and they practise Christian ways; they welcome me, all of them, and are kind to me, for love of our Father Benedict and your own high fame. But in comparison with your Monastery this Palace is a prison, and when I think of the peace there, life here is one hurricane! Only in body am I here; all the mind that is in me is there with you: in your choir, in the refectory, more hungry for the reading than the food, in the round of duties, in the care of the sick and the old—in fact, among the saints in Paradise. Please, dear brothers, *please* keep on asking our blessed common Father and Teacher, Saint Benedict, that by his merits he may prevail with Christ to send me back without delay!" [61]

It is good to think that, nevertheless, the four years of waiting were fruitful. They brought from Paul's pen two

[61] *Epp.* IV, 506ff.

works in prose: a brief History of the Bishops of Metz, written at the request of the prelate then in office there, Angilramn, and, for Charles, an abridgment of Pompeius Festus, *On the Meaning of Words,* a work to which modern students have turned gratefully for its relics of ancient learning.[62] We are more concerned here, however, with Paul's verses, and he wrote many—little letters, composed for Charles and for his own friends, riddles, fables, serious reflections and gay. He was already of some reputation as a poet when he arrived in Frankland, for he had written of the beauty of Lake Como, of the palace and church built by Duke Arichis at Salernum, of the queen of Desiderius, Ansa, who had died in captivity with her husband among the Franks. There were also some touching verses on the death of a young girl, his niece, Sophia, and an entreaty, *Verses of Paul in prayer to the King,* sent to Charles for that brother in an Italian prison. "Scarce any man on this earth," he writes in these twenty-eight elegiac lines, "is sorrowful as I; for, now this seventh year, new cause gives me griefs manifold to shake my heart. My brother lies a captive; his wife begs her bread in the streets; his children starve in rags; our sister, a vowed nun, has wept her eyes out at their misery. Our furniture has gone, and there is no one to help. Have pity, Lord King, and restore him to his home." [63]

Eventually, we may think, the prayer was granted, and Paul's days passed peacefully in study. For his vast erudition—"Is he not like Homer in Greek, Virgil in Latin, and Philo in Hebrew?"—Charles wishes him to instruct in Greek the clerics who are to escort the Princess Rotrud to her proposed home in Constantinople, and sends him many words of

[62] *SS* II, 260ff.; *Epp.* IV, 508.

[63] *PLAC* I, 42f., 44ff., 46ff.; Neff, *Die Gedichte des Paul Diac.: Quell. und Unters. z. lat. Philol. d. Mittelalt.* III, iv, 1908, 1ff. Hauck (II, 166) describes this prayer as "die anziehendste von allen poetischen Produktionen der karolingischen Epoche."

praise, written in trochaics by Peter of Pisa. Paul replies in the same rhythms. Alas! he remembers none of his Greek and Hebrew, except a few syllables gathered long ago at school. But to show that he did once know something he adds a translation of a little Greek poem.[64] He and Peter exchange poems, riddles, and problems of the imagination, often written under the name of Charles. Would Paul, Charles asks in hexameters composed by Peter, rather lie a chained prisoner in a dungeon or be ordered to baptize the terrible Sigfrid, King of the Danes? [65] More interesting are Paul's fables in elegiacs—on the sick lion and the vengeful fox, on the hungry calf and the thin-legged stork, on the gout, menace of rich men, and the flea, bane of poor men, and how these two plagues find their desired end.[66]

A third teacher of literature from Italy had been at the Frankish Court some years when Alcuin settled there,[67] and was to be one of his closest friends. His name was Paulinus, but Alcuin knew him in affection as "Timotheus," [68] called him "the praise of Italy," and loved to receive his letters.[69] In 787 he was again in his native land, where Alcuin's joy, united, as usual, with solemn warning, reaches him on his elevation through Charles to the Patriarchate of Aquileia. "I have always loved you, dear friend," Alcuin writes, "ever since I came to know you. I have inscribed the name of my Paulinus, not on wax tablets where it could be rubbed out, but in my heart for always. Do not forget the name of your Alcuin in your prayers, especially when you consecrate the elements of bread and wine into the substance of the most holy Body and Blood of Christ. I have long been expecting

[64] *PLAC* I, 48ff.: Nos. XIf. [65] *Ibid.* 50ff.: Nos. XIIIf.

[66] 62ff.: Nos. XXVII–XXIX; Jack Lindsay, *Med. Latin Poets*, 1934, 43.

[67] B.M.L. 85, No. 202; Sickel, *Acta* II, 33, K58; *PLAC* I, 222, l. 47.

[68] *Epp.* IV, 103. [69] *PLAC* I, 239ff., 248.

those relics you promised me, of the True Cross, and others. Don't disappoint me and say the distance is too great. Love will find wings. . . . How high God has lifted your name! May your life answer to this great calling. Preach, preach, in season and out of season. Let your throat be as a trumpet of the Lord. . . . A fool I am, trying to carry my wood into your forest, to make your rivers run with my little drops! But, then, the Lord allowed the widow's mites because she loved much. . . ."[70]

It is interesting to compare the pompous and rhetorical language, in which Paulinus reported in 791 to Charles the business transacted at a Council held in Aquileia, with the direct and wrathful prescription of dire penance, sent by him to a man who had killed his wife and dared to make a false excuse for his deed, declaring that she was in love with another.[71]

These three, Peter, Paul, and Paulinus, were leaders of discussion in the humanities for Charles and his kinsfolk at the Palace in 782, the date of Alcuin's arrival. We may turn for a moment to others who were not of its regular teaching staff, but who either lived in the Court or frequently visited it on their official business for Church or State and were an integral part of its life.

Of these perhaps the one who meant most to Alcuin was Angilbert, son of a noble Frankish family. He had been sent as a boy, according to custom, to be brought up, to be made ready for the distinguished career his parents hoped for him, under those best fitted for this charge, the advisers of the King at the royal Court. Many lads were thus destined to become pillars of the Frankish throne.[72] Angilbert listened to the

[70] *Epp.* IV, 70f. For the reference to the Mass cf. *Epp.* IV, 211: *panis, qui in corpus Christi consecratur.*

[71] *Ibid.* 516ff.: Nos. 15f.

[72] *Epp.* V, 7; Halphen, *Eginhard,* 3, note 1.

discourses of Peter, of Paul, and of Alcuin; he placed before their critical eyes his earlier efforts in verse, and, as we have seen, became not only a Court "poet," but a most important figure in the purposes and undertakings of his King. He was sent across the Alps to guide the young Pepin, King of Italy;[73] three times, in 792, 794, and 796, he went to Rome as special envoy for Charles. The King, like all the Court, called him "Homer," a name doubtless bestowed by Alcuin, and held him, as the royal letter to the Pope put it, "the counsellor of my intimate and private ear."[74] Alcuin constantly corresponded with him, from the time when, as it would seem, he was *primicerius,* or leading minister, for Pepin in Italy.[75] He calls him the "son of my erudition," a "faithful and prudent man," begs him to send relics from Rome, and peppers him with sallies of wit.[76] For Angilbert, as Alcuin well knew, like his King, was no ascetic, rather the contrary; and although, after in 790 Charles made this man, lover of his daughter, abbot of St. Riquier near Amiens, Alcuin wrote of him as "now my Father rather than my son," he did not altogether shut his eyes to Angilbert's joy in the lusts and frivolities, as well as in the learning and the beauty of this world. The world owed Angilbert much for the books and the glory of architecture with which he endowed his abbey at Centula, but this did not, in Alcuin's mind, excuse his addiction to pomps and vanities. Yet in his latter days, men said, he was penitent even to holiness, and thus the grave had no power to hurt him.[77]

We have already noticed here and there another dweller

[73] *Epp.* IV, 37.

[74] *ARF ann.* 792, 796; *Epp.* IV, 66, 69, 135, 137; *PLAC* I, 237, 239.

[75] See Hauck II, 180, note 8; Manitius, 543f.; against this theory, Abel-Simson II, 435.

[76] *Epp.* IV, 184, 37, 141; cf. *PLAC* I, 251, 274.

[77] *Epp.* IV, 35; *AA. SS.* Feb. III, 96f.; *SS* XV, i, 179.

in the Court with Alcuin during these years—Theodulf, a Goth, who had penetrated deep into paths of classic culture and of theology in his native Spain, had gained a daughter whom he loved well, had been ordained deacon, and had written much verse concerned with Christian apologetics, doctrines and morals. In his middle thirties, for some reason unknown, he was obliged to leave his country and found an easy refuge with Charles.[78] His verses, his wide reading, and his knowledge of art made him, too, very welcome. He seems never to have been teacher or student in the Palace "academy," nor was he a very intimate friend of Alcuin at any time; he has no special byname. He certainly played his part in its activities, spiritual, intellectual, social, and he was devoted in gratitude to Charles, who, foreigner though Theodulf was, respected his ability so much that about 798 he appointed him bishop of Orléans.[79]

But he, like Angilbert, loved greatly this present life. Among Latin poets he delighted in his Ovid. To the gay, sparkling humour of these two men, now gracious, now biting, but carefree and urbane, Charles turned when at times he wearied of Alcuin's devoted earnestness for the good of this wicked world. To their verses, as to those of Alcuin, we owe vivid glimpses of the people who thronged the halls of the Palace. Theodulf at times looks around in satire at the motley company. How can the swans be heard to sing when the crows make so much noise? Here the magpie sits at the feast, conceited because he imitates human talk; there the parrot is chattering, ruining Angilbert's verse. One would-be poet struts like a peacock, but only his shrill voice is true to character; another calls the cuckoo's note, or tells of rain, like Virgil's

[78] *PLAC* I, 487 (XXV, l. 165); 492 (XXVII, l. 62); 497 (XXVIII, ll. 139f.); 543; 541; 453, l. 31; 481, l. 28; 445ff.

[79] Dümmler, *PLAC* I, 437ff.; Raby, *SLP* I, 187ff.; Manitius, 537ff.; Hauréau, *Singularités hist. et litt.*, 1894, 37ff.

knavish raven, or screeches like the owl that threatens the night.[80]

There are also many pleasant pictures, sketched by Theodulf or other poets at the Court. Father Alcuin, revered and middle-aged, delighting in the moment's interest and surrounded by the young men of his School, now discourses on pious themes, now bursts into lyric lines, now catches the minds of all with the riddles and problems that few can solve, now sits, listening, over his frugal porridge and cheese.[81] Away with porridge! cries Theodulf. A man needs wine and savoury meat if he shall teach and sing good verses! Angilbert is away in Italy; Alcuin and Theodulf will tell of him when he comes back again.[82] Riculf, Archbishop of Mainz since 787, high in the confidential service of Charles, is visiting the Palace, bringing his hands full of poems and quips in verse; Alcuin, who calls him "Damoetas," has a new riddle to exchange with him.[83] Hildebold, bishop of Cologne and arch-chaplain of the Court, blesses the board as priestly Aaron, the name by which he is known to all.[84] From him, his "most familiar bishop," Charles at his dying was to receive the last Sacraments, "to fortify him for his going forth."[85] Ercambald, chief secretary to the King, seizes the two notebooks that hang by his side to take down dictation from the Court officials. A little later he was to be Chancellor.[86] Another scribe, Einhard, living at Court for instruction under wardship of the King, as Angilbert had done, later on to make use of his intimate knowledge as biographer of Charles, is running to and fro, Theodulf writes, like a busy ant upon her important ways; now carry-

[80] *PLAC* I, 490ff.
[81] *Ibid.* 491, 493, 486, 488; 246 l. 49; Raby, *SLP* I, 190f.
[82] *PLAC* I, 246, 487.
[83] Abel-Simson I, 537f.; *ARF ann.* 781; *PLAC* I, 432, 487, 223.
[84] Hauck II, 116; *PLAC* I, 492, 361.
[85] Thegan, *SS* II, 592.
[86] *PLAC* I, 487; Sickel, *Acta* I, 82.

ing books, now darting on errands, a very serious page. He had come from the valley of the Main, had been taught in school at Fulda, and then sent on to Charles by its Abbot Baugulf.[87] Alcuin, who taught him, gave him the name of "Bezeleel," for he was filled with the Spirit of God to devise cunning works of gold and silver and brass in all manner of workmanship. Einhard was a maker of verses, also "skilled in Homeric strains." But everyone, and Alcuin included, called him in play "Nardulus," "Dwarfling," for his little stature. They always added, however, that he had a great mind. Alcuin compared him to the eye that rules the movements of the whole body; so, he jests, does "Nardulus" rule all the Palace.[88]

Nor are the domestic officials neglected. Especially beloved by all was the seneschal, or chief steward, who was made one of the fellowship of the Court by the name of "Menalcas." He could be seen encompassed by squadrons of bakers and cooks, hurrying up the kitchen to send in Father Alcuin's special porridge, wiping the sweat from his forehead, holding as it were a court of law over the menu.[89] Beside him stood "Thyrsis," the royal treasurer and chamberlain. His business it was, among many duties, to admit and arrange the company; now he would usher a guest promptly to his place with a smile and a bow, now another would be bidden wait outside until room could be prepared. Both "Menalcas" and "Thyrsis," whose real name was Megenfrid, respected deeply good verses and made a reverent audience.[90] The wine was poured

[87] Einhard, *Vita Karol.*, Preface by Walafrid Strabo; Halphen, *Etudes*, 68ff.; *PLAC* I, 487.

[88] *Ibid.* 245, 248, 492; Exodus XXXI, 2ff.; XXXV, 30ff.; Halphen, *Etudes*, 70; *Eginhard*, ed. Halphen, 107. Halphen's severity toward Einhard as biographer of Charles (in his *Etudes critiques* and his edition of the *Life*) is criticized by Ganshof, *RBPH* III, 1924, 725ff.

[89] *PLAC* I, 488, 492, 246, 362.

[90] *Ibid.* 486, 492, 362, 246, 269.

by Eppinus, who seems to have been called "Nemias" or "Nehemiah," "restorer of the City"; the fruit was borne around the table by Lentulus, quick of mind but lamentably slow of foot. "Good Lentulus," cries Theodulf, "do walk a little faster!" [91]

In one matter, alas! our Court poets lacked charity. They delighted to pour scorn upon some Irish Scot who lived with them. "Take away his second letter, and you will have his real name," rages Theodulf, "sot," "dumbhead." "Before I, the Goth, make friends with the Scot, the dog shall nurse the hares and the cat run away from the mouse!" [92]

All in all, it was a happy household, with its many guests and visitors, coming and going. We shall hear of more when we come to discuss Alcuin's students and look at his letters. No doubt his spirit struggled within him against acquiescing in the ways of the house of Rimmon; the lusts and loves of Charles and of Angilbert were not his.[93] Rightly or wrongly, however, he must have felt that he could aid, could advise, but could not coerce the power in the land. Protest on his part would only lead to banishment from the work which the Lord, and Charles, had given him to do. It would be better to praise, and to use, the vast good which the King was bringing to pass. After all, the King's leisure time and his private life were his own. And, in any case, "David, the King" in the mind of Alcuin and everyone else was immeasurably greater than this "humble Levite," however remarkable Alcuin's learning and powers of administration undoubtedly proved to be.

[91] *Ibid.* 488, 492, 246, 487.

[92] *Ibid.* 487. His name is not known. On the verse of all these "Poets of the Court Circle" see Raby, *SLP* I, 178ff.; *CLP*, 157ff.

[93] But cf. *Epp.* IV, 174, Alcuin to young Pepin, King of Italy: *Laetare cum muliere adoliscentiae tuae,* and Dümmler's note: *concubina.*

3

When we come to judge Alcuin as head of the Palace School under Charles the Great, it is necessary, first of all, to draw a clearly marked line between his extant writings on education and the man Alcuin himself as we see him elsewhere. In his writings we see a mind which constructed no philosophy, which gave birth to no original thought, which was content to compile from the works of established authorities and to use such dull and dry compilations for the exercise and drill, for the informing and stimulating, of ignorant people, young or old, who came to learn from him and through him.

Into this somewhat dreary picture the careful painter of Alcuin's character from this educational angle will pour life through remembrance of other facts, equally true. It was the Anglo-Saxon Alcuin who came from the land of Bede not only to give its culture to Frankland, but to supply a zest and enthusiasm for learning which was to burn for centuries; to stir up the embers, if the metaphor be allowed, for the blaze of Irish and Frankish philosophers in the ninth century; to found a new era of letters on the continent when the sea-kings from the North had overrun and destroyed English libraries and schools. Eagerness alone, however, does not work miracles. It was, secondly, Alcuin's genius for administration, his minute care for details, united with his vision for the whole, which gave Charles the skilled aid he so badly lacked. Thirdly, Alcuin came from England, not only rich in the experience of forty years as student and teacher in York, but bearing knowledge of many books and, doubtless, copies of some of these; to England he sent later on for others to supply his lack.[94] And

[94] *Epp.* IV, 177.

fourthly, the Alcuin who glows with the warmth of friendship and human feeling in the *Letters* and the *Poems* was the same man who stood behind his dull treatises to teach with living ardour their material to his School. Now and again, even in them, we find a touch of humour, and realize that Alcuin assuredly was friend and fellow of all whom he taught in this informal society of the learned and the learners.[95]

For this reason, this zest for friendship and fellowship, he adopted the method of dialogue, of question and answer. The method in itself was an old one.[96] Perhaps, however, Alcuin introduced it as a new feature in his School; certainly Paul the Deacon, too, used it in his writing on grammar.[97] The informality of procedure in the Palace School is also shown in one of Alcuin's writings in verse. In one part of this picture a teacher is training his pupils to pronounce their words properly in reading; in another, a grammarian holds a class in poetry, with careful instruction in the mysteries of metre and rhythm. Over these the deep voice of Jesse, bishop of Amiens, may be heard giving a lesson to the younger clergy on Holy Scripture. Sometimes, too, when night has fallen, "my daughter," one of the girl princesses, will slip outside to watch the stars in the dark sky, and from her study of astronomy will fall to worship of the Lord who ordered their loveliness.[98]

Since Alcuin arranged his curriculum on the lines of the *trivium* and *quadrivium,* naturally his writings deal with the subjects of these divisions of study; more especially with those of the *trivium*, as many of his students in Frankland were

[95] "With what mixture of poetry, pedantry, and steady common-sense Alcuin managed his strange menagerie is evident in the textbooks that he wrote for it": Waddell, *Wand. Scholars,* 41; cf. Raby, *SLP* I, 186; M. R. James, *CHEL* I, 94.

[96] L. W. Daly and W. Suchier, ed. *Altercatio Hadriani Aug. et Epicteti Philosophi, Illinois Stud. Lang. Lit.* XXIV, 1–2, 1939, 11ff., 42.

[97] Manitius, [illegible]

[98] *PLAC* I, 246 (xxvi)

sadly in need of elementary training. For the same reason throughout his treatises, as in his letters, we find a simple Latin style, clear and easy to understand, after the example of Bede.

First, then, we have from him a work *On Grammar,* in which he does not extend the meaning of the word, as was usual in classical days, to include the interpretation of literary texts.[99] At its opening, a teacher is asked by his young students, exactly as Laelius was asked by his sons-in-law to describe true friendship, to explain to them the various stages of the ladder that leads up to Philosophy. As fire lies buried in the flint, so deep within the human mind lies the desire for wisdom. But, as the flint must needs be struck, so must the mind of a learner be stimulated by a teacher's working upon it.

The master draws his answer from Holy Writ: *Wisdom hath builded her house, she hath hewn out her seven pillars.* This is to be understood, he declares, not only of the seven Gifts of the Holy Spirit, but also of the seven liberal arts: "And no man shall arrive at perfect knowledge save he be uplifted thither by these seven pillars or steps."

Thereupon he proceeds to name in order these seven arts or steps of the ladder of true wisdom, and then to draw from the masters in his field—Donatus, Priscian, Isidore, Phocas, Bede—the matter of his instruction on grammar. To make this a little more palatable, he imagines a discussion between himself, as teacher, and two of his boys, a Frank and a Saxon. "Saxon" is much brighter, perhaps because he is fifteen, a year older than "Frank"; he does much of the talking, helped

[99] *PL* CI, coll. 849ff.; Manitius, 280f.; West, 93ff.; Frey, 1ff.; Hagen, *Anecd. Helvet.* CCLVIIff.; Alcuin, *Vita,* 195. On Alcuin's educational writings see also J. W. H. Atkins, *English Literary Criticism: The Medieval Phase,* 1943, 51ff. For Alcuin, *De Musica,* see *Alc. Vita,* 194; L. Delisle, *Le Cab. des MSS. de la B.N.* II, 1874, 444, 34; Manitius, 277, note 4. For music in the Palace School, cf. *PLAC* I, 246, ll. 38ff.

out by Alcuin, while "Frank" asks routine questions.[100] But the conversation must have needed all Alcuin's vigour to keep it going, for it deals exclusively with the parts of speech and their proper treatment in words, from mouth and from pen. The only interest here for us is the essential place given by Alcuin to secular learning as the handmaid of Divine Wisdom; for him "the steps of grammatical and of philosophic disciplines lead to the summit of evangelical perfection." [101] For the generations to come in Frankland, however, his *On Grammar* was a masterpiece that left its models altogether in the shade.[102]

Alcuin's *On Orthography* will interest us even less, except for its illustration of the changes taking place in the Latin language. It is a list of words, arranged in alphabetical order after the fashion of Bede's work on the same subject, and intended to teach the proper forms, declensions, and usages according to traditional custom.[103] Thus students shall themselves speak and write correctly in order to understand the Latin manuscripts of former days. Mediaeval error, however, finds its way into Alcuin's own spelling, and his explanation at times is seriously amiss. Among the pitfalls which he correctly points out for the writer we notice constantly the con-

[100] See, however, Dietrich Gerhardt, "Über Bruchstücke von Alkuins Grammatik," *Thüringisch-Sächsische Zeitschrift f. Gesch. und Kunst* XXVII, 1940, 31ff.

[101] Möller-Hahn, 368; Emile Bréhier, *La Philosophie du M. A.*, 1937, 46f.: "Alcuin insiste avec une force singulière sur la nécessité des arts libéraux; il sanctifie ces arts, en montrant leurs relations avec la création divine." Cf. Ueberweg-Geyer, 158f.; Schmitz, 18; Bastgen, *HJ* XXXII, 1911, 812ff. As Ernst Curtius reminds us, however, this thought of Alcuin goes back to Cassiodorus: *Europ. Lit. und lat. Mittelalt.* 1948, 447. Cf. for influence of Cassiodorus upon Alcuin, Lehmann, "Cassiodorstudien," *Philologus* LXXIV, 1917, 363ff.

[102] Page 310 *infra*.

[103] Keil, *Gramm. Lat.* VII, 295ff. We may note the definition of caelebs (299): *qui sibi iter facit ad caelum et caelebs caelestium ducens vitam:* West, 102f.

fusion of b and v; again and again he stresses the difference between such words as *acerbus* and *acervus, habena* and *avena, albus* and *alvus, bile* and *vile*. Be very careful, he warns, of initial h: *ara* means an altar, *hara* a pigsty! On the whole, the work might still be used with profit as a brisk quiz on grammatical forms. It was duly presented to King Charles, with a poem declaring it was but a plucking of the flowers of the ancients for the instruction of pupils in a kind of game. Its sources, in addition to Bede, were Priscian and Cassiodorus, with a little of Alcuin's own devising.[104]

Cicero provided most of the material for the *Dialogue on Rhetoric and the Virtues,* carried on between Alcuin and the King, who is represented as craving assistance in correct style for the many addresses and writings of his official life.[105] "Alcuin did the talking, Charles, busy as he was, found time to approve it." [106] Occasionally there is a bit of Alcuin himself, as when he makes Charles wonder why Christians fall below the standard of ethics reached by the heathen philosophers, or brings him in trepidation to a *reductio ad absurdum*. But, if the busy King really approved this dull work step by step, one must admire him for the record of his own enthusiastic words: "I *do* want to see what you are going to say about 'rebuttal'!" [107]

Nor did Alcuin's *On Dialectic* do anything but bring the teaching of previous writers, such as Cassiodorus, Boethius,

[104] Keil, 225; Manitius, 281f.; *PLAC* I, 253f. (No. XLII). Cf. Lot, "A quelle époque a-t-on cessé de parler latin?": *Bull. du Cange* VI, 1931, 144ff.

[105] Halm, *Rhet. lat. min.* 525ff. The sources are Cicero, *De Inventione, De Oratore;* Julius Victor, *Ars Rhetorica;* Cassiodorus. For text, translation, sources, MSS. and educational value consult Wilbur S. Howell; cf. R. McKeon, *Speculum* XVII, 1942, 13f. and Lehmann, *Philologus* LXXIV, 364f.

[106] *PLAC* I, 299f. (LXXX, i, ii).

[107] Halm, 549, 543, 541.

Cicero, Julius Victor, and Pseudo-Augustine on the *Categories* of Aristotle, before the mind of Charles and his more cultured subjects.[108] We may pass over this with a glance at its definition of philosophy—"The searching of Nature, the learning of things human and divine, so far as is possible for man"—and look at a more interesting work, *A Discussion of the Royal and Most Noble Youth Pepin with Albinus (*Alcuin*), the Schoolmaster.* It consists of a hundred and one questions, problems, and riddles exchanged between Alcuin and this boy, no doubt the younger son of Charles. They are concerned with things of Nature, with the Universe and with Man, his virtues and his appetites; at the end the riddle, so characteristic of Anglo-Saxon writings, again appears. Alcuin was no exception among his compatriots, and riddles formed an important part of his educational practice and theory, as a lightening of the burden of learning for his disciples.[109]

Three sources may be traced in this *Discussion*: a Latin version of the *Sentences* of Secundus, probably the Greek philosopher of the time of the Emperor Hadrian; the *Altercatio Hadriani Augusti et Epicteti Philosophi,* of uncertain date, but known by Alcuin on certain evidence; the Latin *Riddles* of Symphosius, so dear to his fellow-countryman Aldhelm.[110]

Some idea of the work may be given by quotation of some of its questions and their answers. Alcuin and his pupil take turns, on both sides; Pepin starts, with simple problems:

[108] A. van de Vyver, *RBPH* VIII, 1929, 430f.

[109] *PLAC* I, 281ff.; West, 106f. Cf. H. Reuschel, "Kenningar bei Alkuin," *Beiträge z. Gesch. der deutschen Spr. und Lit.* LXII, 1938, 149: "Ebenso wie seine rätselfreudigkeit mag auch Alkuins kenninggebrauch heimatliches erbe sein." For the subject see H. van der Merwe Scholtz, *The Kenning in Anglo-Saxon and Old Norse Poetry,* 1929.

[110] Daly and Suchier, 44ff.; W. Wilmanns, *ZDA* XIV, 1869, 530ff.; *Epp.* IV, 133; *PLAC* I, 248 (XXIX, ii).

	Pepin	*Albinus*
1.	What is writing?	The guardian of history.
2.	What is speech?	The revealer of the spirit.
3.	What gives birth to speech?	The tongue.
4.	What is the tongue?	The lash of the air.
5.	What is air?	The guardian of life.
6.	What is life?	The joy of the blessed, the sorrow of the sad, the looking for death.
7.	What is death?	An inevitable happening, an uncertain pilgrimage, the tears of the living, the basis of last wills and testaments, the thief of man.
8.	What is man?	The bondsman of death, a passing wayfarer, a guest sojourning on earth.
9.	To what is man like?	To an apple on a tree.
10.	How is he placed?	Like a lantern in the wind.
30.	What are the lips?	The doors of the mouth.
31.	What is the throat?	The devourer of food.
39.	What is the stomach?	The cook of food.
49.	What is day?	The stimulant of toil.
51.	What is the moon?	The eye of the night, the giver of dew, the foreteller of storms.
65.	What is spring?	The painter of the earth.
67.	What is autumn?	The barn of the year.

Then Alcuin begins his riddles. Here are two:

89. I saw the dead give birth to the living, and the alive consumed unto death by the living's wrath.

Pepin, doubtless with great pride, answers: "Why, the

cooks know the answer to that! It is Fire, born from the friction of dead trees."

The other was a well-known question:

97. There were three men. One was never born and died once, the second was born once and never died; the third was born once and died twice.

The answer is: Adam, Elias, Lazarus.

After this same character is another little writing which has come down to us under Alcuin's name, although we are not certain that he wrote it. However, as it has well been said, "whether he did really do so, or whether copyists attributed it to him, is a matter of little moment, for it well represents the character of the teaching of the time." [111] It is called *Problems for sharpening the Wits of Youth,* and contains fifty-three puzzles which would speedily now be solved by short methods of arithmetic or algebra. But Alcuin painfully and slowly worked them out from first principles of the most elementary calculation. We will look at two:

37. Six labourers were hired to build a house; five of these were experienced, one was a lad, an apprentice. The five men were to divide between them as payment 25 pence a day, less the payment to be made the apprentice, which was to be half an experienced worker's daily wage. How much did each receive a day?

Alcuin's answer runs: Take 22 pence; give 4 to each man, and the half of this, 2, to the boy. Three pence remain. Divide each penny into 11 parts, making 33 in all; give 6 of these to each man, making 30, and 3, the correct amount, will be left for the boy.

42. A ladder has 100 steps. On the first sits one pigeon, on the second two, on the third three, and so on up to the hundredth. How many pigeons in all?

[111] West, 109ff.; *PL* CI coll. 1145ff.; M. Cantor, *Vorles. über Gesch. d. Math.* I, ed. 3, 1907, 836ff.; Manitius, 286.

The reckoning here recalls to us, of course, arithmetical progression, a process unknown as such to Alcuin. But he calculates:

On step one and step 99 combined sit 100 pigeons, similarly on step 2 and step 98, and so on. Step 50 and step 100 have no pairs.

So his answer is: $49 \times 100 + 50 + 100 = 5050$ pigeons.

Sometimes a problem runs into nonsense, "for the teasing of the boys." Of this kind is No. 43:

Three hundred pigs are to be killed on three successive days, an uneven number on each day—an impossible feat.

It shows, at least, that Alcuin had need of humour, however elementary, among his ill-assorted learners.

Occasionally, also here, the "riddle" element is found, as in No. 17:

Three brothers had each a sister. As the six were travelling together, they came to a river which they were obliged to cross. There was but one boat, which would hold only two persons, and ethics demanded that no one of the women should cross alone with one of the men, unless he were her brother. How did they proceed?

Alcuin solves it thus (we may substitute, for his long-winded Latin, ABC = the men; A′B′C′ = the women):

A and A′ cross; A returns and stays. B′ and C′ cross; A′ returns alone and stays. B and C cross, C disembarks, B returns with B′. A and B cross and stay; C′ returns, picks up A′ and takes her over. B′ is now alone at the starting-place; B returns to escort her over.[112]

A modern Psychology test would probably allow one minute for its solving!

[112] So in No. 18, where the problem is to carry safe and sound across a river a wolf, a goat, and a head of cabbage, in a boat which will only hold two of these together.

Chapter IV

THE WORLD OUTSIDE THE COURT

CHAPTER IV

THE WORLD OUTSIDE THE COURT

I

As THE right-hand man of King Charles in work for Church and State, Alcuin, of course, often turned his eyes from the Palace and its School to wider fields of Frankish activities.

First, he became deeply concerned in the education of the clergy. The prevailing ignorance among them had troubled the King long before 782. About 769, in his first General Edict, he had proclaimed: "Any priest who, after repeated admonition from his bishop, shall neglect to acquire the learning needed for his ministry, shall surely be inhibited and removed from his cure; for those who themselves are ignorant of the law of God cannot declare and preach to others." [1]

His zeal for the education of his Frankish priests received, we must think, fresh stimulus and hope with the arrival of Alcuin. Moreover, when Charles had returned from Italy in 774 he had brought with him as gift of Pope Hadrian an amplified collection of the canon law of the Roman Church, based on that made by Dionysius "Exiguus." This, in his desire to order anew and to invigorate with fresh life after the pattern of Rome the organization, spiritual and secular alike, of his realm, he had carefully studied and drawn upon in his future pronouncements. On March 23, 789, another edict, a

[1] *Cap. reg. Franc.* I, 46 (16). This "First Capitulary" of Charlemagne is declared "not genuine" by Ganshof, *Speculum* XXIV, 1949, 528, note 3, following F. Lot, *Ecole Pratique des Hautes Etudes, Sc. hist. et phil., Annuaire,* 1924–1925, 7ff. It is cited by Amann, 77.

"General Admonition," appeared in immense detail. It dealt with bishops, priests, deacons, monks, and it was largely culled from Councils of the past. There was within it, however, matter freshly composed;[2] and among these newer orderings Charles ruled, no doubt in consultation with Alcuin and others:

No. 70. "That bishops diligently examine their priests throughout their dioceses, to the end that they hold the right Faith, observe Catholic baptism, and understand well the prayers of the Mass; that they measure rhythmically and with due reverence the psalms according to the divisions of the verses; that they both understand the Lord's Prayer and teach its meaning to others, so that every man may know what he is asking of God. . . ."

72. ". . . That there be schools to teach boys to read. Correct, we command you, with due care the copies of the psalms, the written signs, the chants, the calendar, the grammar in each monastery and diocese, and the Catholic books, because often people wish to pray to the Lord, but do so badly, because the books are at fault. And do not allow your boys to corrupt the books by their own reading or writing. If a copy be needed, of the Gospel, or Psalter or Missal, let men of ripe age write it out with all diligence."

78. "Likewise let no false writings and doubtful narratives, records which entirely contradict the Catholic Faith, and that most evil and lying letter which in the year past some, themselves deceived and misleading others, declared had fallen from heaven—let not such documents be believed or read, but destroyed by fire, lest they lead people into error. Only the canonical books and Catholic treatises and the sayings of sacred writers are to be read and delivered."

[2] *Cap. reg. Fr.* I, 52ff.; de Clercq, 171ff. The collection is called the *Dionysio-Hadriana.*

80. "Let all clerics learn thoroughly the Roman chant and let this be observed in all Offices of Night and of Day, in accordance with the ordinance of our father, King Pepin of blessed memory, when he abolished the Gallican chant for the concord of the Apostolic See and the peace of God's holy Church."

This enforcement by Charles of his father's ruling looks back to the year 754, after Pope Stephen the second had been escorted by Chrodegang, bishop of Metz, from Rome to his meeting with Pepin in Frankland. Inspired by Roman influence, Pepin had ordered Roman chant for his realm. Upon returning home, moreover, Chrodegang, now Archbishop, had introduced on his own account into his diocese of Metz the Roman use of chanting and ritual.[3] Pope Paul the first had sent, as we saw,[4] an Antiphonal and a Book of Responses from Rome to Pepin. He had also sent Simeon, high in office in the Scola Cantorum there, to teach the monks of Remedius, bishop of Rouen, to sing the psalms properly. Later on, the Pope had been obliged to recall Simeon, and Remedius, much upset because his monks had not yet acquired the skill he desired, had only been comforted when Paul had allowed him to send some of these monks to Rome to finish their training in the School.[5] The Roman manner of chanting, therefore, had gradually been replacing the Gallican in Frankland, and Charles was now confirming the change.

82. "You are likewise to take care, beloved and venerable shepherds and governors of the churches of God, that the priests whom you send throughout your dioceses to rule and to preach do so rightly and honourably; that you do not permit

[3] Paul. Diac. *De Episc. Mett.: SS* II, 268. For the ruling of Charles here cf. *Libri Carol.* I, c. 6: ed. Bastgen, 21.

[4] Page 63 *supra; Epp.* III, 529.

[5] *Ibid.* 553f.; *DACL* III, col. 306 (Leclercq); Batiffol, *Hist. du Bréviaire rom.*, 1895, 80f.; Klauser, *HJ* LIII, 1933, 176f.

them to invent and teach to their people things new, of their own imagining, in accord neither with the canons of the Church nor the Scriptures."

Entirely after Alcuin's own heart, if not—as well may be—bearing the marks of his own composition, was that most important Letter, addressed by Charles some time between 794 and 796 particularly to Baugulf, abbot of the monastery of Fulda in Hesse-Nassau, but intended for the serious attention of all bishops and abbots in his realm. Under the title, *Karoli Epistola de Litteris Colendis,* it has been printed and translated frequently. Its content, however, is so important for the understanding of Alcuin's working with the King that it must again find place here:

"Charles, by Grace of God, King of the Franks and of the Lombards, and Patrician of the Romans, to Abbot Baugulf and all his community, and to our faithful fellow-Christians: In the Name of Almighty God, Loving Greeting.

"Be it known to your devotion, pleasing to God, that we, together with these faithful, have judged it expedient that throughout the monasteries entrusted by the grace of Christ to us for governance, in addition to the following of the Regular Life and the discipline of holy Religion, monks who by the gift of God are able to learn should also give due care to the teaching of letters, according to their individual capacity; to the end that even as the Regular Life fosters in monks uprightness of manners, so perseverance in teaching and in learning may order and adorn in them literary form; that those who seek to please God by rightful living may not neglect to please Him also by correct speaking. For it is written: *By your words you shall be justified, or by your words you shall be condemned.* It is better, in truth, to do well than to know; yet knowing is prior to doing. Therefore each man must learn that which he desires to carry out, and the soul will more fully understand its duty when the tongue declares the praises of Almighty God without offence of falsities.

"Now falsities are to be avoided by all men; but much more, so far as is humanly possible, by those who are openly called to this one thing, the singular serving of truth. Of late years writings have frequently been sent to us from monasteries, telling us that the brethren are diligent for us in holy and pious prayer. Yet in many of these writings we have perceived goodly feeling clothed in rough writing; the faithful dictation of the heart could not find correct expression in words because of lack of learning.

"We began to fear, therefore, lest this might lead to lamentable want of understanding of the Holy Scriptures, and we all know well that, dangerous as are errors in form, errors of understanding are far more to be feared.

"Wherefore we exhort you, with most humble effort pleasing to God, not to neglect the study of letters, but to learn eagerly for this end, that more easily and rightly you may penetrate the mysteries of the Divine Scriptures. For when figures of speech, metaphors and the like, are found amid the sacred text, none can doubt that each reader is the quicker to gain spiritual understanding as he shall have been the better instructed beforehand in grammar.

"Let men, then, be appointed for this work, willing and able to learn and keen to teach, and let this be done with that same energy with which we now bid the same. For we would that you, as becomes the soldiers of the Church, should be both inwardly devout and outwardly learned, pure in goodly living and cultured in goodly speaking; so that whosoever shall visit you, for the Name of the Lord and the repute of your holy life, may both be edified, as he looks upon you, at your outward aspect, and instructed in wisdom, as he listens to you, through your skill in reading and in chant. So shall he who came only to see return home inspired both by sight and by hearing, giving joyful thanks to Almighty God." [6]

Alcuin's interest in the political history of Frankland was naturally not so keen as in its progress in education, sacred and secular, especially during the earlier years, when he had not yet determined to stay in permanence. His letters during these years were largely directed to his friends in England. There had not yet been time and occasion for forging those intimate bonds which were to hold him so firmly in touch with various men on the continent. Yet no one, and certainly no one as sensitive and quick to respect and admire as Alcuin, could live for even a short while near King Charles without being drawn into his world of political thought and doings.

In 782 the war against the Saxons, after a momentary lull, was again drawing the King's energy into full tide.[7] A great Assembly at Lippspringe—the source of the Lippe, near Paderborn—had brought out the Saxons in their multitude for the making of peace, together with envoys from that chieftain so formidable to Alcuin and his friends, Sigfrid the Dane, and from the Avars, as well. Only the Saxon Widukind was absent, in his obdurate refusal to yield the submission rendered to the Frankish conqueror by so many of his people. It was a great triumph; and Charles even dared in his confidence to raise some of the Saxon leaders to the office and work of Count after the manner of Frankish administration.[8]

As before, he was over-sanguine. Below the Süntelgebirge,

[6] *Cap. reg. Fr.* I, 78f.; P. Lehmann, *Fuldaer Studien, SBM* 1927, 2. *Abh.* 8f. (the text used here). For its influence see Curtius, *Europ. Lit.* 55f.

[7] *ARF ann.* 782ff. On Alcuin in regard to the Saxon War see Hilde Mühlner, *Hist. Stud.* 308, 1937, 11ff.; Rüngeler, 40ff.

[8] *Ann. Lauresh.* = *Chron. Moiss. ann.* 782; Hauck II, 392f.

the range running on the bank of the Weser between Hameln and Minden, his army, despatched against the rebel Sorbs, was suddenly attacked by the Saxons under Widukind. Nearly all the Franks were killed, including two *missi*—or special administrative envoys, Adalgis and Geilo by name—four counts or grafs, and twenty leading nobles.[9] Charles hastened to avenge this disaster, and came up with the Saxon enemy at the meeting of the river Aller with the Weser. Once again they declared submission, yielding to him those of their number who had taken part in the recent attack.

The victory was marked by horror. Tradition, supported by excellent historical evidence, declares that forty-five hundred of these captives were beheaded by his orders on one day at Verden on the Aller.[10] Widukind again escaped to the shelter of the North.

The next two years saw renewed rising of the enemy, and Charles in spite of the death of his wife, Queen Hildegard, and of his mother, drove himself and his Franks forward ever more furiously for the ending of the long struggle. At Detmold in Lippe, and on the Haase, a tributary of the Enns, he conquered the rebels—only to face, in the next year, 784, another wave of attack from Saxons and Frisians combined. Now he drew his son Charles, a boy of twelve, into the campaign. After a concentrated effort in Saxony against the tribes of both east and west, and a winter spent in the enemy's country, where Fastrada, his Queen since the autumn of 783, and his children joined him, the summer of 785 at length saw him master of these Saxon peoples. Their forts and settlements lay in ruins, their fields were deserted and ravaged, their chieftain Widu-

[9] *ARF ann.* 782; Halphen, *Etudes,* 163ff.

[10] *ARF, Ann. S. Amandi, Chron. Moiss. ann.* 782; Hauck II, 394. Wiedemann, 22, explains this mass execution as caused by the King's loyalty to his slain friends. Some authorities suspect exaggeration in the number; cf. Fichtenau, 30, 42.

kind found himself caught on all sides and forced to submit. At the royal country-house of Attigny in the Ardennes the victory attained its desired end in the solemn baptizing of this chieftain and his supporters.[11] "Then the whole of Saxony was subject," and Pope Hadrian wrote in ecstatic congratulation to his "spiritual co-father and most excellent son Charles": "By Divine inspiration you have brought that whole Saxon race to the holy font of baptism! So much the more do we give praise to the Divine Mercy because in our and your time the people of the heathen have come beneath your royal sway into true religion and the perfect Faith." Three days of public thanksgiving were decreed throughout the dominion of the Church of Rome to mark this triumph.[12] Henceforward the King of the Franks had to deal with rebellion of the Saxon peoples, not with their conquest.[13]

Sometime between 775 and 795, probably within the period 782–785, Charles issued a General Edict in regard to the peoples of Saxony.[14] Its provisions relate principally to the Catholic religion, its practice and its obligations for these new subjects of the Frankish King. Death was the penalty prescribed for burning a Christian church; for theft of any of its content; for wilfully eating meat in Lent; for killing any one of the clergy; for celebrating pagan ritual; for refusing Christian baptism; for conspiring against Christian men; for disloyalty toward the Lord King. It might, indeed, be remitted, by witness of a priest, for the guilty who should of their own accord confess

[11] *ARF, Chron. Moiss. ann.* 785. For discussion of the baptism of Widukind for political, not religious reasons, see Wiedemann, 24ff.

[12] *Epp.* III, 607f.

[13] Cf. M. Lintzel, *Hist. Stud.* 227, 1933, 44ff.

[14] *Capitulatio de Partibus Saxoniae,* ed. von Schwerin, *Leges Saxonum,* 1918, 37ff., and ed. von Richthofen, *MGH Leges* V, 1889, 34ff. Halphen, *Etudes,* 180, dates the *Lex Saxonum* (ed. von Schwerin, *ibid.* 17ff., ed. von Richthofen, *ibid.* 47ff.) at the same time (785) as this *Capitulatio*. For varying opinion on this *Capitulatio* see Halphen, *Etudes,* 171ff., *Charlemagne,* 68f.; Calmette, 87f.; Ketterer, 226.

to him their offences and submit to penance; fugitives to the sanctuary of a church were also to be granted life, and left for sentence to the King's clemency.

On the material side this legislation was equally severe. All Saxons, high and low alike, were to give a tenth of their property and labour to their churches and their priests.

Revenge came eventually. A small rising on the Elbe in 792 was followed by a general Saxon revolution.[15] As the pious annalist of the Franks put it: "The Saxons showed right clearly what had been lurking in their heart. As a dog that returns to its vomit, so did they return to the paganism they had once spewed forth, again forsaking Christianity, lying both to God and to the Lord King who had bestowed on them many benefits, joining themselves to the pagan peoples that were round about them. . . . They laid waste all the churches that were on their borders, with pillage and fire, casting out bishops and priests; some they seized, others they slew, and fully turned themselves again to the worship of idols."[16]

Charles was equal even to this conflagration. Although war against the Avars was engaging his soldiers and he could not move in force until 794,[17] in that year he sent Prince Charles westward against the Saxons by way of the Rhine at Cologne, while he himself advanced from the south. On the plain of Sendfeld near Paderborn they all turned to surrender, "conquered without a battle."[18] When, however, they failed to send him the aid he needed in 795 for his other campaigns, he exacted from them "so great a number of hostages as had never before been known in all the days of the Frankish kings."[19]

[15] *Ann. S. Amandi, ann.* 792; B.M.L. 135, No. 317b; Halphen, *Etudes,* 184ff.

[16] *Ann. Laureshn. ann.* 792.

[17] Halphen, *Etudes,* 189.

[18] *ARF* ("Einhardi"), *ann.* 794.

[19] *Ann. Lauresh., Alamannici, Maxim. ann.* 795. Cf. Dawson, 219: "The religion of Charles was like that of Islam, a religion of the sword, and his private life, in spite of his sincere piety, resembled that of a Moslem ruler."

The treatment of these Saxons did not fail to impress Alcuin. Ravaging, massacre, and bloodshed, indeed, mattered little, even to his mind, compared with conversion. In 790 he wrote cheerfully to Colcu, that Irish teacher he had known in York: [20] "First of all, dear friend, I must tell you that by the mercy of God His holy Church in Europe is at peace, is advancing and growing. For the Old Saxons and all the tribes of the Frisians by the power of King Charles, working on some by rewards, on others by threats, have been converted to the Faith of Christ." [21] The same spirit is shown in a letter to "Damoetas"—Riculf, Archbishop of Mainz—with King Charles in Saxony, apparently in 794: "I am worried about your leaving for the enemy's country; so many dangers threaten. All the same, he who has just cause in his journey and his fight for God can trust in His aid. May His angel protect you in all troubles, and do pray that He may bring home David, His beloved, and all of you in joyful victory." In 795 he wrote to the community in his beloved York: "I have not forgotten your prayer that I would come to you. But the King has gone to lay waste Saxony, and I could not leave without his permission. A friend such as he is not to be scorned by one like me. By grace of God my friendship with him has helped many people. Not for greed of gold—He Who knows my heart is witness—did I come to Frankland or stay in it, but for the need of the Church and the firmer knowledge of the Catholic Faith." [22] There is also a letter from him to Queen Liutgard, asking her for news of the King and of the "Christian army": "Where is he spending the winter and when will he be back?" The same year he remarks that he is starting to meet Charles on his return from Saxony.[23]

Yet nothing must be done unwisely which might hinder this

[20] Page 29 *supra*.
[21] *Epp.* IV, 32.
[22] *Ibid.* 66f., 88f.; cf. 90 (No. 44).
[23] Ibid. 93f.

same excellent conversion, and therefore a different note is sounded in Alcuin's letters of 796. To Arno, bishop of Salzburg, he writes as one clearly worried: "Do you be a preacher of righteousness, not an exactor of tithes, because a new spirit must be nourished with the milk of apostolic kindness until it grow and become strong for the receiving of solid food. The tribute of the tenth, they say, is upsetting the faith of the Saxons. *Why* must a yoke be placed on the necks of ignorant men which neither we nor our brethren could bear?"

So strong was his feeling that he sent letter after letter on this matter to the Court. He begged Megenfrid, the King's treasurer, to use his influence with Charles: "Those who receive money in return for preaching ought carefully to consider age, place, time, each particular individual. If the light yoke of Christ and His pleasant burden were to be preached to the hard Saxon people as insistently as the rendering of tithes and legal retribution, exacted by the edict for each little fault, perhaps they would not reject the sacrament of baptism. Really, do let our leaders of the Faith take a lesson from the Apostles; let them be revealers, not stealers." [24] The King himself received the same entreaty in regard to conquered Saxons and Avars: "What glory shall be yours, most happy King, in the Day of eternal retribution, when all whom you have turned from idols to knowledge of the true God shall follow you, standing in blessedness before the judgment-seat of our Lord Jesus Christ! See with how great devotion and kindness you have toiled to soften the hard hearts of the unhappy Saxon people, for the increase of the Name of Christ! But, because election in them seems not yet to have been of God, there still remain many of them to be damned with the devil in the filth of most evil practice. . . . Give these conquered peoples teachers who shall feed them with the milk of babes.

[24] *Ibid.* 154, 159ff.: *praedicatores, non praedatores;* Addison, 50ff.

Tithes, surely, are good. But better to lose these tithes than the faith of souls. And remember the teaching of Saint Augustine: First, let a man be taught and brought to faith. Then, and only then, shall he be baptized."

His urgings, however, availed little, and he wrote sadly again to his friend Arno: "And so the wretched Saxons have so often lost the grace of baptism because they never had the foundation of faith in their hearts. What avails baptism without faith? A man can be driven to baptism, but not to belief." [25]

The Saxon war brings us again into touch with Willehad, Alcuin's young kinsman, whom Alcuin himself had seen solemnly sent out from Northumbria about 770 to work for the conversion of the Frisians. This he had done at Dokkum, known for the martyrdom of Boniface in 754, also in the region across the river Lauwers, and in the province of Drenthe, where he himself almost suffered the same end. His renown, in course of time, reached Charles, ever eager to find missionaries for his newly-conquered heathen; and the King sent him in 780 to carry on his ministry among the Saxons throughout Wihmode, the district lying between the estuaries of the Elbe and the Weser.[26] Much had been done, churches were rising

[25] *Epp.* 157ff., 164; cf. 289 (dated 799, Alcuin to Charles): *Componatur pax cum populo nefando, si fieri potest . . . Olim vestrae sanctissime pietati de exactione decimarum dixi: quia forte melius est, vel aliquanto spatio ut remittatur publica necessitas, donec fides cordibus radicitus inolescat; si tamen illa patria Dei electione digna habetur. Qui foras recesserunt, optimi fuerunt christiani, sicut in plurimis notum est. Et qui remanserunt patria, in faecibus malitiae permanserunt. Nam Babylon propter peccata populi daemoniorum deputata est habitatio, ut in prophetis legitur.* These are strong words; see Wiedemann, 29f., 35ff., and cf. Moss, 227; Viard, 93f.; Rüngeler, 40ff.; Kleinclausz, *Charlemagne,* 139f. The capitulary of Charles, dated Oct. 28, 797, showed important lightening of penalties for the Saxons: *Cap. reg. Fr.* I, 71f.; Kleinclausz, *Alcuin,* 136; Glotz I, ii, 457.

[26] Anskar, *Vita S. Willehadi: SS* II, 380ff.; Halphen, *Etudes,* 170; Levison, 110. See O. H. May, *Regesten der Erzbischöfe von Bremen* I, 1937, 1ff.

and priests were being ordained to serve them, when the rebellion of Widukind and his Westphalian Saxons drove Willehad from the land to take refuge, first with Pepin, King of Italy, and then in Rome. Encouraged by the sympathy of Pope Hadrian, he returned to Frankland and lived for two years in retirement at Echternach, by invitation of its abbot, Beornred, friend of Alcuin. After the submission and consequent baptism of Widukind, he resumed his work. In 787 he was consecrated at Worms bishop over Wihmode and adjacent lands, with his "bishop's stool" at Bremen. There he dedicated his cathedral of Saint Peter on the first of November, 789, and died a week later of fever.

Alcuin still remembered in Frankland the student and priest he had known in Northumbria. In a letter, written shortly before Willehad died to a friend in Saxony, he sent a message: "Give a thousand greetings to my Willehad, the Bishop. I am so sorry that I left him. I wish I may see him again."

The same letter continues: "Do write and tell me how the Saxons are taking your preaching. Is there any hope of the conversion of the Danes? Are the Wiltzi, that people the King has lately conquered, learning the Faith of Christ? What *is* going on there, and what is the King going to do about the enemy Huns?" [27]

By "Huns" Alcuin here means the Avars, barbarians akin to the Huns and regularly confused with them by the Franks. In the past they had long raided the lands of the Byzantine Empire and had reduced its Emperor to payment of rich tribute. They roamed over Hungary and what is now Yugoslavia, over the plains stretching from the Save and Drave to the Theiss. There, far remote from civilization, lay their great

[27] *Epp.* IV, 31. For the bishopric of Bremen cf. Tangl, *MOG* XVIII, 1897, 65. Hauck (II, 388, note 5) sees in Alcuin's words concerning Willehad evidence of some share in Willehad's mission.

and mysterious city, the *Ring*, fortified by its mighty circular walls, of which tradition numbered nine.[28] Here they had piled through the centuries the plunder they had carried off, and the glamour of their unreckoned treasure was told everywhere among men. Now they had ceased to menace Constantinople and were turning their eyes toward the Frankish Empire. Alcuin wrote, in that letter of 790 to Colcu: "The Avars, whom we call the Huns, have blazed out against Italy and, conquered by the Christians, have returned home in shame. Yes, and they have raided Bavaria, too, and here, also, they have been defeated and scattered by the Christian army." [29]

Their two inroads, into Italian Friuli and into Bavaria, were met then, for the moment. But Charles was not the man to let the menace grow unchecked. Was not this, moreover, another crusade ready to his hand? In 791 he marched against these heathen Avars, reached the river Enns, where he sent off to his Queen Fastrada the letter we have noticed, telling of the success of young Pepin, his son, and from thence advanced to the Raab. His delight in victory, however, was sorely dimmed by a plague which attacked his horses and left only one out of every ten alive. So, at least, the old annals declare.[30] Nor was victory at once complete, since the Saxon war was exacting too much toll for a final blow here. But in 795 the soldiers of Eric, Duke of Friuli, with the aid of the Slavs, dared to penetrate the innermost stronghold of the Avars, killed their Lord, the Khagan, broke into the great *Ring,* and captured vast treasure. The same year an Avar prince or "tudun," only second in dignity to the Khagan, sent word to Charles that he was ready to submit to Frankish orders and Christian baptism. Pepin, King of Italy, followed Eric's army in 796 to finish the

[28] Monach. Sangall., ed. von Knonau, 33f.
[29] *Epp.* IV, 32; *ARF ann.* 788.
[30] *ARF* (see both versions) *ann.* 791.

destruction of the *Ring* and to carry off further loads of plunder. The "tudun" was duly baptized at Aachen with his followers, although, it must be confessed, his new loyalty was but skin-deep. Trains of wagons arrived there, bearing to the King all the spoil. Congratulations were clearly in order.[31]

Alcuin, certainly, did not spare his pen. Duke Eric visited him shortly after the victory, it would seem, perhaps in escorting his wagons to the Court, and Alcuin wrote to thank him for this honour and to wish lasting success to his "brave arm against the adversaries of the Lord's holy Name." He wrote of his joy to Paulinus of Aquileia, also, full of eagerness to know what the Patriarch was going to do for the souls of these barbarians, so near to his land: "The eyes of so many are upon you, good Father." To Arno, bishop of Salzburg, went a word of blessing, for he was setting out on a mission to the Avars, to prove the truth of their submission: "If God's grace shall look upon their kingdom, who may dare to refuse to them the ministry of salvation?" And Charles received again Alcuin's cry of thanksgiving: "Christ has brought beneath your soldiers, fighting for His glory, the peoples of the Huns, dreaded for their savagery and their courage from old time." At the same time he begged for mercy and for prudence in the work of conversion among these Avars.[32]

From the enormous booty splendid gifts, originally intended for Pope Hadrian, were despatched to Rome. But Hadrian

[31] *ARF, Ann. Lauresh. ann.* 795, 796; Sym. Dun. II, 57; *PLAC* I, 116f.: *De Pippini regis victoria Avarica* (anonymous poem, "inconditum sed vividum": Dümmler); cf. Raby, *SLP* I, 210f.

[32] *Epp.* IV, 142f., 154, 157, cf. 162ff., 173f.; Theodulf, *Ad Car. Reg.: PLAC* I, 484, l. 39. For the influence of Alcuin's pleading upon Paulinus see Halphen, *Charlemagne,* 85f.; cf. Paulinus himself (*Concil. aevi Kar.* I, 174): *Haec autem gens bruta et inrationabilis vel certe idiota et sine litteris, tardior atque laboriosa ad cognoscenda sacra mysteria invenitur.*

by this time was dead. The offering, therefore, went to his successor, with a letter from Charles telling both of his sorrow and of his thanksgiving for the uninterrupted intercession to Heaven from the Chair of Saint Peter.[33] Queen Liutgard sent from her share a gift to Paulinus of Aquileia, announced by Alcuin in writing to this friend of his in Italy: "My daughter, the Queen, a woman religious and devoted to God, has forwarded to you two armlets of gold, asking you to pray for her with your priests." [34]

The other campaigns mentioned by Alcuin in the letters written before 797 may be briefly described. The Welatabi, whom the Franks called Wiltzi, lived beyond the Elbe, and thus had been brought close to the empire of Charles after his conquest of the Saxons. In 789 he crossed the river, laid waste their country, and received the submission of their chieftain Dragawit and his nobles.[35]

Alcuin's hope that the terrible Sigfrid, King of the Danes, might be baptized was, so far as we know, never fulfilled. Sigfrid prudently sent envoys to discuss peace; but he did all he could to aid the enemies of Charles and of Christianity.[36] There is no mention in Alcuin's letters of Tassilo, Duke of Bavaria, that cousin of Charles who, under Pepin, had struck for independence. Under Charles he had given much trouble, also, and had finally been deposed in 788, to face weary days as prisoner in the monastery of Jumièges. Alcuin must have seen his misery when in 794, clothed in monk's habit, he appeared again to plead for mercy at the Synod of Frankfurt.[37]

In one of his letters from the Court Alcuin mentions the Saracens: "The leaders and officers of our Most Christian King have taken a great part of Spain from the Saracens, about

[33] *ARF ann.* 796; *Epp.* IV, 136f. [34] *Ibid.* 140.
[35] *ARF ann.* 789. [36] *Ibid. ann.* 782.
[37] *ARF* and *Reginonis Prum. Chron.* ed. Kurze, *SRGS ann.* 788; *Cap. reg. Fr.* I, 74 (3); *Chron. Moiss. ann.* 794.

three hundred miles along the seacoast. But, the shame of it! those same accursed Saracens, also called Agarenes, hold control all over Africa and much of greater Asia." [38]

There is also here a passing reference to the Greeks of Sicily, once again rising against the Frankish power under the lively encouragement of the progeny of Desiderius: Adelchis, his son, always eager to return from his exile in Constantinople, and Adelperga, his daughter, wife of the ambitious Arichis, Duke of Beneventum.[39] Beneventum, indeed, had given Charles deep concern and had sent him again across the Alps to Italy in 786. At Rome the next year, 787, after keeping Christmas in Florence, he had discussed matters with Pope Hadrian and had decided to march against Arichis in person. Arichis, however, did not live to see the end of this campaign, and finally his younger son, Grimoald, was installed as Duke of Beneventum after swearing homage to Charles as overlord.[40] The Pope had disapproved heartily of this step, but the event proved its wisdom. "The Greeks came upon Italy with their fleet," wrote Alcuin, of a Greek expedition in 788; "but they were conquered by the King's generals and fled to their ships. They say that four thousand of them were killed and a thousand captured." The people of Beneventum at this time remained loyal to their Frankish bond.[41]

Often, too, Alcuin's thoughts during his years at the Frankish Court, from 782 to 796, must have turned to Constantinople itself, especially since much friction had developed between that city and the kingdom of the Franks when the long-standing

[38] *Epp.* IV, 32. Alcuin is referring here to the surrender of the city of Gerona to Charles: *Chron. Moiss. ann.* 785; Abel-Simson I, 510f.

[39] Page 74 *supra.*

[40] *ARF ann.* 786f., 788; *Cod. Carol.* Nos. 78, 80, 82f., 84: *Epp.* III, 610ff.; Abel-Simson I, 603ff.; Poupardin, *Le Moyen Age* XIX, 1906, 254ff.; Erchempert, *SRLI* 236.

[41] *Epp.* IV, 32.

engagement between the young Emperor Constantine and the Frankish Princess Rotrud had been broken. The Frankish annals declare that Charles himself forbade the marriage, to the great wrath of the Empress Irene; [42] but the Greek account holds her responsible.[43] According to this narrative, Constantine, who had been romantically in love with his dream of his far-off betrothed, was heart-broken when, at the end of six years, his mother suddenly forced him to wed a woman of Armenian race, named Maria. In any case, he was politically no match for this Empress, his co-ruler, and her minions, especially her chief minister, the eunuch Stauracius. Irene was entirely determined to be "Emperor" in her sole right, without partner and without control. "And so he, though strong and able, found himself exercising no authority. And it pained him to see Stauracius, the Patrician and Logothete, controlling all things, and all men coming to Stauracius and no one daring to seek out himself, the Emperor."

At last he could bear it no longer. In 790, with three men who were his friends, he planned to arrest his mother, send her off to Sicily, banish Stauracius, and be master himself in Constantinople. For a while he was successful, and both Irene and her supporter retired from the scene. Fundamentally, however, he was weak and undecided; and in 792 he gave up and let his mother remain in power. He also did himself much harm some years later by banishing his detested Armenian wife to a convent. Other report declared, indeed, that the Lady Irene was secretly guilty in this, because she wanted to make him unpopular among the people. Constantine, perhaps in a desperate effort at self-assertion, horrified the Church in

[42] *ARF* ("Einhardi"), *ann.* 788; Abel-Simson II, 423; cf. *Gesta s. Patr. Fontanell. coen.*, ed. Lohier and Laporte, 1936, 85f.

[43] Theophanes, 463. Jealousy of her proposed daughter-in-law may well have moved her: Amann, 446.

795 by wedding "in unlawful union" Theodote, a lady-in-waiting in the Palace, and by crowning her as his Empress.[44]

2

In the midst of all his particular work in the Palace School and his general concern for the evangelization of the heathen, Saxon or Dane, Avar, Slav or Sorb, Alcuin found time to carry on a never-ceasing correspondence with men and women of all ranks and callings. Popes, prelates, monks and nuns, scholars and students, good, bad, and indifferent, received his sympathy, his rebukes, his congratulations, his counsel. To a spirit of intense interest in his fellow-men this was entirely necessary; and the toil of dictating or of penning that multitude of letters from which some three hundred have been saved for us, largely through the care of his friend Arno,[45] was to him as nothing compared with his need of friendship. We cannot, indeed, imagine how many must have been written in all, especially to King Charles and to Arno himself, the two men who meant most to him in his later years.

To Pope Hadrian he wrote as Chief Pastor of the Church: "Surely I know that the devotion of Your Holiness is ever interceding for the Christian people of all the world, yet in more special act for those who with larger faith flee to the prayers of so great a power. By my baptism I was brought into the fold of that Shepherd Who commended His flock to Peter, and you, Father, I confess as heir of that power. Here, then, is a little sheep of your charge, sorely sick with many sins. And so I offer myself to that healing which is yours, loving Father, handed down in long succession from Christ the Lord." [46]

When toward the end of Alcuin's stay in Aachen Hadrian

[44] Theophanes, 470, 484.
[45] Sickel, *Alcuinstudien* I, 8f., 19; Dümmler, *Epp.* IV, 3.
[46] *Epp.* IV, 68f.

died, on Christmas Day, 795, King Charles commanded an epitaph to be inserted in letters of gold upon marble for the adorning of his tomb in Rome. There was keen competition among the Court poets for the honour of authorship of these verses, and Alcuin, it seems, was victor, defeating Theodulf. The successful competition was duly inscribed. Then Alcuin wrote, as in duty bound, to Hadrian's successor, elected immediately as Leo the third: "Always have I loved, so far as was in me, the princes and shepherds of the See of Rome, desiring to be numbered by their intercession among the sheep of Christ. Draw us, the sons of Holy Church, by your prayers and your letters, within its firm and lasting fold." [47]

Arno, or Arn, was usually described by Alcuin as "Aquila," "The Eagle," in translation of the German. This he explained thus: "Your parents, albeit ignorant of God's working, gave you a prophetic name. For He ordained you to minister the Mysteries of heaven, and with piercing spiritual vision, poised above the waves of this world's stormy sea, to pluck men as fish for everlasting life." [48] "The Eagle" was Bavarian by birth, very probably of Italian descent, as Alcuin refers twice to his "black hair." [49] He was ordained priest in 776 and then left his native country to become one of the community of St. Amand, in Elno. This monastery, founded in the seventh century by the monk whose name it bears, missionary to the regions of Ghent and Maastricht, was famous afterward among seekers of his relics.[50] It lay on the rivers Elnon and Scarpe, where now the busy Saint-Amand-les-Eaux offers its mineral springs for bodily ills. Alcuin wrote some verses in

[47] Seppelt, 184; *Ann. Lauresh. ann.* 795; Sym. Dun. II, 56f.; *PLAC* I, 101, 113f., 238, 245, 247, 254f.; *Epp.* IV, 138f.; cf. Theodulf, *PLAC* I, 489f.

[48] *Epp.* IV, 163. Old Germ. *arn* = *aquila*. On Arno see Hauck II, 430ff.

[49] *Epp.* IV, 321, 384.

[50] Hauck I, 325.

praise of its Founder; also inscriptions, both for the church built by its Abbot Gislebert, the bishop of Noyon at a later time, who died in 782, and for various works of beautifying and enlarging carried out there by Arno. Arno was installed as abbot of St. Amand on the Feast of Pentecost, three days after Gislebert had gone to his reward, and he always loved it, even after he had left it in 785 by the desire of King Charles that he should return to Bavaria as bishop of Salzburg. He enlarged its crypt, raised twelve arches in honour of Saint Michael, restored the tomb of St. Amand, and made a new shrine for the resting of its departed brethren, "because he could not bear the ugliness of the old one." [51]

At Salzburg he worked hard for both loveliness of material building and for culture of mind. The tradition of his predecessor, the famous Virgil, had left high renown to its school of learning. In the scriptorium at Salzburg, it was said, more than one hundred and fifty books were copied under Arno, and young men were attracted there as students and teachers. The adornments he made for the glory of its Church of Saint Peter, dedicated by Rupert, the Founder-Saint of Salzburg, were also told by Alcuin, in verses written for the honouring of its many altars and chapels.[52]

But Arno's energy found time also for political service to his secular leaders. In 787 Tassilo, Duke of Bavaria, sent him on a mission to Pope Hadrian to seek peace between the Duke and King Charles; and Charles himself often used the urbane wisdom of Arno in the same way.[53]

Alcuin writes, in these earlier years, of his longing to see his friend: "My waiting has gone for nothing, my hope is all empty. Oh! if only I had you here instead of hoping for you, how full my joy would be! Hope is good in absence, but

[51] *PLAC* I, 305ff., 338.
[52] *Ibid.* 335ff.
[53] *ARF ann.* 787.

better is love in real presence. Well, we must have patience. . . . But my mind is tossed in a sea of thoughts, longing for you as a harbour of steady confidence, driven in the surge and no haven in sight. I loved your gifts; only they make me feel worse because you are not here." [54]

Riculf, who succeeded Lul at Mainz, we have already seen as "Damoetas," writing verses for Alcuin. He, too, was known for his building. The Church at Mainz of Saint Alban (not the martyr of England, but one who suffered death in Riculf's city) was raised by him.[55] To him, also, Alcuin tells of disappointment: "How miserable it is that the people one loves are nearly always absent! But, then, I do what I can, remembering you before God." Another time Riculf has sent him a comb, and he returns "as many thanks as my present has teeth, of the most beautiful ivory." Then, as always, he goes on to plead: "Dear son, amid all the distractions of the world, don't forget yourself. Stay your mind in God by prayer while you comfort your body, tired out by travelling. God keep you wherever you go." [56]

Another Riculf, bishop of Cologne, had become known to Alcuin during his travels in Frankland before 782.[57] His successor, Hildebold, who attained the pallium as Cologne's Archbishop, we have seen as intimate friend of Charles. The King asked permission of the Pope that Hildebold might be absent from his cathedral to fulfil "the needs of the Church" at the Court and petitioned the Church at the Synod of Frankfurt in 794 to confirm the Papal assent.[58] Alcuin marked his adorning

[54] *Epp.* IV, 102f.; cf. *PLAC* I, 239f., 260f.

[55] *PLAC* I, 431.

[56] *Epp.* IV, 77, 67f.; cf. 29f.; *PLAC* I, 223.

[57] Page 35 *supra.*

[58] *Cap. reg. Fr.* I, 78 (55). Hildebold was "bishop" in 794, but "Archbishop" in 795: Perlbach, *NA* XIII, 1888, 161, No. 32; Ketterer, 182; Hauck II, 212, note 4.

of the cathedral at Cologne by some verses; and about 794 Charles wrote to him and to the bishops of Rouen, Constance, and Eichstätt a theological letter, of the kind that the King delighted to think out with Alcuin, on the sevenfold grace of the Holy Spirit.[59]

More interesting, perhaps, is Alcuin's correspondence with Ricbod, whom he called "Macharius." Ricbod, abbot of Lorsch and bishop of Trier,[60] had once been a student of his; and Alcuin duly honoured him, too, for his gifts to the house of the Lord. But there were words of complaint as well as of praise. He has not come to see Alcuin for a very long time, has not even written to him for a whole year. "I would almost rather have you poor, with me, than rich, away from me. What care I whether you are rich, if I don't see you? Your power is only sorrow to me. Where is that pleasant talk of ours? That discussion of sacred books which I miss so badly? What has your Father done, that his son should forget him? What the Master, that his student has held him in neglect? Is it that you have become too great in the world to remember him who taught you?"

There is, however, worse to come. "Or is it *Virgil* who has made you forget me? Flaccus" (the name by which Alcuin himself was called in the Palace School) "has gone, Virgil has come, to build his nest in the Master's place. I am angry with you. I pray that the Four Gospels, not the Twelve Books of Aeneas, may fill your mind!" [61]

Like Willibrord, and like Boniface, Alcuin loved to stay in the peace of the monastery of Echternach, especially under the hospitality of his cousin, the Anglo-Saxon Beornred, its abbot for twenty years. Since Charles readily endowed his

[59] *Epp.* IV, 529ff.; *PLAC* I, 334.

[60] Very probably Archbishop. See for him Hauck II, 214, note 3; Levison, 235, note 5.

[61] *PLAC* I, 305, 248f.; *Epp.* IV, 38f.; cf. 93, 119f., 318.

prelates with more than one charge of souls, this Beornred, or "Samuel," who also served the King well as diplomatic envoy, remained ruler of Echternach even after he was appointed first the bishop, and afterward the Archbishop, of Sens.[62] Alcuin writes him from Echternach: "You had better stay at Sens. Here we are all hungry and there is nothing left for you, holy bishop. Don't forget me as you sit warm by your fire, and don't forget to say grace when the rich feast comes into your dining-hall!" But Beornred was no idler. He loved his grammarians, Priscian and Phocas, and he read and copied for himself Alcuin's Commentary on Saint John's Gospel long before it came to publication.[63]

Among other bishops who received letters were Remedius of Chur, whom Alcuin thanks warmly for his gifts, "I am delighted that you keep me in mind," and Agino, that prelate of Constance with whom Charles the King discussed theology. Alcuin, like most men of his time, had a great desire for relics of the saints, and he reminds Agino of a promise to send him some. Angilbert was passing Constance in making one of those journeys to Rome for Charles, and would bring them: "I will humbly and gladly accept whatever you care to send, and will repay you as I can, when I know what you would like." [64]

Among other monasteries in Frankland connected by letter with Alcuin during these years were those of St. Denis, Corbie, St. Riquier, St. Martin's at Tours, Nouaillé, Fleury, and Aniane. For Fulrad, veteran statesman and arch-chaplain of the King as well as abbot of St. Denis, he wrote an epitaph after his death in 784, and another for Maginar who succeeded him in office.[65] The next abbot, Fardulf, merits special

[62] *Cat. abb. Ept.*: *SS* XIII, 738; *Epp.* III, 632; B.M.L. 152, No. 343.
[63] *Epp.* IV, 93.
[64] *Ibid.* 117ff.
[65] *PLAC* I, 318f.; cf. *Hibern. Exulis Carm., ibid.* 404; Sickel, *Acta* I, 77, note 1.

note because he was a foreigner, that Lombard captive who revealed to Charles in 792 the plot of his eldest son, Pepin the Hunchback. For his loyalty he was rewarded by appointment to St. Denis.[66] This he acknowledged in verses, for he was one of the minor poets of the time. He showed his gratitude to the King in more solid form by building for his royal usage as guest of St. Denis a great hall "after old Frankish pattern," and by carrying the relics of St. Denis on campaign with him to bless the King's crusade in Saxony.[67]

From Angilbert of St. Riquier Alcuin also asked relics. In honour of Magulf, abbot of St. Benoît-sur-Loire, Fleury, he composed metrical inscriptions to mark the oratory this "son of Benedict" had built and the refectory table he had bought for the glory of his Benedictine house. Similar lines from Alcuin's pen record the restoration at Nouaillé, in the diocese of Poitiers, of its Church of the Mother of God by its abbot Ato.[68]

Itherius, another recipient of Alcuin's letters, was abbot of St. Martin's, Tours, from about 775 until 796. He was high in rank and in esteem both in Church and in State. Waifar, Duke of Aquitaine, had given him as a noble hostage to King Pepin. Charles had repeatedly sent him, in company with Maginar of St. Denis, to Rome on missions for his service. "Itherius and Maginar," the Pope writes to Charles, "religious abbots, have asked us what penance should be meted out to Saxons who have renounced their conversion to Christianity." And again, "Your Excellence promised me a thousand pounds of tin for the restoration of the roof of Saint Peter's, and Itherius, your faithful envoy, has promised to send me through

[66] *ARF* ("Einhardi"), *ann.* 792.

[67] *PLAC* I, 352ff.; *AA. SS.* Oct. IV, 933.

[68] *Epp.* IV, 37; *PLAC* I, 328f., 323, 325f. For the honouring of our Lady by Alcuin in his work see S. Beissel, *Gesch. der Verehrung Marias in Deutschland während des Mittelalters,* 1909, 39f., 58f., 307.

your generosity another thousand." [69] Alcuin knew Itherius when he was old and drawing near his death: "Pain during earthly time brings health for eternity," he wrote him. "But don't delay now. Do what you mean to do, of your own free will; don't wait till necessity compels. I write, God knows, of my love and desire for you. I know that I shall have no friend like you hereafter at St. Martin's. We have served the world well enough these many days. Let us live unto God in the few that remain. Now read this with joy, begin with decision, fulfil in blessedness, and God be with you forever." [70]

Adalhard, abbot of the monastery of Saints Peter and Paul, Corbie, was of the royal family, a cousin of the King. Alcuin knew him well and called him "Antony," for he was taught as child and youth in the Palace School. His brother, Wala, too, and his sister, Gundrada, were present at its discussions; and Alcuin acknowledged their part in its fellowship by renaming them "Arsenius" and "Eulalia."

"Antony" seems to have shared in the family characteristics. After drinking in all the learning the Frankish Court could give him, he left the world to become a monk at Corbie. Not unworldliness alone moved him; he was bitterly opposed to the King's repudiation of his marriage with the Lombard princess and to his union with Hildegard. After some years Adalhard went on to Monte Cassino; but Charles, who knew that the young religious was a man of shrewd sagacity and practical genius for administration and diplomacy, in matters secular as well as spiritual, recalled him to Frankland and made him abbot of Corbie. As such Alcuin found in him, on his arrival from England in 782, a congenial companion who

[69] *ARF ann.* 760; *Epp.* III, 564, 609f. See Bouquet V, *index* s.v. Hitherius, Maginarius.

[70] *Epp.* IV, 96. Itherius seems to have been planning the foundation of Cormery; cf. Vaucelle, *La Collégiale de S. Martin de Tours,* 1908, 56; Sickel, *Acta* I, 77f.

frequently visited the Court, one with whom he could discuss problems of literature and theology. But friendship suffered because of Adalhard's many practical interests. He did not have that leisure for correspondence which Alcuin held indispensable: "Please don't mind writing," Alcuin begs of him, "because I do so love to read your letters. It only costs you a little, and it gives me such joy." Abbot Adalhard's pupil, Paschasius Radbert, describes his sharp, clear manner of speaking, his unceasing energy, his many interests, his zealous teaching. His students sat on the ground around him while he lectured: "And," Paschasius wrote long afterward, "I never saw anything more terrible, Father, than the fire which blazed from your eyes," a touch which seems too real a memory to be entirely the conventional detail of a monastic biographer.[71]

If Adalhard was a little remote from Alcuin's love of intercourse with his fellows, so, in a different way, was Benedict of Aniane, who was, however, to be of great aid to him in his later years.[72] Benedict, too, had been "entrusted by his father to Pepin's Queen to be taught among the pupils in Pepin's Court." He was the son of a Gothic chieftain in Septimania, on the border of Spain, and his name originally was Witza. As he was "quick and useful in all things," he entered the military service of Charles and fought for him against the Lombards in Italy. There a narrow escape from drowning in a river, raging with flood, turned the course of his life; and in 774 he entered the monastery of St. Seine l'Abbaye near Dijon, where for some years he led a life of intense self-denial and discomfort. Only under direct obedience to his abbot would he relax his rigorous practices. The

[71] Paschasius Radbert: *SS* II, 525, 531f.; *Epp.* IV, 35; Hauck II, 179.

[72] Ardo, *Vita Benedicti Anian.: SS* XV, i, 200ff.; W. Williams, *Monastic Studies*, 1938, 84ff.; Hauck II, 588ff.

Rule of Saint Benedict, he declared, was laid down for novices in Religion and for the frail; he himself aimed at the heights of blessed Basil and of the Rule of Pachomius!

His abbot, being a wise man, made him cellarer, and used his abounding desire for work in providing for well and sick, guests and children, poor and beggars. In these multifarious duties he did so excellently that when their Superior died, nearly six years later, the brethren unanimously chose Benedict for his place. But he, "perceiving that there was no sympathy between his ways and theirs," left Dijon to go south, and built for himself and a few like-minded ascetics a little hermitage on the banks of the stream called Aniane, where he and his father owned some land in the district of the Herault, Montpellier.

Here life was by no means easier, and nearly all who came to try their vocation under him, writes his biographer, retreated hastily from its "unheard-of abstinence, like pigs returning to their mire." Benedict was so disturbed in mind by his failure to induce permanence in his aspirants that he mounted his beast and went off to tell a neighbour hermit, who was living a life "religious, but not Regular," that he was returning forthwith to St. Seine l'Abbaye. The friend administered caustic rebuke, and Benedict stayed on the Aniane. He and his monks had no vines, no sheep, no cattle, no horses, only that one donkey on which they took turns to ride when they had to journey forth. Occasionally women of the district brought them milk, but they lived mostly on bread and water. The very blanket that covered the donkey, their drinking cup and the metal parts of the mill with which they ground their little patch of corn, were carried off in the night by a traveller to whom they had given lodging. Benedict told his disgusted sons to be sorry for the poor, ignorant man.

Little by little, however, the community grew in number

until it became needful to build a larger house near by, "dedicated to Mary, Mother of God." In 782, when Alcuin arrived to stay in Frankland, Benedict was raising a great monastery of Saint Saviour, with the aid of Frankish "dukes and counts." In spite of his own asceticism, much splendour went into the making of its church, without and within. Eventually he gave all into the keeping of King Charles, and received in return a charter of freedom from outside interference.[73]

The lives of Alcuin and of Benedict ran on very different lines; yet they ran to the same end, and often they touched one another. "Of all monks," we are told, "Benedict was nearest to Alcuin in friendship, and often he would come hurrying to seek Alcuin's counsel for himself and his brethren." In his verses Alcuin pictures this "great shepherd of monks" leading before the judgment-seat of God the sons whom he has begotten by his teaching and guided by his prayers. "My life surges with distractions, pray for me," he writes to Benedict. "Thank you for that physic of herbs. As you care for my body's health, so do I long for your soul's good in your community. That longing is one we share in common, even though the merits of our works are so unequal. I hope to see you soon." And, in another letter; "Where you are, there am I, and God with us for always. Write whenever you find some one to bring your letter. Don't let the light of your friendship shine the less on paper because of that 'countrified style' of yours for which you are always apologizing." [74]

On the continent outside Frankland Alcuin's letters went, above all, to Italy, especially to his beloved Paulinus, now back in his own land and installed as Patriarch of Aquileia. "You know how the earth longs for showers of rain on a boil-

[73] Hauck (II, 591, note 2) would place this building shortly before 792.

[74] *Alc. Vita,* 192; Ardo, 219; *Epp.* IV, 100f.

ing hot day? That is how I feel when I am waiting to hear from you. Every single minute I say to myself, again and again, '*When* shall I see that writing and be sure that he still keeps my name in his heart?' And now it has come! I took it in both my hands—What would it say? And I broke the seal and ran my eyes eagerly over every line. It was so good to know you are well!" Then joy passes swiftly into sadness. "But I am afraid—I cannot bear to say it—that we shall not meet again. The road of my life, so far from yours, is getting difficult, and I walk through this valley of tears to an end I know not. The flesh returneth whence it came and all its glory withereth, struck by the burning wind. Man goeth home for evermore and his spirit returns to God who gave it. . . . I am thinking my own miserable thoughts while I dictate this. You need not set me right, it isn't necessary; but do help me with your prayers to return home to my Father, as I sit here feeding the swine of all my foul desires." [75]

"Quicker than the East wind would I cross the Alps to you, could I only fly," Alcuin writes to Peter, Archbishop of Milan. To the monks of the Holy Saviour, at Montamiata in the diocese of Chiusi, he sends word that he has brought their petition before Charles, with the support of Queen Liutgard; to Abbot Morald and the community of Farfa in the Sabina he sends a prayer that they will receive him into their fellowship: "not as unknown, but as a brother. For, though I have never seen you with bodily sight, yet with eyes of the heart I seem to see and keenly to esteem you and your honourable life." [76]

3

But even more constantly, in these years of indecision as to his future, Alcuin's thoughts turned back to his English land of Northumbria, the more so because some of its students

[75] *Epp.* IV, 128ff.

[76] *Ibid.* 126, 134f.

had followed him across the Channel to teach and to learn further under him.

In a letter written from the Frankish Court to Riculf, Archbishop of Mainz, he remarks: "I am here like a father bereft of his sons. You are in Saxony, Homer has gone to Italy, Candidus back to Britain. Martin has stayed sick at St. Josse. Do please pray he may get well." [77] Candidus was Alcuin's Latinized name for the English Witto, who had come to him in 793 from the schoolroom of Higbald, bishop of Lindisfarne. Alcuin wrote to Higbald about this boy, "the son we share together." He advised his return home, after a year in Frankland: "But if you like to send him back to us, I will gladly give him all I can, for the good of your Church in Lindisfarne. It makes me so happy to give whatever I have learned to the people of our English race." [78] Candidus later did return to a busy life in Frankland, and to work with Alcuin and others. And Martin, another English boy, now at St. Josse, was to be Alcuin's friend long after these years at Court.[79]

Far more comforting, however, was the thought that Liudger of Frisia and his friend, the Irish Joseph, were both on the continent. We last saw Liudger retreating from England to work under his abbot Gregory in Utrecht. His future life was full of adventure. He was sent by Alberic, Gregory's nephew and successor, to find the body of Lebuin (Leafwine),[80] an Anglo-Saxon priest who had been told by the Lord in a "terrible and thrice-repeated admonition" to preach

[77] *Ibid.* 66.

[78] *Ibid.* 65. Alcuin sometimes called Higbald "Speratus": *Epp.* IV, 181, 443; Dümmler, *Alchvinstudien,* 504.

[79] Charles had lately, about 792, made Alcuin ruler, "for hospitality toward pilgrims and strangers," of the "cell" or little community of St. Josse-sur-mer on the Canche in the Pas-de-Calais. See Servatus Lupus, ed. Levillain, 1927, I, 103f.; Hauck II, 134, note 4; *PLAC* I, 402.

[80] Altfrid, *Vita S. Liudgeri: SS* II, 408.

Christianity in Holland, on the banks of the Ijssel. At Deventer, which was to honour him afterward as its patron saint, Lebuin had built a church, and upon his death had been buried in it. Then the Saxons, in one of their frequent raids, wrought destruction through that region and the precious relics were lost. Liudger, however, in beginning to rebuild the ruined church, had his own vision, and found, as he was directed, the body of Saint Lebuin "under the south wall." [81]

Later years found Liudger in Dokkum. Alcuin wrote verses to commemorate his building of a church at the place where Boniface was martyred.[82] From there the rising of Widukind drove him, too, into refuge at Monte Cassino. Then Charles, doubtless stimulated by Alcuin, sent him, first, to convert the Frisians on the Lauwers, where the raiders again fell upon his work, and afterward to the East Saxons. As Abbot Gregory had told him in a dream, "he was to be clothed in three priestly vestments." By gift of Charles he became abbot of Lotusa in Frankland; [83] soon after 800 he was consecrated first bishop of the see which the King had founded at Münster; and he himself fulfilled the longing of a lifetime and the hope of his study at Monte Cassino by founding the abbey of Werden on the Ruhr. The old story tells that the counsel of Heaven bade him build it in the heart of impenetrable forest and that he sat down in despair. Then, remembering that with God all things are possible, he stole out at night under its outlying trees for secret prayer. Twice an inquisitive cleric who, as usual in monastic records, hoped to see a miracle, was sent back to bed. But he persevered in his disobedience and saw the hope of Liudger rewarded, as once that of Scholastica, sister of Saint Benedict. The clear night clouded

[81] *Vita Lebuini antiqua: SS* XXX, 2, 789ff.; Hucbald, *Vita S. Lebuini: SS* II, 361ff.

[82] *PLAC* I, 304.

[83] Its exact situation has been disputed; see Hauck II, 417, note 3.

over, a terrific hurricane blew up, trees were uprooted right and left, the needed space was cleared, and next morning Liudger fell to work.[84]

"Joseph of Ireland," one of the first of Alcuin's students from the York School to arrive in the Frankish Court, was a poet and wrote verses about Liudger. For Charles the King, too, he concocted some of those elaborate acrostic structures which so often filled the leisure hours of the Anglo-Saxons, and dedicated to his "Master," Alcuin, a long commentary on Isaiah, drawn from Saint Jerome. One record inscribes him as "abbot"; if truly, we do not know of what monastery.[85] Before many years had passed Alcuin was writing to sympathize with his "dear son" in sickness, and to record his delight in the restoration of churches which Joseph had begun. The sickness soon ended in death, for before 796 Alcuin was bidding the bishop of Chur "to pray for the soul of Joseph, whom I taught." [86]

Other English youths who followed Alcuin to the continent while he was still at the Palace School were Sigulf and Fridugis. Sigulf had attained Holy Ordering as priest and was constantly with "the Father." Fridugis was a deacon, "both skilled in learning and well taught"; [87] Alcuin called him "Nathanael." Concerning other lads who were Alcuin's students in Frankland, we know less. One, Osulf, entered the service of the younger Charles, son of the Frankish King. If Alcuin's biographer is to be trusted here, Osulf caused the Master much anguish, for some reason unexplained.[88] So did a young man called Dodo, probably the same whom Alcuin

[84] *SS* II, 420.
[85] *PLAC* I, 149ff.; *Epp.* IV, 483f.
[86] *Epp.* IV, 40, 119.
[87] Theodulf, *PLAC* I, 487, ll. 175f.; Alcuin, *ibid.* 259 (?); *Alcuini Vita,* 191.
[88] *Alc. Vita,* 191f.

sorrowfully thought of as "Cuculus," "The Cuckoo," because he fled the haunts of religion and learning in the springtime of his youth. Will he some time return, Alcuin asks, as the cuckoo does every year afresh, when the cowslips bud again in the meadow and the leaves upon the bough? "Dear little son of mine," he wrote after him, "late in time did I receive you and quickly are you lost, before you have ripened beneath my care." There follow many words of warning against the life of sin and wanton pleasure: "I meant to write a few lines, but I dipped my pen again and again in the ink of love and wrote more than I thought—no, not more than I would. Whenever you read this, know in your heart that it is I who speak to you, and please read once more." Then, because prose cannot tell all he would say of their common loss, he writes to yet another boy whom he calls "Daphnis" and who has shared with Dodo the Father's teaching. To this Daphnis he sends verses that tell of his searchings of soul, of his fear for their friend, whom wine and the wiles of the devil have lured from their fellowship. So, also, Arno, "The Eagle," writes to this same fleeting child of passage: "Remember now your promise to me. Up and come back to us! The angels are longing to hear again your voice, dear bird of ours." [89]

In 786 Alcuin himself was once more home in England. His brief stay there was of special importance. In that year two legates from Pope Hadrian, George, whom we know already as bishop of both Ostia and Amiens, and Theophylact, bishop of Todi,[90] visited England formally to hold Councils for carry-

[89] *Epp.* IV, 107ff., 109f.; *PLAC* I, 269f.; trans. Waddell, *Med. Lat. Lyr.* 79, 81. For Dodo = Cuculus, see Dümmler, *Epp.* IV, 109, note 4. Cf. also *Epp.* IV, 101f.; *PLAC* I, 243 (XXII); p. 297 *infra.* Other students, mere names in Alcuin's letters, are "Mopsus" and "Gallicellulus": *Epp.* IV, 66, 123.

[90] Levison, 127f.; *PLAC* I, 242 and note 1.

ing out certain reforms in matters of the Church. Two of these Synods assembled in 786; Alcuin, with Pyttel, whom we last saw travelling in his company across the Channel to Frankland, attended both, the first in Northumbria, the second in Mercia.

We learn of their proceedings from the detailed report which Bishop George sent to the Pope at Rome. He begins by declaring the object and aim of these two legates: to root out utterly the tares and to establish the good grain still standing of the harvest sown in England by blessed Gregory through the mouth of Augustine. He and his companion, Theophylact of Todi, have duly arrived, though sorely set and hindered by many perils, especially of contrary winds.

After being welcomed by Jaenbert, Archbishop of Canterbury,[91] and making a short stay for necessary conference with him, they then travelled on to the court of Offa, ruler of Mercia. Offa was now the most powerful king south of the Humber; on the lands in this part of England he impressed his will as he would; he held himself brother and equal of Charles the Great. Pope Hadrian himself described him as "King of the English people" when he wrote to Charles concerning the "incredible rumour" that Offa had suggested that Charles hurl him from the Chair of Saint Peter and place within it a Frankish Pope. It was good that the Frankish King had vigorously denied this "most impious" purpose.[92]

Offa, in fact, held Saint Peter in special reverence,[93] and at the moment he desired a special boon of the Pope. Whether, as he declared, because of the vast extent of Mercia's subject lands, or, perhaps more truly, because he had no goodwill toward Kent and its Archbishop,[94] the King of Mercia was

[91] 766–792 A.D.
[92] H. S. III, 440ff.; *Cod. Carol.* No. 92: *Epp.* III, 629f.
[93] Levison, 30f.
[94] H. S. III, 522, 524; Birch I, 397; *Epp.* IV, 188.

very eager that yet another metropolitan see should be established in England to share honour and responsibility with Canterbury in the south, and that its archbishop should sit and govern at Lichfield, in Offa's own Mercia.

Such matters were duly discussed in Offa's Palace. Then the visiting bishops, with Abbot Wigbod, an envoy from King Charles,[95] proceeded to the Northumbrian Synod, in which King Elfwald of Northumbria, Eanbald, Archbishop of York, and all the dignitaries, spiritual and secular, of the North were gathered. It was a very distinguished occasion, since no Papal Legate had been sent to England by Rome from the days of Augustine.[96]

Among the twenty lessons and reforms commanded by the Pope at this Synod for the English people of this late eighth century and declared by his ambassadors, certain details stand out as showing manners and characteristics of the time. No man, Rome ordained, born of unlawful union, might be appointed King; no one thus born might even "hold lawful claim as his father's heir." Priests must celebrate holy rites with proper reverence. None might say Mass bare-legged; the People's Host should be of decent bread, not of fragments and crust; the chalice and paten should not be made of the horn of an ox, for this was not seemly for the pure Sacrifice. Bishops should not discuss worldly matters in their councils.

Two sections are of special interest. In one of these, houses of canons in England were formally acknowledged: "Bishops are to take due care that all their canons shall live according to the rule for canons, and their monks and nuns according to monastic rule, so that the distinction be clear between the canon, the monk, and the layman, both in manner of living and in outward appearance of dress." By the other ruling,

[95] Levison, 128, note 9; *PLAC* I, 88; *Epp.* IV, 20, note 7.
[96] *Ibid.* 20ff.; Stenton, 214; cf. Levison, 16.

tithes were henceforth required from all men for the service of the Church. In this latter command, therefore, Alcuin now saw in force, at least theoretically, for the people of his own land the imposition against which he had protested on behalf of the conquered Saxons.[97] The Papal Capitulary ended on a stern note: "If anyone, which God forbid! depart from this life without penitence and confession, for him prayer shall not be made. Repent ye therefore and be converted, for death tarries not. . . ."

At the end of the Northern Council, when signatures of bishops, King, nobles, and abbots had been inscribed upon the document providing these ordinances, the Papal Legates, accompanied by Alcuin and Pyttel as representatives of Church and State in Northumbria, travelled south and held a second Synod in Mercia, attended by its King Offa, by Jaenbert, Archbishop of Canterbury, and by bishops, clergy, monks and secular dignitaries of the southern province. The same rulings were read, both in Latin and in the Old English understood by the people; the same documents were marked by sacred sign and witness.

Thus ran the report to Rome in regard to this mission, of which it was recorded in Northumbrian annals that its legates came "renewing the ancient friendship between the Apostolic See and Britain, and returned home in peace with great gifts, as was meet and right." [98] Alcuin, also, returned to Frankland.

King Offa obtained from Pope Hadrian his wish. The Archbishopric of Lichfield was allowed in the next year, 787, at a "contentious synod" assembled at Chelsea: "Archbishop Jaenbert gave up part of his See and Higbert was elected by

[97] Stenton, 155.

[98] Sym. Dun. II, 51. The Northern Synod has been identified with a Council held in 787 at "Pincahala," and the Southern with that held the same year at Cealchythe (Chelsea). See H. S. III, 443, and, against these theories, Stenton, 216, note 5; cf. Levison, 16, note 3, 127.

King Offa." The election was confirmed by the Pope, the pallium was sent from Rome to Higbert, and the south of England held two archbishops for some fifteen years.[99]

The "great gifts" included a promise from Offa to contribute to the Church of Rome three hundred and sixty-five mancuses, one for every day in the year, "for the support of the poor and the making of lamps." [100]

Shortly after these high matters were arranged, in 788, Elfwald, the "good and just king" of Northumbria, was murdered by Siga, one of his own nobles, at "Scytlecester-on-the-wall," perhaps Chesters near Chollerton, on the line of the Roman Wall. He was buried at Hexham, "with great company of monks and dirge of clerics," in the Cathedral of Saint Andrew. Osred the second, a son of the former King Alchred, now held the throne briefly. In a year's time he was deposed, again by conspiracy of Northumbrian thanes, forcibly tonsured at York, and driven to flee for his life into exile on the Isle of Man. Then King Ethelred, in exile since 779, "by grace of Christ" returned from his banishment to rule Northumbria.[101]

In this year, 790, Alcuin once again won consent from Charles that he should visit his own land.[102] From England he wrote to Joseph toward the end of the year: "Blessed be God, who only doeth wondrous things. Ethelred, son of Ethelwald, has lately come out of prison to the throne, from misery to majesty. I have been detained here by the beginning of his rule, though I did want to return to you. Please write to me about our Lord King Charles. Is he on campaign or at home? Is there peace or is there war? Tell me all the news. Send

[99] *A-SC ann.* 785.

[100] *Epp.* IV, 188f.; Chadwick, *Studies on A. S. Institutions,* 1905, index s.v. *mancus.*

[101] Sym. Dun. I, 50; II, 52, 54; *A-SC ann.* 789; Allen Mawer, *Place-Names of Northumberland and Durham,* 1920, 44.

[102] *Alc. Vita,* 190.

me, too, the things I need for my journey across the sea. Send clothes of goat's hair and of wool, suitable for young men, lay and cleric, and linen for my own use, and cloaks, black and red, if you can find them, and much pigment of good sulphur and colours for painting. . . ."

Life in England, however, still had its troubles for one who knew the gay hospitality of the Frankish Court, and the letter goes on: "But, O woe! There is death in our pot, O man of God! The wine in our bins is all spent, and sour beer rages in our stomachs. So, then, as we have it not, do you drink for us and spend a joyous day; sad for us, because we have not that which maketh glad the heart, and scarcely bread to strengthen. . . . Vinter, the doctor, promised me two loads of wine, good and clear. Send me one! God keep you well with your friends. How far away you are! And how I wish you were near, still that young goat among the vines!" [103]

Later on, to Abbot Adalhard of Corbie, Alcuin's trouble told of higher things: "But I have to tell you, dear brother, that I found things rather disturbed in my country, and the new King not disposed as I hoped and wished. However, I gave him and others some of my advice, and at the moment we are working hard against injustice." [104]

Another matter that weighed upon his mind in England was a quarrel between the two Powers of the time, Offa and Charles. About 789 the Frankish King had sent Gervold, abbot of Fontenelle in Normandy, upon a mission to Offa, seeking one of Offa's daughters as bride for his son Charles. Offa, however, had declined to consider this proposal unless King Charles would give his daughter Bertha in marriage to Egfrith, Offa's son. In 787 Offa had associated Egfrith with himself in rule over Mercia by solemn enthronement and anointing, presumably in emulation of the rite celebrated for

[103] *Epp.* IV, 33f.; Waddell, *The Wandering Scholars,* 41.
[104] *Epp.* IV, 35f., 49ff.

the sons of Charles by Pope Hadrian.[105] In 790 we find Alcuin writing to his Irish friend Colcu: "I don't know what will happen to us. For some dispute, fanned by the devil, has risen lately between King Charles and King Offa. In consequence, trade has been forbidden to merchants on both sides. Some people say that I am to be sent as a mediator for peace." [106]

Neither marriage took place, since Charles would not yield his daughter. But after some years and much effort on the part of Alcuin and Abbot Gervold, friendship was restored between the two kings. Matters in Northumbria, however, turned again to evil. Recently, according to rumour, a leading chieftain, Eardwulf, had been led to execution by order of King Ethelred outside the gates of Ripon Abbey. Fortunately the axe miscarried, and the "corpse," borne with Gregorian chanting by the Abbey brethren for funeral rites into their church, in the middle of the night suddenly came to life. Men said, too, in their gossip, that dire fate had befallen the late King Elfwald's two sons, that they had been dragged by the King's men from York, beguiled from sanctuary by false assurances and drowned in Windermere. The horror of people at talk of such deeds and the support of some Northumbrian nobles tempted Osred to return from his exile on the Isle of Man. But his soldiers failed him; he was caught by Ethelred's officers and promptly put to death. Ethelred's popularity waned; and in 792 he grasped at security by wedding Elfled, a daughter of the all-powerful Offa of Mercia.[107]

[105] *Gest. s. Patrum Fontanell. coen.* ed. Lohier and Laporte, 86f.; *A-SC ann.* 785; Stenton, 217ff. Moreover, Charles welcomed to Frankland Egbert of Wessex, driven from England by Offa: Stenton, 208. On the ceremony of anointing of kings in Frankland and in England see Levison, 118f.

[106] *Epp.* IV, 32, cf. 35. Sickel, *Alcuinstudien* I, 66, note 1, suggested that Alcuin was to go from Offa in England to Charles; Jaffé preferred the reverse; see *Epp.* IV, 32, note 10.

[107] Cf. Sym. Dun. II, 52ff.

Alcuin returned to Frankland in 793, and the same year the wrath of God, as he believed, visited his sinful land of England in punishment for its crimes. On June 8 the Vikings from the North came in their ships to strike and to destroy Cuthbert's church and monastery upon Lindisfarne. "Think you," Alcuin wrote to Ethelred and his chieftains, "all but three hundred and fifty years have we and our fathers dwelt in Britain, and never has such a terror appeared as now we have suffered from a heathen race. Never did we imagine that such a sailing of ships could come to pass![108] Think you, think of the church of holy Cuthbert bespattered with the blood of the priests of God, despoiled of all its glories—this place, more reverend than all in Britain, given to pagan peoples for ravaging! And there, where first after the departure of Paulinus from York the Christian religion took its beginning among our people, from there has arisen the onset of misery and disaster! Think carefully, brothers, whether this unwonted and unheard-of evil has not been merited by evil habit. I do not say that sins of fornication were not found among our people in olden time. But from the days of King Elfwald, fornication, adultery, incest have flooded the land. What shall I say of greed, plundering, and dooms of violence? Surely, as saith holy Scripture, for crimes of this sort kings have lost their kingdoms and folk their fatherlands.

"And there have been signs that foretold these things. What meant that raining of blood which, in time of Lent, in the city of York, in the Church of Saint Peter, the head and capital of all the realm, we saw falling in threatening manner on the north in fair weather from the topmost roofs? Did it not foretell that retribution of blood was coming upon our people from the North? Consider well the wanton dress, the arraying

[108] See M. Bloch, *La Société féodale* I, 1940, 89, 92, on the lack of the seafaring spirit and of the spirit of resistance, implicit in Alcuin's letters of this time; cf. Traill-Mann, *Social England* I, 1901, 308; Jerrold, *Introd. to the Hist. of England to 1204*, 280f.

of the hair, the excesses of our nobles and people! Have you not willed to follow the heathen in the fashion of your hair and beards? What also of your immoderate lavishness in fashion, beyond the necessities of human use, beyond the custom of our ancestors? Some are bowed by enormity of extravagance, others perish of cold. Dives clad in purple is drowned in delights and feasting; Lazarus dies of hunger at his gate. Behold! a judgment from the house of God, the house in which the lights of all Britain rest, marches upon you with great dread! What must be feared for other places, seeing that the Divine judgment has not spared even this most holy seat?"[109]

Letters of grave counsel and exhortation follow, dictated by him to the monks of Wearmouth and Jarrow, to Higbald, bishop of Lindisfarne, to Cudrad, a priest of Lindisfarne, to whom Alcuin writes in thanksgiving that Cudrad's life was saved in the raid. Let him, therefore, whether in a solitary cell or in community, persevere in secret prayer and diligent fast. To the monks of Wearmouth and Jarrow he bids not only constant reading and explanation of the Rule of Saint Benedict, and in Anglo-Saxon for the understanding of all, but also intent study from tender years: "He who does not learn as a boy, does not teach when he is old. Remember the priest Bede, the most renowned teacher of our time. What joy he had in learning, what praise he now has among men! So sit beside your teachers, open your books, peer into their letters, understand their sense, so that you may both feed yourselves and give to others the food of spiritual life."

Here, as again and again in his letters, to monks and priests as to layfolk, Alcuin warns against sins and lusts of the flesh, elaborate and frivolous array, foolish and unrestrained laugh-

[109] *Epp.* IV, 42ff.; cf. 49ff., 71f.; Sym. Dun. II, 54ff. Alcuin also wrote verse on the tragedy: *De Clade Lindisfarnensis Monasterii: PLAC* I, 229ff. See J. E. A. Jolliffe, *Constit. Hist. of Medieval England,* 1937, 43, and Lester K. Born, *RBPH* XII, 1933, 589ff., on Alcuin's view of an English king's office and responsibility, emphasized at this time.

ter, manners, and words, bizarre fashions following the secular mode of the day, secret feastings and stolen joys of wine and strong drink. Some of his warning was no doubt due to his own intense dread of evil: "Tell your boys not to dig out fox-holes or follow coursing hares. How wicked to leave the service of Christ for a fox hunt!" [110]

It would be tedious to list all the names of Alcuin's correspondents, clerical, monastic and lay, in his native land. Perhaps we may single out two or three more. Ethelbert, bishop of Hexham, is bidden to study and teach: "Teach your boys and young men the knowledge of books that they may pray for you, their leader on the road to God. For the prayers of the living help us when we come to die." The priest Hechstan receives counsel as "my son Altapetra"; the priest Monna (Man) as "Anthropos." A pang of conscience, born of thought of his comfortable life in Frankland (for, as we have noted before, Alcuin admittedly enjoyed good eating, drinking, and the beauty of craft and art in man and Nature), makes him burst out to another English priest, Eada: "You hold in your hands what I long ago thought to hold. But the waves of the world have hurled my little boat on stormy winds into the surge of riches. Try by your kind prayers to call me back to the haven of peace. I, too, want this, but I *do* nothing about it. Poverty is tranquil, and you have loved it happily so long." A pleasant letter commends a penitent to the charity of Wulfhard, an English abbot: "Do not drive away by harshness this little sheep whom Christ in His mercy has brought back to Himself. If he has sinned ten times, have not we, a hundred? But, then, you know this all the more surely than I, because you keep it better." [111]

King Offa and his family, as is natural, occupy a large place in these letters. To the King himself Alcuin writes: "I have sent you back my dear son, as you asked. I beg you, treat him

[110] *Epp.* IV, 53ff., 56ff., 59f. [111] *Ibid.* 73, 79ff., 97, 113f.

well until, if God will, I come to you. Don't let him wander loosely or fall into drink. Give him boys to teach, and see that he teaches them with energy. I know he can, because he was a good student." Seemingly the young man was one of Alcuin's problems, perhaps Osulf or Dodo. The letter continues on a more personal note: "I am so glad you have made a strong resolution to read in order that the light of learning may shine in your kingdom; it is being extinguished in many other places. You are the glory of Britain, the trumpet of preaching, a sword against enemies, a shield against assailants." [112]

Offa's son and fellow-ruler, Egfrith, also received good advice upon his assuming kingship over Mercia; much was hoped from him, Alcuin wrote to his father. Offa's daughter, Ethelburga, Abbess of Fladbury in Worcestershire, was one of Alcuin's regular correspondents. Another nun, living for some reason in Offa's Court, is encouraged to keep her rule amid the busy life of the Palace; and through her Alcuin sends greeting to Offa's wife, Queen Cynethrith: "I would have written a letter of counsel to her if she had not been too much concerned with the King's affairs to read it. She may be quite sure, however, that I am loyal to her lord with all my power." [113] The assurance of his loyalty, arising probably from the dispute be-

[112] *Ibid.* 107, note 1.

[113] *Ibid.* 104f., 148f., 77f., 105f. Alcuin's name for Ethelburga was "Eugenia": *Epp.* IV, 78, 458. The tradition of Queen Cynethrith is highly conflicting. Alcuin wrote (*Epp.* IV, 105) of her "piety, charity, sobriety of life." One tradition declares that she persuaded King Offa to murder King Ethelbert of East Anglia (e.g. Flor. Worc. *ann.* 793: *Mon. Hist. Brit.* I, 546; cf. *A-S C ann.* 792); another that she herself did the deed without Offa's knowledge; see the dramatic story in the *Life of Offa II* appended to Matthew of Paris, *Hist. Major* (23f.). But here it is impossible to separate truth from legend. See for interesting detail and suggestion Bruce Dickins, *Proc. of the Leeds Philosophical Society* (*Lit. and Hist. Section*) IV, 1936–1938, 54; R. W. Chambers, *Beowulf,* 1932, 38; Levison, 30, 251; Stenton, 209; M. R. James, *EHR* XXXII, 1917, 220ff.; Edith Rickert, *Mod. Phil.* II, 1905, 327ff. King Ethelbert became the patron saint of Hereford.

tween Offa and King Charles, was repeated by Alcuin in writing to a priest named Beornwin: "Never was I disloyal to King Offa or the English people. Just as I serve faithfully these friends whom God has given me here, so will I those whom I left in my own country." [114] Yet another nun, once a queen, to whom Alcuin wrote much exhortation was the Lady Ethelthrith, widow of Ethelwald Moll and mother of the reigning King Ethelred. His instructions here show that she was abbess of some "double" cloister, ruling men as well as women.[115]

Thus time ran on, and we reach the early nineties of the eighth century. They were difficult years in many ways for Alcuin. He was growing very weary of the manifold distractions of life at the Frankish Court, teaching, travelling, talking, making merry with the energetic King and his innumerable officials, visitors, and friends, attending constantly Court functions here and there. On the other hand, life in England was now so full of turmoil and disaster, under no settled rule, robbery, murder, and disorder were so common, that he could not contemplate returning to pass his last days in that uneasy home. He had reached his sixtieth year, and he craved peace, to pray, to prepare his passage hence to that unknown destiny beyond death, to help, warn, and encourage his uncounted friends, as before.

The event that finally decided his future fell on April 18, 796, when King Ethelred was killed "by his own people." For twenty-seven days Osbald, a Northumbrian thane apparently high in Ethelred's court, held the throne by support of his fellow-nobles; then, suddenly deserted by all, he fled to Lindisfarne and thence to the King of the Picts. That leader in

[114] *Epp.* IV, 124f.

[115] *Ibid.* 120ff.; page 26 *supra.*

Northumbria, Eardwulf, whom King Ethelred had condemned, was recalled from exile and raised to kingship, hallowed in the Cathedral of York. He was to maintain his crown against rebel and assassin for eleven stormy years.[116]

Soon after this last detail of violence and bloodshed had reached Frankland, Alcuin wrote to Offa:

"First, I would have you know that our Lord King Charles has often spoken gracious and loyal words to me concerning you; in him you have altogether a most faithful friend. He is sending envoys to Rome and to Canterbury and gifts to you. Also he is sending offerings to the bishops of Mercia, and asks you to bid them pray for himself and the head of the Apostolic See.

"Likewise for King Ethelred he had forwarded gifts to the bishops of Northumbria. But—the horror of it!—when these gifts and accompanying letters were already in the hands of his envoys, there arrived news of the treachery of Ethelred's people and of his slaying. At once the Lord Charles withdrew his gifts and burst out into so great wrath against the Northumbrians, 'that perfidious, perverse people, murderer of its Kings, worse than the heathen,' that truly, had I not pleaded for them, he had taken from them all the good he purposed and done them every evil in his power.

"Indeed, I had myself made ready to come back to you with the gifts and to settle again in my fatherland. But now it has seemed better to me to remain here, a pilgrim in a foreign country. For what would I do in Northumbria, where no one is free from fear, where no one can devise any healthful purpose? The holy places laid waste by the pagans, the altars defiled with falsehood, monasteries profaned with adultery, the

[116] Sym. Dun. II, 57f.; *A-SC ann.* 794. Alcuin had written a long letter to King Ethelred and "Osbald Patricius" and other Northumbrian chieftains: *Epp.* IV, 49ff.

earth stained with the blood of rulers and kings! And if your letter, Sir, tells truly that this iniquity came from the leaders of the people, where, then, are surety and faith to be sought?

"Unworthy though I be, the rule of the Abbey of Saint Martin's, Tours, has of late come into my hands, not of my own will but somewhat through necessity, and devised by counsel of many men."

So, too, Alcuin wrote to Offa's daughter, his friend Ethelburga, the Abbess of Fladbury: "The treachery of my country horrifies me so much that I am afraid to go back. What could I do for it except mourn for its coming doom? And you, too, must have wept for your dear sister, thus made a widow. It were best to advise her to enter a nunnery. Queen Liutgard has sent you a mantle as a little gift, and I have sent you, dear lady, an ampulla and a paten to offer in your hands to the Lord God. When you look on them, say, 'Christ, have mercy on Alcuin, Your humble servant.' I wish that you would make every day your offering at the altar. We have the authority of the Apostles for this custom and therefore it should diligently be followed." The "dear sister" was, of course, Elfled, that other daughter of Offa, whom Ethelred had married five years before.

Alcuin also sent his sympathy to the murdered King's mother, Abbess Ethelthrith: "Many are the mercies of God. I am sure that He has left you living after your son's death so that by your prayers and alms He may have mercy upon him. Perhaps he did die in his sins; but the Divine Mercy can give him life. Do not mourn for him, for you cannot call him back. And if he is with God, then do not grieve for him as lost, but be glad that he has gone before you into rest. When there are two friends, the death of the one who goes first is happier than that of the one who follows after; for he who has gone has some one to pray for him every day."

A similar thought appears in a letter sent about this time with individual gifts from the Frankish king to all the bishops of Britain. It came from Alcuin's pen: "Of your charity remember that King Charles earnestly desires your prayers, both for himself and for the welfare of his land, for the spreading of the Christian Faith, and for the soul of our Holy Father, Hadrian the Pope, since loyalty toward a friend that has passed hence is judged exceeding good." [117] Perhaps, indeed, Alcuin took comfort in picturing the mighty treasure of those conquered Avars moving toward so excellent an end.

The new king, Eardwulf, had long been a friend of Alcuin, who now sent him good wishes for the realm "given him by God," bade him be grateful for his safety amid the perils of its late years and never to forget the crimes for which his predecessors had lost both throne and life. To Osbald, now in exile, came a sterner word of counsel: "I am vexed with you, because you did not obey me when I told you in a letter two years ago to leave the lay world and serve God, as you promised. Now a worse reputation, a more unhappy motive, has upset your life. Return, return, and fulfil your vow. So may you not perish with the unrighteous, if you are innocent of the blood of your King. If indeed you *are* guilty, in consent or in purpose, confess your sin, be reconciled to God, and flee the company of crime. Do not add sin to sin by ravaging your country, by bloodshed. Think, how much blood of kings and chieftains and people has been poured out by you and yours! Free yourself, I beseech you by God, that your soul be not lost for eternity. And if you can persuade the people with whom you live in exile toward their salvation, neglect it not, that more speedily, by the grace of God, you may come to your own."

Evidently there was a strong suspicion abroad that Osbald

[117] *Ibid.* 147f., 149, 151f., 150; cf. 152f.

had had part in the slaying of Ethelred and that he was scheming to regain the throne of Northumbria. Alcuin heard later that he did become a monk, even an abbot. He died in 799 and was buried in Alcuin's own cathedral at York.[118]

On July 26 in this same year, 796, Offa of Mercia also departed this world. Two letters sent to him by Charles may be noted here as of some interest. In one Charles wrote to his "beloved brother and friend, King Offa," that a "reprehensible Irish priest in the diocese of Hildebold, bishop of Cologne," so it was rumoured, had been eating meat in Lent. His fellow-priests, indeed, had refused to condemn him, because the evidence was insufficient. Yet they could not allow him to stay in his cure, "lest the good name of the priesthood should be disgraced among the unlettered crowd, or lest, perhaps, busy chatterers might use this precedent to urge the breaking of prescribed abstinence." Would Offa, therefore, kindly get this priest sent back to his own country whence he came, for judgment there?

The other document was also concerned with ill-doing, but on the part of laymen. It was written in 796, shortly before Offa's death, and reminds him of "the ancient bond" between him and Charles. Its complaint was laid against merchants who posed falsely as pilgrims in order to enjoy the exemption from custom dues granted to these devout travellers. Such, if they are caught, Charles writes, are to pay the full taxes. The letter goes on to discuss certain blocks of black stone which Offa had asked the Frankish King to send him for building purposes. Charles will be delighted to do so, and he would be equally happy to receive woollen cloaks for the comfort of himself and his friends, "such as used to come to us in former times. . . ." "From the treasure of human riches which the

[118] *Ibid.* 155f.; Sym. Dun. II, 62, where a chieftain, Aldred, is named as Ethelred's murderer.

Lord Jesus yielded to me of His free affection, I have sent somewhat to the Archbishoprics in England. To you, dear brother, in my joy and thanksgiving I have forwarded a belt and a sword of Avar workmanship, also two mantles of silk. Please pray for us all." [119]

Offa was succeeded by his son, Egfrith. Egfrith was to live but a few months, and it was still 796 when his crown passed to a cousin far removed, Cenwulf, destined to rival Offa in the fame of his power.[120]

Of all places that nearest to Alcuin's heart was still the ancient City of York, and most intimately remembered by him of all its shrines was that house of God and Saint Peter in which he had spent most of his years. Again and again he wrote to its brethren, in thanksgiving, in joy, in counsel, in warning: "You are they who cared for me as a mother when I was a little child, who patiently endured the wayward boy, who brought me by your teaching and training to the full strength of man. You, my fathers, when you gather for holy Office, or when you pray alone in secret, keep Alcuin, your son, in your hearts and on your lips. And you, too, who are my sons in age, but my fathers in merit of holiness, I beseech, forget not in your pleadings him who taught you there." [121]

Eanbald had been Chief Pastor of York for fifteen years when, in 795, Alcuin heard that he longed to retire from his episcopal duties to the peace of leisure. He wrote to the Archbishop: "I have been sick with fever, and the King has been kept in Saxony, so that I could not come to you, as I longed to do. I hope and pray that I may find you still in office. Yet, should you decide to retire, I ask that you allow no coercion to be wrought upon the Church, but give the brethren free power of election." To Eanbald's clergy he wrote, also, con-

[119] *Epp.* IV, 131, 145f. [120] Sym. Dun. II, 58.
[121] *Epp.* IV, 85f.

cerning this same danger of evil preferment: "I beseech you, proceed faithfully and wisely in the election of a Bishop, should this have to be before I can come. Again and again I entreat that you allow no one to gain appointment by the sin of simony; for he who sells this office shall receive his gold but shall lose the kingdom of God. Hitherto the Church of York has remained pure of guilt in this respect. See to it that she be not defiled in your days." [122]

[122] *Ibid.* 90, 92.

Chapter V

ALCUIN IN FRANKLAND, 782–796: WRITINGS FOR THE CHURCH

CHAPTER V

ALCUIN IN FRANKLAND, 782–796: WRITINGS FOR THE CHURCH

I

MORE IMPORTANT to the world of Alcuin's time and of the future than his work as teacher of the young Franks, as counsellor of Charles the Great, and as friend and correspondent of men and women innumerable, were the letters, treatises, manuals and service-books which have come down to us and which still cause his name to be remembered in the annals of the theology and doctrine, of the liturgy and worship of the Church.

Two "errors" in matters of the Faith and its practice felt his hand under the direction of the Frankish king.

The first was the heresy of Adoptionism.[1] This found its nursery in Spain, a land remote from the vivid centres of that Catholic life and teaching seen in Frankland and in Italy, a land where the tradition of Arius on the one hand, and of Theodore of Mopsuestia on the other, still sowed tares among the wheat. Yet this particular aberration from sound doctrine, paradoxically enough, seems to have raised its ugly head amid the passionate outpourings of a Catholic prelate, Elipand, Archbishop of Toledo, in defence of his Church's belief regard-

[1] See, among secondary sources, Hauck II, 297ff.; Menéndez Pelayo, *Hist. de los Heterodox. Esp.* II, 1947, 14ff.; Hefele-Leclercq III, 2, 985ff., 1001ff.; *DTC* s.v. *Adoptianisme* (Quilliet); Amann, *L'Epoque carol.* 129ff., and *RSR* XVI, 1936, 281ff.; von Schubert, 376ff.; Grössler, *Die Ausrottung des Adoptianismus im Reiche Karls des Grossen,* Eisleben, 1879.

ing the Holy Trinity. Just about the time when Alcuin left York to live in Frankland, Elipand had come across some extraordinary teaching of a certain Spaniard named Migetius, to the effect that the Second Person of the Blessed Trinity had never existed before the Incarnation and that the One Christian God had been manifested Incarnate in time under three forms: those of David, of Jesus Christ, of Saint Paul.

The Archbishop of Toledo was a peppery old gentleman, and he regarded himself and his See as pillars of orthodox tenets. Promptly he rushed off a long letter to Migetius: "I have seen, yes, I have seen," he shouted at the offender, "and I have laughed to scorn your idiotic, mad declaration. Get you behind me, Satan, you who bark your insane words against the Holy Mystery of the Trinity. And you, Migetius, learn of holy Gregory to think before you dare to teach!" [2]

Unfortunately, however, in his wrath Elipand himself fell backward. He was well over eighty; the Spanish ecclesiastical atmosphere was not very clear, Toledo itself being under control of the Saracens; and in his burning desire to uphold the glory of the Logos, the Eternal Word, he wrote more than the truth concerning the Son Incarnate. For he made untrue distinction between the Eternal Sonship of the Lord Divine and another Sonship, rising not by Nature but by grace, from the adoption of the Christ in the flesh.[3] Therefore, in his turn and to his exceeding horror and indignation, he found himself attacked for unCatholic teachings, by Beatus, priest and abbot of Liébana, in the region of the Asturias, Northern Spain, and by Heterius, pupil of Beatus and bishop of Osma in the modern Archdiocese of Burgos. "Never," he wrote to his friend, the abbot Fidelis, in October, 785, "has it been heard

[2] *PL* XCVI, coll. 859ff.

[3] He believed that he found support for his error in the Mozarabic liturgy in use in Spain.

of that men of Liébana should teach those of Toledo! The whole world knows that this See of Toledo has been famed from its very foundation for its sound doctrine, that never has aught of schism flowed from it. It will be a disgrace to me if this evil be inscribed in its annals! So take young Heterius and teach him better things than he has learned from that ill-named Beatus." [4]

The letter was sent to Fidelis under the seal of secrecy, but he made no scruple of discussing its content with Beatus and Heterius when he met them some months afterward at a religious ceremony, the veiling of a Spanish widow queen.[5] By this time the matter was widely known, and Beatus and Heterius held it well to launch a formal rebuke of Elipand in two long books: "Not only through the Asturias, but through the whole of Spain and as far as Frankland it is spread abroad that two arguments have arisen in the Asturian Church. And so there are now two peoples, two Churches, contending with one another concerning the One Christ. You and your faction declare that Jesus Christ Incarnate is in His manhood the Son of God only by adoption; and we declare that both as God and as Man He is the one, true Son of God, not by adoption but by begetting and by Nature, which is the Catholic creed of the whole Church. Yet you in your error call us liars, heretics, disciples of Antichrist." [6]

Naturally, this division among the clergy of Spain reached the ears of Pope Hadrian, who wrote, supported by witness from many Fathers of the Church, a stern admonition to the Spanish bishops "that they be not poisoned by this serpent's venom." [7] But Elipand, in his turn, feeling it advisable to gain weighty support for his teaching, wrote off to one of the most

[4] *PL* XCVI, coll. 918f.
[5] Adosinda, widow of Silo, King of Leon, 774-783.
[6] *PL* XCVI, coll. 893ff., 901f., 919.
[7] *Epp.* III, 637ff.

able men in Spain, Felix, bishop of Urgel in the Pyrenees, a diocese then included in the dominions of King Charles as part of the Spanish March. Felix was respected far and wide, not only for his learning, but for his Christian character and devotion. So far had his reputation reached that Alcuin, always keen to live in touch with those whose saintliness he revered, introduced himself to him in a letter, about 789: "You are so well known to me for your piety, if not in person, through the praise of some of my brethren, that I venture to commend myself to your prayers. Please let me be one of your friends in this fellowship of intercession." [8]

No doubt Felix was delighted that the Archbishop of Toledo should consult him on a matter of doctrine. He readily declared himself an adherent of the Adoptionist belief and thereby gave immense impetus to its circulation.

This now concerned not only the Pope but King Charles, for the evil was already flourishing in his own realm, and he was a sworn Defender of the Faith. He did not dare to use his secular power for its suppression, lest the Saracens might seize such occasion of discontent among the people of Toledo and the Spanish March and start a revolution. The King preferred instead to leave the uprooting of this noxious weed in his vineyard to the powers ecclesiastical. Accordingly, as its growth was advancing with formidable rapidity, he summoned in 792 to his palace in Regensburg, Bavaria, where he had spent the winter, a Synod of bishops from Frankland and from Italy. Alcuin was absent in England at the time. To this gathering Felix was called to argue his case; but to no purpose, for the "Felician heresy" was condemned with solemn anathema. Felix himself was convicted of grievous error, admitted his wrongdoing, and was sent under escort of Angilbert for further judgment to the presence of the Pope at Rome.[9]

[8] *Epp.* IV, 30. [9] *ARF ann.* 792; *PL* CI, coll. 251f.

Here, as one under penance, he was held in prison, until in Saint Peter's he once again confessed his guilt and promised adherence to the true Faith in a written document, placed within the Apostle's shrine for permanent witness.[10] Then he was allowed to return to Urgel, but whether to his bishop's throne or not, we are uncertain, since our sources differ on this point.[11] At any rate, he soon renounced his penitence, real or assumed, and fled from Frankish power to the shelter of Spain, probably to Toledo and its Archbishop.

It was time, Charles decided, that his leader of the "Palace School" should return from England to head his battle against heretics. Once back in Frankland in 793, Alcuin sent another letter to Felix, "with the pen of love, not with the prick of contention, in desire for my brother's welfare, not for bitter rebuking." "It is no light matter," he now wrote, "to care for the soul's health of one's fellows. Once I longed for your friendship, simply because I had heard of you; now I long for it more eagerly, that we may be one in Catholic union. Revered father and dear brother, with humility I dare to beg you, if your foot has slipped and you have stumbled in the way, regain your standing, come back bravely to fight the battles of the Lord. Do not follow new inventions, contrary to the Faith, lest, if the Holy Church throughout the world cast you forth, God refuse to hold you hereafter in His eternal peace. Think how great is her authority, what terror lies upon those who depart from her! You shall find in me your faithful fellow-labourer for your happiness, so far as I have power; nay, I would not hold it below me to learn, myself, at your side things that are true and of Catholic belief." [12]

[10] Mansi XIII, 857, 1031; *ARF, Ann. Fuld. ann.* 792.

[11] *Poeta Saxo,* ed. P. von Winterfeld: *PLAC* IV, i, 33 (*ann.* 792, ll. 21f.); *PL* XCVI, col. 868.

[12] Alcuin, *Adv. Felic.* I, c. 1: *PL* CI, col. 127; *Adv. Elip. ibid.* col. 251; *Epp.* IV, 60ff. For the answer to this letter see page 234 *infra*.

The Adoptionist heresy, however, by this time had taken firm hold of many bishops in Spain. With high resentment they wrote both to King Charles and to the bishops of Frankland against "the foul, misnamed Beatus, impious priest, false prophet." Let Charles beware of the fate of the Emperor Constantine, once converted to the Christian creed, then turned by the guile of his serpent sister to Arian heresy and lost in hell! Let the Frankish bishops condemn Beatus for his "pestilential viperous teaching and sulphurous, stinking doctrine." [13]

The King sent these letters to Rome and asked counsel of Hadrian in his difficult situation. At the same time he judged that another Council was in order, more comprehensive and authoritative than that of Regensburg. He had kept the Easter of 794 at Frankfurt. From its Palace he now called an assembly of bishops, representative priests, deacons, and layfolk to meet there as the summer drew on.

On the first of June [14] they began their sessions; and Charles rose to deliver his harangue against evil and false doctrine to the reverend audience of Frankish and Italian prelates, surrounded by a wide ring of lesser clergy and secular dignitaries. Mediaeval record describes this Synod as "universal," because the presence of two Papal legates, the bishops Theophylact and Stephen,[15] endued it with authority from the Holy See. Alcuin was now present, and was formally welcomed into membership of its body. Delegates had also been summoned by Charles from England.[16]

When the King, as president, had asked the will of the Council, it divided into two companies for deliberation, and each produced its own reasoned argument and decision. The one, of the bishops of North Italy, was written by Paulinus

[13] *PL* XCVI, coll. 867ff.; CI, 1321ff.; *Concil. aevi Karol.* I, iii, 121.
[14] *Ann. Mosell. ann.* 793 (*recte* 794). [15] *ARF ann.* 794.
[16] *Cap. reg. Franc.* I, 78 (56); *Conc. aevi Kar.* I, 159.

of Aquileia, entitled *Libellus Sacrosyllabus* and based on witness from the Scriptures. The other, known as the *Epistola Synodica,* contained evidence taken from the Church Fathers by the Frankish episcopacy of Gaul, Germany, and Aquitaine. Both condemned the beliefs of Elipand and Felix, and both were approved by the whole assembly.[17] Charles had not yet left Frankfurt when he received from Hadrian the counsel he had sought, written in the form of another letter to the bishops of Spain. This he sent on its way to them, together with copies of the two treatises presented by the recent Synod and, finally, a strongly worded ultimatum from himself.[18]

All, it would seem, had been done to quench this stubborn *ignis fatuus.* Yet it continued to blaze up during Alcuin's last days at the Court, and dared to lap with its blighting tongue the nearer regions of Frankland proper. "Alas!" he wrote to Charles soon after the Synod had dispersed, "the error has secretly crept, it seems, into the minds of even some of our faithful teachers," and, in 795, to his English friends at York: "Many now are bold to tear apart the seamless robe of Christ, which even the soldiers near the Cross did not dare to harm." [19]

This problem having been dealt with to the satisfaction of the orthodox, the Council of Frankfurt now proceeded to hurl condemnation against a second "error," wrapped around in even more delicate and complicated detail, both ecclesiastic and political. It was the iconoclastic trouble which now again came to the front.

[17] *ARF, Ann. Lauresh. = Chron. Moiss., ann.* 794; Paul. Aquil.: *PL* XCIX, coll. 151ff.; *ibid.* CI, 1331ff.; Mansi XIII, 863ff.; *Cap. reg. Fr.* I, 73; *Conc. aevi Kar.* I, 130ff., 142ff.

[18] *PL* XCVIII, coll. 899ff.; *Conc. aevi Kar.* I, 157ff., 122ff.; Hauck II, 311ff.

[19] *Epp.* IV, 84, 89.

The Empress Irene, as we have noted, had learned in her Greek home to reverence deeply sacred pictures and statues. The campaigns waged against these and their cult by her predecessors on the throne of Constantinople were utterly abhorrent to her heart and conscience. For some time after assuming, in 780, what amounted to sole rule through the minority of her son, Constantine the sixth, she could do little, as her energies were fully occupied by revolution within and war outside her City. In 784 Paul, the Patriarch of Constantinople, laid low on a bed of sickness, openly declared himself penitent for his persecution of those who reverenced images, and, directly he could gather strength, fled his office to become a monk. The Lady Irene was much pleased at this change of heart. "Would I had never sat on the high seat of the Church of Constantinople!" he said to her, and to her senators and nobles, "If there shall not be called an Ecumenical Synod for the righting of this error in your midst, you shall have no salvation." [20]

The same year a layman, Imperial secretary of the Empress, Tarasius by name, was consecrated Patriarch in Paul's place, and, shortly before this consecration, an Imperial letter, officially known as *Divalis sacra,* went from the two sovereigns, Constantine and Irene, to Pope Hadrian. Irene wrote that, after due consultation with her subjects and well-learned priests, she had decided to call a Synod to deliberate on this matter of the holy pictures and statues. Would not the Pope grant his presence for this purpose at Constantinople? He would be welcomed with every conceivable honour.[21]

In October, 785, the Pope replied. He rejoiced to hear that the Imperial rulings in Constantinople had turned from

[20] Theophanes, 457; Bury, *Lat. Rom. Empire* II, 494f.

[21] *AA. SS.* Feb. III, 578f.; Mansi XII, 984f.; *PL* CXXIX, coll. 199ff. (Latin translation by Anastasius Bibliothecarius); Amann, 114; L. Bréhier, *Le Monde byz.* I, 89.

heresy concerning the sacred images to godly belief and practice in their respect. Surely there would once again arise a new Constantine, a new Helen, in the present faithful sovereigns! Let them, he bade and besought, restore these same images in all care and continue to cherish them, in obedience to the Church's tradition. But let them, further, duly venerate the head of the Church Universal, the See of holy Peter and of his Catholic and Apostolic successors. He, the present holder, was still awaiting the restoration of lands and possessions wrested from this same See by those lawless iconoclastic Emperors. Victory, he had no doubt, would crown Constantinople under the protection of Saint Peter, even as Charles, King of the Franks and Lombards, Patrician of Rome, who wholeheartedly followed the counsels of the Pope and had richly endowed the Church, was now conqueror over his enemies far and wide. If a Council really were necessary, the Holy See would send envoys. But let it begin its work by anathematizing the action of that image-breaking Council held at Constantinople in 754.[22]

The inveterate hostility of the army, however, brought speedily to an end the gathering of a Synod within Constantinople in 786, and it was not until September, 787, that the seventh Ecumenical Council of the Church opened its sessions at Nicaea in Bithynia, where, it was hoped, reverent thoughts of the great debate held in 325 would inspire the assembled contenders. Constantine and Irene did not appear in person, but they were officially represented.[23]

The proceedings of the iconoclasts of 754 were promptly nullified, and exposition of their iniquities proceeded apace. At length, in the seventh session at Nicaea, a final decision

[22] Mansi XII, 1055ff., 1073ff.; *PL* XCVI, coll. 1215ff.; Caspar, *ZKG* LIV, 164f.
[23] Mansi XII, 992, 1000.

was declared: "Emblems of the holy Cross and likenesses—painted, carved, or in whatsoever fashion wrought—of Jesus Christ, of His Immaculate Mother, of Angels and Saints, shall appear lawfully on vessels, vestments, walls, buildings, and roads, for the recalling in men's minds of those whom they represent, for the encouraging of desire to imitate their originals, and for the showing toward images of due respect and veneration—προσκύνησις. This, however, the Council declared, was entirely different from the worship and adoration—λατρέια—due from men to God alone. Incense and candles may properly witness to this veneration of sacred images, as offered in honour of the person represented. Anyone guilty of irreverence toward these symbols, or toward holy vessels, relics, or monasteries, shall be deposed, if in clerical orders, or excommunicated, if of the lay people."

All present signed this decree, crying, "This is the one faith, the faith of the Apostles! Anathema to them that believe it not!" At an eighth session, held in the Imperial Palace at Constantinople, the Acts of the Council were signed and approved by Emperor and Empress, and the tidings of good cheer were forwarded to Hadrian at Rome. The time of a new bond between Rome and Constantinople had arrived. It would have been, indeed, far stronger had word of restitution of Papal lands, of declaration of Papal primacy, been part of the document now forwarded to the Pope. But of these matters not a word.[24]

The scene now changes to Frankland, where relations between its King Charles and the East were not happy at the moment. Perhaps the cult of holy images professed so warmly by the Empress Irene was an important factor in the breaking-off of the betrothal of Irene's son Constantine and the Princess

[24] Ostrogorsky, *Gesch.* 126f.; Mansi XIII, 373ff., 413ff.; Hefele-Leclercq III, 2, 772ff.; Haller II, i, 5ff.

Rotrud. No doubt this break meant alienation of Charles from the East; no doubt his sore feeling was deepened by the descent of the Greek fleet upon Italy, even though this had been thoroughly defeated. We may also think that Charles resented the fact that the Pope had not urged his taking part in a solemn Council, attended by Papal legates, to discuss important matters of Church faith and practice, as well as the fact that it had been called together by a woman.

In any case, he received in no mood of contentment the Acts of the Second Council of Nicaea,[25] translated into Latin. His dissatisfaction flamed into anger when he read the pages of this document. For the translation was so seriously in error that it recorded the Synod as denouncing all who should not render "adoration" to the holy images as to God Himself, One in Three Persons.[26]

Scholars have interpreted in various ways the treatment meted out by the King to this Latin record of the Nicene Acts. Certainly he summoned the chief authorities among his clergy to study its details; with them he discussed, criticized, examined paragraph after paragraph with concentrated scrutiny. From these conferences—and Charles felt always as warmly toward theological and ecclesiastical debate as he then felt cool toward the Greeks—two writings issued, fruit of the united labours of the King and his advisers. One was a list of eighty-five criticisms, briefly noted; the second was an elab-

[25] Hincmar of Reims: *PL* CXXVI, col. 360; XCVIII, col. 997.

[26] For the errors and "unreadability" of the translation, which forced Anastasius to make another in the 9th century, see Mansi XII, 981; *Epp.* VII, 416ff.; *PL* CXXIX, col. 195. Anastasius himself, however, uses the word *adoratio,* which must therefore have been variously interpreted in early mediaeval days: Hefele-Leclercq III, 2, 1079, note 2. The suggestion (Hauck II, 327) that the iconoclasts in Constantinople made a deliberately corrupted Latin translation lacks evidence: Hampe, *NA* XXI, 1896, 85f.; Kleinclausz, *Charlemagne,* 244, note 2. For a Latin translation made in Rome by a worker lacking in culture, see von den Steinen, *QF* XXI, 1929–1930, 11, 18, 91; Caspar, *ZKG* LIV, 183f.

orate treatise, dealing in four divisions with the same points, but not in the same order, and called the *Caroline Books*.[27]

Three theories have been advanced: (1) that the list of criticisms under eighty-five headings—*quaedam capitula*—was made informally at the royal conferences and was afterward enlarged and worked over to make the Caroline Books;[28] (2) that the *Caroline Books* were written first and the *quaedam capitula* were a summary of points taken from them;[29] (3) that the *capitula* and the *Caroline Books* represent one work,[30] made at one and the same time. Of these three theories the first is to be preferred.

Charles forwarded his list of criticisms to Pope Hadrian at Rome by the hand of Angilbert, probably in 792,[31] "that through his judgment and authority these might be corrected." [32]

The Papal See was now sailing in stormy straits, between the Scylla of the East, at last orthodox in this matter of iconoclasm, but impenitent in its obstinate retaining of Papal lands, and the Charybdis of the Franks under Charles, now railing against the Second Council of Nicaea, approved by Papal blessing.[33] A letter from Hadrian assured the King that his envoy Angilbert had been received with all courtesy and affection, as one bearing the royal words, that loyalty to the Church

[27] See bibliography s.v. *Libri Carolini.*

[28] von den Steinen (see note 26 *supra*), 1ff.; Hampe, *NA* XXI, 1896, 98; Caspar, 184; Knabe, *Hist. Stud.* 292, 1936, 35; E. J. Martin, *A History of the Iconoclastic Controversy,* 229.

[29] Petau, *Theolog. dogmat., De Incarnat.* XV, c. 12, 8; Hefele-Leclercq III, 2, 1086ff.; Hauck II, 337.

[30] Bastgen, *NA* XXXVI, 1911, 637; XXXVII, 1912, 476ff.; cf. Caspar, 185.

[31] *ARF ann.* 792; Hauck II, 337; *Epp.* IV, 615; E. J. Martin, 230, note 1. For 791 see Hampe, *NA* XXI, 1896, 100f.; Caspar, 184f., 198; cf. von den Steinen, *QF* XXI, 72ff.

[32] Synod of Paris, 825 A.D.: *Conc. aevi Kar.* I, ii, 481; *PL* XCVIII, coll. 997, 1300.

[33] Dawson, 220f.

of Rome would surely bring victory to the King's campaigns, that in response to this "kingly and mellifluous" list of points of detail the Pope was sending another list. Perusal of this by no means soothed Charles' mind; for it confronted each "Reprehension" of his by a Papal "Refutation." [34]

At the end of the long succession of Frankish chapters the Pope, however, had found one with which he himself was entirely in harmony. For it upheld and followed the teaching given to Serenus of Marseilles by Gregory the Great, that sacred representations were to be accorded neither irreverence nor the worship meet for God alone.[35] So different was this, Hadrian declared, from the grievous content of those Frankish criticisms which he had, one by one, vigorously opposed, that he was sure it was the particular and special contribution of the King himself and set forth Charles' own royal and orthodox belief, as distinct from the erring opinions of his advisers.

Finally, the Pope added that he had as yet sent no letter to the rulers of Constantinople, Irene and her son, in regard to the Council of 787. They had, indeed, recalled their Empire from error in one respect, in bidding reverence and restoration for the sacred images; in another, their refusal to restore Papal patrimonies, they were adhering to former wrong, an act of heresy.[36]

In 792, it would seem, the same faulty Latin translation of the Acts of the Second Council of Nicaea was sent across the Channel by Charles to Alcuin, at that time in England. The English Church was horrified to think that the leading theologians of the East, with three hundred or more bishops, should be asserting their belief that images ought to be "adored," and Alcuin at once composed a letter in stern con-

[34] *Epp.* V, 5ff. (dated here, by Hampe, c. 791 *in.*); *PL* XCVIII, coll. 1247ff., 1300; Jaffé, *Mon. Alc.* 246f.

[35] Page 50 *supra.*

[36] *Mon. Alc.* 247f.

demnation.[37] This, approved and confirmed by bishops and kings, he brought with him when he returned to Frankland the next year.

The letter, now lost, was distinct from the *Caroline Books.* These strongly condemned both the order of the Council of Constantinople in 754, to destroy the sacred images, and also the supposed order of the Second Council of Nicaea in 787, to "adore" them. The *Books* appeared under the name of Charles.[38] But they were written and composed for his inspection and approval by some man, or men, near to him in his realm. Whether Alcuin was this author, or one of these authors, has long been debated. On the one hand, it has been contended that their vehemently bitter tone of opposition to the East and its Empress Irene, their criticisms of the writings of the Pope himself in his "Refutations," are fundamentally unlike the humble, charitable, Catholic Alcuin; that Alcuin was absent in England; that one better acquainted with the Mozarabic-Spanish Psalter, perhaps Theodulf of Orléans, should be held as author, from the language of their quotations. Argument on the other side points out that Alcuin looked upon defence of orthodox belief as his particular work and wrote unflinchingly against Felix of Urgel; that certainly, whoever was the writer of these *Books,* his work was criticized, edited, and flavoured by the mind of his autocratic King, holding himself lord over bishops, theologians, churchmen, as

[37] Sym. Dun. II, 53f.; *Vet. Ann. Nord. ann.* 792: *SS* XIII, 155; H. S. III, 468f.; Thomas Fuller, *Church History of Britain,* ed. Brewer, I, 277: "These canons . . . were sent by Charles the Great . . . to be received of the English; who notwithstanding generally distasted and rejected them, the aforesaid Alcuinus writing a learned epistle against the same."

[38] On the making of the *Libri Carolini* and on MS. Vat. lat. 7207, showing corrections in their text, and marginal notes by King Charles himself, see Bastgen, *NA* XXXVII, 1912, 51; Tangl, *NA* XXXVI, 1911, 752ff.; von den Steinen, *NA* XLIX, 1932, 207ff.; De Bruyne, *RB* XLIV, 1932, 228f.

over generals and statesmen; that Alcuin could have worked on these *Books* in England and finished them at the Court of Charles; that Spanish influences had penetrated Church circles in Frankland;[39] that the use of secular science, the treatment and style of the *Books,* are in keeping with Alcuin's method and manner; that Alcuin, as the author of the letter from the English Church, might well have been also the author of the larger work.[40]

The last chapter in this unhappy story, so far as Alcuin was concerned, unrolled its solemn sentences in 794 at the Council of Frankfurt. There he and British delegates, in union with the general assembly and in the presence of the two Papal envoys, definitely declared that the commandment of the Council of 787, to pay "service and adoration" to the images of the saints as to the Divine Trinity—so they interpreted it—was herewith held in scorn and condemned.[41]

Thus the evil of untrue translation continued to live. Nevertheless, in trying to judge the whole matter, we shall do well to hold in mind that, if the Latins differed from the Asiatic-Greek tolerance of obeisance toward sacred persons and symbols, so, and in far greater measure, did the Franks and Saxons of northern countries. Both Charles, with his fellow-Franks, and Alcuin, with his fellow-English, had inherited

[39] Cf. Cabrol, *Les Origines liturgiques,* App. D, 216.

[40] Against Alcuin's authorship see Hampe, *NA* XXI, 1896, 101; Hauck II, 329; Allgeier, *HJ* XLVI, 1926, 352; von den Steinen, *NA* XLIX, 1932, 207, 232, note 1 (assigns the work to Theodulf of Orléans; cf. Seppelt, 179, Voigt, *Staat,* 341); Kleinclausz, *Alcuin,* 295ff. For Alcuin see Amann, *RSR* XVI, 1936, 302, note 3; Bastgen, *NA* XXXVII, 1912, 507ff.; *HJ* XXXII, 1911, 815; Delius, *Die Bilderfrage im Karolingerreich,* 1928, 22f., and cf. de Ghellinck, 95. Ganshof (*BHR* IX, 1947, 16, note 4) holds that Alcuin did important work in its preparation; so also Liutpold Wallach, *Speculum* XXIV, 1949, 589. In general, see Laistner, 238f.; Hefele-Leclercq III, 2, 1065, 1242, and, for a detailed description of content, E. J. Martin, 231ff.

[41] *Cap. reg. Fr.* I, 73f.

the cooler, more practical temper of their race, and, at least instinctively, would understand the attitude and feeling of iconoclasts rather than those of iconodules.[42] The Council of Paris in the ninth century was still of the same mind.[43] The King of the Franks had emphasized his view of the matter at Frankfurt in the presence of Papal legates; the advantage lay with him. The Holy See continued to look to the Frankish ruler for the strong support of his secular arm.[44] But at the moment, in 794, and for long years to come, relations between Frankland and Constantinople were definitely hostile in tone.

2

We turn now from heresy to the prayers of the faithful. As Charles worked and commanded, in his conception of his God-given kingship and in its widening sphere, to bring barbarians and heretics alike into one ordered and orthodox body of State and Church within his lands, so as king and ruler he desired harmony and uniformity within the ecclesiastical use and service of the Frankish Church. Here was a problem at hand that to his eyes was equally pressing, in its own place. It troubled him greatly that, at the time when he was stirring the clergy and people of Frankland by the work of Alcuin, there was no one and the same Mass-Book in official use throughout his many dioceses. Different bishops and priests were following texts which differed, one from another, in lesser detail, which held more or fewer offices, celebrated more or fewer feasts, and contained varying forms of prayer. A brief tracing of events may help to explain the gradual growth of this disorder, so intolerable to the controlling vision of the King.[45]

[42] Cf. Haller II, i, 10; Dawson, 220.
[43] Note 32 *supra*.
[44] See Ostrogorsky, *Gesch.* 127.
[45] See, in bibliography, Bishop, Cabrol, Dix, de Puniet.

In the course of centuries the Christian Liturgy, one and the same in its basic form, had among the various peoples of Christendom naturally taken into itself special details—feast days, and prayers designed for these; prayers for the specific rulers; rites of distinctly national origin. In no country was this more true than in Frankland, for its people differed essentially in character and in tradition from that of Rome. The Franks, as "barbarians," were a younger race, more childlike, freer and warmer of expression than the Romans, who had inherited from ancient days a strong feeling for legal formality and precise order. This national Frankish character was reflected in the Gallican Liturgy of the churches of Frankland of the fifth and following centuries.[46]

The liturgical Book of Rites in use at Rome during the early years of the sixth century is known to us by the name of the "Gelasian" Sacramentary. The connection of Gelasius, Pope from 492 to 496, with its text is uncertain; it was called simply the "Book of the Sacraments of the Church of Rome." [47] Its use, of course, was not confined to Rome itself, and, as might be expected, in other parts of Italy this Roman "Gelasian" Book was reproduced in many copies to which were added, here and there, different prayers in keeping with the local tradition of saints honoured in each district.

Before the end of this same sixth century this "Gelasian" Book of Sacraments, in a text, very possibly made in Central or Southern Italy, found its way across the Alps into Frankland,[48] settled there, and became the parent of many copies. As time went on, more and more of these copies omitted

[46] Probst, *Die abendl. Messe,* 298, 305, 332ff., 354.

[47] de Puniet, *Pont. rom.* I, 22ff.; Probst, *Die ält. röm. Sacr.* 143ff.; S. Bäumer, *HJ* XIV, 1893, 300f.; Frere, *Studies* I, 53f.; Wilson, *Gelas. Sacr.* lviiiff.

[48] Mone, *Lateinische und griech. Messen,* 1850, 112ff.; Dix, 566; Sinclair, 142ff.

Roman features and showed Frankish material, introduced from the Gallican Liturgy as suitable for some particular parish or diocese. One of these copies, dated in substance about 700 and still extant, shows enough of this "de-Romanizing," pro-Frankish influence to indicate that the "Gelasian" text must have been long in use in Frankish churches.[49]

About the year 600 Gregory the Great, Pope from 590 to 604, decided that the time had come for a revision of the text of the Liturgy in the service-books of Rome. With that care revealed in his *Letters,* both world-wide and individual, for the needs of the souls of men—priest or religious, Christian or pagan, Roman or barbarian—he worked to bring the Roman Book of the Sacraments into more intimate touch with the hearts and minds of his people as they prayed at Rome.[50]

During the seventh century this revision of the Roman Liturgy by Gregory the Great met a twofold destiny. It underwent constant use in Rome and churches under Rome, where its copies, also, were augmented by the addition of material that it lacked—collects and prayers for Masses that had been omitted by Saint Gregory.[51] And in its turn it, too, travelled to Frankland, where it was not only itself enlarged, but also contributed from its content to the texts of the Liturgies, Gallican and "Gelasian," which it found already there. We find evidence of this influence in copies of these, still available

[49] *Vat. Reg.* 316; Frere, *Studies* I, 36ff.; Muratori, *Lit. Rom. Vet.* I, coll. 493ff.; Wilson, *The Gelasian Sacramentary;* Leroquais I, XIVf. The word "Gelasian" is used to describe a Roman liturgy with Frankish additions; cf. Frere, *Studies* I, 53; Duchesne, *Christian Worship,* 1919, 129.

[50] Bishop, 14; Dix, 570ff. and bibliography cited there; de Puniet, *Pont. rom.* I, 27ff.

[51] Wilmart, *RB* XXVI, 1909, 281ff. (Monte Cassino fragments: *Cod. Casin.* 271); Dix, 572f.; Mohlberg, ed. *Die älteste erreichbare Gestalt des Liber Sacr. anni circuli der röm. Kirche* (MS. of Padua, D 47), *LQ* 11-12, 1927, XXXVIf.

to us, from the eighth century.[52] This influence of Roman tradition was also seen in Frankland during this seventh century by the various approaches to Roman use and ritual made by the bishops of Rouen and of Metz and by Pepin, King of the Franks.[53]

It was this confusion of rites, Gallican, "Gelasian," Gregorian, which Charles was determined to replace by an ordered and uniform rite for the churches of his dominions. During his stay of 781 in Rome he had been much impressed by the difference between the text prescribed there and the lack of conformity enjoyed by the Frankish peoples and their priests in regard to their missals. Autocratic and dictatorial as he was in the consciousness, ever in his mind, of his surpassing power in Europe, yet he always saw in Rome the appointed centre of man's search after God through the Church. And so, soon after his return home, he sent a request across the Alps to Pope Hadrian. Would the Pope please forward to him a copy of the Book of the Sacraments officially at this time in use there?

The letter of the Frankish King is lost, but we have the Pope's answer, dated sometime between 784 and 791. After considerable delay, Hadrian wrote, he was now sending to Charles by John, abbot in Ravenna, a copy of the Sacramentary of Rome as revised and sanctioned by Pope Gregory the Great, without supplementary material. This last statement was not literally correct in every respect, for some additions were present, incorporated in Gregory's book after his

[52] For the influence of the Roman Liturgy upon the Gallican Liturgy, see Dix, 574; for its influence upon the "Frankish-Gelasian" texts, see de Puniet on the Sacramentary of Gellone (*saec.* VIII), *EL New Series* VIII, 1934, 4f.; cf. Bishop, *DR* XXXVII, 1919, 5ff.; Leroquais I, 1ff., Pl.IIff.; Leclercq, *DACL* s.v. Gellone, and the *Sacramentary of Angoulême* (*saec.* VIII or IX *ineunt.),* ed. Paul Cagin, 1919.

[53] Page 123 *supra;* Mönchemeier, *Amalar von Metz,* 1893, 5f.; Frere, *Studies* I, 51; Leroquais I, XV; Klauser, *HJ* LIII, 1933, 170f.

death, such as prayers for Feasts of our Lady, for some days in Lent, and for a Day in honour of Gregory himself. Moreover, in the eyes of the Franks there were many serious omissions in this book which now reached them. Its lack of material, indeed, has caused keen debate among scholars, who have questioned whether it did represent in substance a text sanctioned by Gregory, or a well-pruned text edited by Hadrian.[54] Upon its arrival Charles handed it to Alcuin, who by his long experience of Roman liturgy and usage in England was ideally, as well as *ex officio,* the man to prepare, on this Gregorian basis, a Sacramentary which the King should prescribe for usage among his people.[55]

Alcuin found this charge neither easy nor simple. In the first place, the copy of the book which had been sent to Charles had been hastily made, held many errors, and, as we have noted, was extremely incomplete. Alcuin had to begin his work with a thorough revision and correction of its text by the aid of Gregorian manuscripts already current among the Franks. Those parts of it, moreover, which had been introduced after Saint Gregory's time he marked by a sign in the margin. At the end of this corrected text he placed a warning in his own words, that "none may reject it without peril to himself."

These words formed part of a "Little Preface," as he called

[54] *Epp.* III, 626. Its text was copied in MS. Cambrai (159) 164, dated 811 or 812: Sacramentary of Hildoard, bishop of Cambrai, 790-816. See Leroquais, 9; Wilson, *The Gregorian Sacramentary;* Lietzmann, *Das Sacrament. Gregorianum.* For varying explanation of its lack in Sunday Masses, and of its relation to Popes Gregory and Hadrian, cf. Dix, 579; Sinclair, 152f.; Frere, *Studies* I, 54f.; de Puniet, *Rom. Pont.* 20f.; Lietzmann, XX; Wilmart, *RB* XXVI, 298; Probst, *Die ält. röm. Sacr.,* 317; Bäumer, *HJ* XIV, 1893, 251, note 2, 264ff.; Klauser, *HJ* LIII, 1933, 181f.; Andrieu, *RSR* IX, 1929, 372.

[55] Bäumer, 259f. For the constant honouring of the pure Roman tradition in England from 600 to the latter part of the 8th century, cf. Knowles, *The Monastic Order in England,* 1949, 548.

it,[56] introducing a Supplement which contained material added by Alcuin himself, as editor, to the book he had received. In this he did what had been done in Italy; he filled up a lack of material in this "Gregorian" book by including prayers for Masses not provided in it, especially for Sundays after the Epiphany, after Easter, and after Pentecost, gathering them, here and there, "like spring flowers of the fields." These were readily available for him in other texts, Gallican—"Gelasian"—"Gregorian," now familiar in Frankland. From these same sources he added, next, other prayers, for votive Masses, for episcopal offices, for special occasions, until he hoped that he had made what might well be used among the Franks as their Book of Sacraments.

Yet, as he examined the Sacramentaries already in use around him, especially those of Gallican origin, as well as those "Gelasian" or "Gregorian" texts which had received numberless local additions since their arrival in Frankland, as he talked with the Frankish bishops of dioceses and with parish priests, he felt that his Supplement was not yet complete. The Franks, as a people, loved their own Frankish saints; they were accustomed in their liturgies to make special and detailed remembrance of their dead;[57] as we have already seen, they differed deeply in their thought before their altars from the more restrained, more traditionally-minded people of Rome. And so at last Alcuin felt he must enlarge this Supplement to contain yet other prayers and rites dear to the Frankish heart, gathered from Frankish and Spanish sources for those who would otherwise sorely miss their presence in this Book of Rites to be appointed for the subjects of King Charles. This, accordingly, he did.

[56] It is called the *Hucusque* Preface, from its first word.

[57] Bishop, 100f. and *DR* XXXVII, 12ff.; Neale and Forbes, *Ancient Liturgies of the Gallican Church*, 1855–1867, 3, 9, 16.

But his liturgical mind moved very carefully. His "Little Preface," he assures all, has been purposely placed between the two parts—the necessary Book of blessed Gregory, and his own optional Supplement—so that the line between them may be entirely clear. Let those, who will, use the prayers of the Supplement, added by him with no feeling of arrogance, but only in the desire for the happiness of all; those who do not feel them needful, will use only the first part. All may be certain that nothing has been included which has not been wrought by the labour of most experienced, most learned men. Much has been brought together from many sources for the service of many. At the end of the Book a collection of Proper Prefaces will be found; please, let these be happily chanted by those who like them, left alone with equal charity by those who either do not understand their use or do not care for these particular forms. Further, Alcuin has included some benedictions which bishops may use for their people, and some forms of ordination to lesser orders in the Church, not given by Gregory the Great in his Book. Will all who use or copy this Book, as edited by Alcuin, pray to the Lord for him? He has worked hard and eagerly. And, finally, will copyists be very careful, lest by their errors they offend the ears of the learned and cause the simple to go astray? For indeed, as said blessed Jerome, it avails nothing to amend a book unless it be well preserved in the work of those who reproduce it.[58]

Alcuin's *Book of Sacraments,* with its Gregorian heart, its

[58] The MS. tradition of Alcuin's Book, in addition to Cambrai (159) 164, derives from *Vat. Reg.* 337 (Frankish, 9th cent.) and *Vat. Ottob.* 313 (9th cent., perhaps of Paris). For the Book see Wilson; Lietzmann (note 54 *supra);* Brou, *EL* LX, 1946, 299f., note 26; Alcuin's Preface, from *Cod. Ottob.:* Wilson, 145f., Lietzmann, xix. See also Lietzmann, *JL* V, 1925, 79. For Spanish-Mozarabic elements used by Alcuin see Bishop, 167f.; Cabrol, *Les Origines liturgiques,* 216f.; for the Spanish liturgy, Férotin, ed. *Liber Mozarabicus Sacramentorum, Mon. Eccles. Lit.* VI, 1912.

Gallican, "Gelasian," and Spanish members, was at last ready, shortly after 794, and was approved by Charles. The part preceding the Supplement was prescribed by his order for uniform use throughout Frankland, to the exclusion of other rites; [59] the Supplement might be used, if desired. The freedom of devotion allowed by this Supplement undoubtedly aided immeasurably in the general adoption of the book, although we have evidence that other Mass-books, especially the "Gelasian," were still in service in Frankish churches thirty years later.[60] As time went on, the "Little Preface" was omitted from copies, and the two parts, so scrupulously separated by Alcuin, became fused; moreover, as was natural, prayers made their way from outside sources, "Gelasian" and Gallican, into its pages.[61]

Use of the Book, thus enlarged, spread far and wide in Western Europe. Later in the Middle Ages the charity and wisdom of its editor bore unexpected fruit, when his Sacramentary, with a wealth of added matter, took the place of the Roman *Gregorianum* in Rome itself and became parent of the Missal now in use in the Roman Church. Every Catholic under the obedience of Rome owes a debt of gratitude to Alcuin every time he hears Mass at the altar, to this deacon and teacher who in his eagerness for the life of souls laboured without haste and without rest to give men what they needed and, with this, what they desired.

[59] *Cap. reg. Franc.* I, 234, No. 116, 4 and 7. Cf. the instructions given to monks by Charles to follow the Use of Rome in the Choir Office: *Chron. Moiss. ann.* 802; B.M.L. 175, No. 390a; Bishop, 53f.

[60] *Chron. S. Richarii, Mon. Centul.* III, 3: *PL* CLXXIV, col. 1261; Wilson, *Gelas. Sacr.* liv. On the feelings of the Frankish people, deprived, as it was, in this book of part of their beloved ritual, see Wilmart-Bishop, 201f.; Ellard, *Ordination Anointings in the Western Church before 1000 A.D., MAA*, 1933, 35f.

[61] Wilson, *Greg. Sacr.* XXVII; Dix, 582f.; Leroquais I, 22, 30.

3

Of Alcuin's other official works in the service of the Church little is known, even in regard to their date. Two, however, may be briefly described here, as they, too, belong to that campaign for order which he directed under Charles.

The earlier, perhaps, in time was a collection of homilies or sermons. That Alcuin did make such a collection has been held in doubt, especially since it is well-known that Charles commissioned Paul the Deacon to gather passages from the writings of the Fathers for reading as Lessons in the Night Office of Frankish monasteries. The book which resulted from Paul's study was sent by him to the King after his return to Monte Cassino in 786, and its use was formally enjoined by Charles upon the monks in his dominions by a "General Letter," usually dated between 786 and 801.[62]

The *Life of Alcuin,* however, written some twenty years after he died, states that "he collected two volumes of homilies from many works of the Fathers." [63] Evidence from manuscript has been brought forward in support of this claim, showing a collection of sermons characteristic both of Alcuin's time and of his manner, and attributed to him by marginal note of a later century. The series starts with the four Sundays of Advent. It continues through the year and includes an address for the *Depositio S. Mariae,* the Falling Asleep of our Lady, placed in January. The observance of this Feast in this month was characteristic of Gallican ritual of Frankland in the eighth century, as was also the absence, noted in the same series, of Feasts of the Annunciation, Nativity, and As-

[62] *Cap. reg. Fr.* I, 80f.; *PLAC* I, 68 (XXXIV); Manitius, 259, 266f.
[63] *SS* XV, i, 195.

sumption of blessed Mary. Toward the end of the century these Feasts gradually won observance throughout Frankland; that of the Falling Asleep in January was then replaced by celebration of the Assumption in August. The subject matter of this series of sermons shows traces of Alcuin's method, in its erudition and in its careful dwelling on the significance of words and number.[64]

The other work, held likewise in doubt by some authorities, has also been assigned to Alcuin by others in recent research. It consists of a revision of the *Comes* or Book of Lessons to be read at Mass, and contains two hundred and forty-two passages from the books of the Old Testament and from the Epistles, Acts, and Revelation, of the New, in a text carefully corrected in regard to grammar and spelling.[65] Its chief interest for us lies in the witness it eventually gave to the importance of Alcuin's work on the Frankish Sacramentary. For not long after Alcuin's death this revision of the Lectionary by him was itself held in need of reshaping, and the author of this second revision, very probably Helisachar, chancellor under Louis the Pious, followed Alcuin's example in adding a supplement and a preface.[66] Both by his matter and his word-

[64] See Morin, *RB* IX, 1892, 491ff. But, among papers relating to Alcuin given to me by the generous courtesy of Mr. C. J. B. Gaskoin, there are two written to him by Dom Germain Morin, remarking that further research into the matter of the homilies attributed to Heiric should be made, for comparison with those attributed to Alcuin. Cf., on these homilies, Cabrol, *RHE* XIX, 1923, 510f., and *DACL* s.v. *Alcuin,* coll. 1077f.; Leclercq, *ibid.* s.v. *Gallicane (Liturgie),* coll. 506f.; Hauck II, 259f.; Levison, 158; Lietzmann, *LQ* III, 1921, XX. Alcuin's collection differed from that of Paul in being made for general use.

[65] Ed. Tommasi (*Opera,* ed. Vezzosi V, 297ff.), reproduced by Ranke, *Das kirchl. Pericopensystem,* app. II, ivff.; see also 154ff.; Morin, *RB* XXVII, 1910, 74; Godu, *DACL* s.v. *Épitres,* coll. 300ff.; Leclercq, *ibid.* s.v. *Lectionnaire,* col. 2284; Frere, *Studies* III, 40ff.; Wilmart, *EL* XI, 1937, 136ff.; *PLAC* I, 299 (LXXIX).

[66] This later preface is known, also from its beginning, as *Hunc codicem:* Ranke, 154; Wilmart, *RB* XXIX, 1912, 341ff.

ing he showed here how deeply Alcuin in his edition of Saint Gregory's Book of Rites influenced liturgists of the ninth century.[67]

In 796 Alcuin was well past his sixtieth year. It was time that Charles should heed his repeated longing for freedom from these many duties for King, Court, "School," Church and State. More and more he was finding it harder to tear himself away from the brief seasons of retreat which now and then he allowed himself, especially at the monasteries of Saint Peter at Ferrières and of Saint Lupus at Troyes, both of which had been given him by the King for his charge and ordering.[68] Even here, however, he was pressed by problems of law and rule and gladly sought peace at times in Echternach. For its Abbot Beornred, at his request, Alcuin wrote a *Life* of its Saint Willibrord, the kinsman they shared together, in a double version, prose and verse, following the precedent set by Sedulius in his *Paschale* and by the Anglo-Saxons, Aldhelm in his *De Virginitate,* and Bede in his *Life of Saint Cuthbert.* He records that "it was dictated in stolen hours of the night, because I was so busy during the day." [69] Of himself Alcuin knew that he was speaking, in the words of exhortation which escorted on its way to his old friend, Abbot Rado, his revision of the *Life* of Saint Vedast,[70] patron of Rado's monastery at Arras: "White hair tells that one's last

[67] Bishop, describing this influence upon Helisachar and upon Benedict of Aniane (in the preface to the *Concordia Regularum*) wrote: "It is hardly too much to call the preface *Hucusque* a State Paper of the time": *Lit. Hist.* 53, 333ff., 344ff.

[68] *Alc. Vita,* 190.

[69] *Epp.* IV, 175; cf. page 15 *supra;* Verbist, *S. Willibrord,* 285f. For editions and translation see bibliography *infra,* s.v. Alcuin. At the end Alcuin prays as usual for the intercession of the saint. The work, like Alcuin's other essays in biography, aims, not at recording of history, but at edification of souls; cf. Kleinclausz, *Alcuin,* 222ff.

[70] Modern Saint Vaast.

day is hastening. So see that you stand ready every hour for the meeting with your God." [71]

And now Abbot Itherius of Tours died, and the King, as we have seen, conferred upon Alcuin the rule of its Abbey of Saint Martin, in the assurance that this new Abbot would still be available to him for counsel and collaboration in time of need. To Alcuin this held out exactly what he so long had craved: a home among brethren united by religious rule, in which, removed from immediate contact with the Court and its calls, he might serve God and men in comparative peace.[72]

[71] *Epp.* IV, 116. *The Life of St. Vedast* here reshaped by Alcuin was written by Jonas, author of the *Life of St. Columban;* see *SRM* III, 399ff.; Levison, 161.

[72] Nevertheless, what Alcuin felt in leaving his friend and King he told in a letter to Arno (*Epp.* IV, 309): *in lacrimis lacrimans dimisi eum; cupiens perpetuam laetitiae illius memoriam animae meae inscribere.*

Chapter VI

ALCUIN IN TOURS: EARLIER YEARS

CHAPTER VI

ALCUIN IN TOURS: EARLIER YEARS

I

In August, 796, the body of Eanbald, Archbishop of York, was borne through great crowds to its resting-place in his Cathedral of Saint Peter.[1] "Bid prayers for his soul," Alcuin wrote to his friend Arno of Salzburg. "He was fellow-student with me under my master, and now I am left alone." Without delay another Eanbald, once Alcuin's pupil in the School of York, was chosen in his place and consecrated on Sunday, August 14.[2] The following year envoys travelled to Rome to ask the Archbishop's pallium for this new Pastor. They were supported by a letter from Alcuin to Pope Leo: "because the authority of the sacred pallium is exceedingly needful in Northumbria to repress the perversity of wicked men and maintain the authority of Holy Church." [3] The dignity was granted, and Eanbald the second was solemnly confirmed in office on the Feast of our Lady's Nativity, September 8, 797.[4]

Letters, of course, came one after another from his former teacher to counsel and warn the Archbishop. "Praise and glory be to the Lord God Omnipotent," was Alcuin's cry of joy in 796, "Who has given this to me, that I should see the exaltation of my dearest son, that I, the least of the servants of the Church, by His grace should prepare one of my sons to

[1] Einhard, *Vita Karol.* c. 19 (see Halphen, *Eginhard,* 61, for criticism); Sym. Dun. II, 58; *A-SC ann.* 796.

[2] *Epp.* IV, 162; *Ann. Lindisf. ann.* 796.

[3] *Epp.* IV, 184.

[4] *A-SC ann.* 797; Sym. Dun. II, 58; cf. *PLAC* I, 255, l. 40.

be a worthy dispenser of the Mysteries of Christ, to labour in my place, in the church where I was reared and taught, to preside over the treasures of wisdom to which my master, Archbishop Aelbert, left me heir.

"Now you have by God's gift all that mortal man could hope, even more than our littleness could dare to hope. Only do now bravely the work of a true man. Fulfil the task of the Lord which you have in hand, for the rewarding of our soul and the salvation of many."

These counsels of holy living then take a practical turn: "Do all things in order. Settle a time for reading; let prayer have its own hours; let the celebration of Masses find their proper season. Hold not yourself lord of temporal possessions, but their dispenser. Let not the number of your kinsmen make you grudging in generosity, thinking you must gather for their inheritance; no heir is better than Christ. Give your alms, first, in saving souls; secondly, in aiding the bodies of the poor.

"See to it that your clergy do not chatter idly, nor shout and run to hunt foxes in the fields. Bid them rather ride with you in pleasant chanting of Psalms. See to it that your deacons serve you in due ritual, with, also, all ranks of the sevenfold ministry of the Church. Let each rank have its own appointed station and vestment. For if the use of seniority and rank is to be maintained in the banquets of this world, how much more in the Church of Christ? And, with decent habit of office, let your clergy chant with moderation of voice, striving to please God rather than men; to raise the voice beyond measure is a sign of conceit. Moreover, they are not to refuse to learn the rites of Rome, so that, following the head of the churches of Christ as far as they may, they may merit eternal blessing from holy Peter, whom our Lord Jesus Christ placed as head of his chosen flock. Be ye like unto bees, and learn, by proving, all things which are honourable; thus by your choice shall you hold fast what appears best.

"Provide diligently masters for the boys in your School, and let them be taught in separate classes, for reading, for the study of chant and song, for writing. Each class should have its own teacher, that your boys may not be left idle to wander where they will, to play silly games or give themselves to other foolishness.

"You know that I am always most ready to help you in every way, even though I live in a foreign land.

"Bid, also, the providing of hostels for the receiving, day by day, of the poor and of pilgrims, and let them have comfort from our substance.

"But, for me, I am weary with two heavy burdens, old age and frail health. It may be the dread day is coming upon me in which the pitcher shall be broken at the fountain and the golden fillet shrink back; then shall the dust return to its earth and the spirit to God Who gave it. And I am frightened and afraid of that weighing, in which it must be judged. Please, my son, labour for the soul of your Father, now tarrying in this dust, then hastening to judgment, that he may find rest and forgiveness.

"Have regard, too, to all my sons, brethren and friends, those with me in this land abroad, or those with you in the home country. Hold them as your own, and not as strangers.

"Keep this letter of mine, and have it copied in a better script, so that your Father may often speak with you, my dear son in Christ." [5]

So much counsel, indeed, passed from Tours to York that Alcuin wrote later on: "I can find nothing new to add to my

[5] *Epp.* IV, 166ff.; H. S. III, 501ff. The method of "separate classes" was doubtless practised under Alcuin at Tours, introduced by him from York: Hauck II, 195; *Versus de Sanctis,* ll. 1433ff.

devotion of the past." [6] At another time he bids: "Wherever you go, let the *Pastoral Book* of holy Gregory go with you. Read and re-read it, that you may see as in a mirror how a bishop should live and teach.[7]

"And do not grow soft of spirit in the flattery of chieftains, nor slothful in the correction of those under you. The times are dangerous in Britain, and the death of kings is a sign of misery." [8]

The kings of whom Alcuin was writing here were Ethelred of Northumbria and Offa of Mercia. A more ominous note was struck in a letter of 797 to Osbert, a noble of Mercia, once a member of Offa's council.

"I have heard, my friend," Alcuin wrote, "that many things have happened of deep concern, not only to you, but to your whole kingdom, a source of anxiety also to my people in Northumbria, through the treachery of evil men. It is for you to take thought under God for yourself and for all the peoples of the English. Times of tribulation are now everywhere in our land, as faith wanes and truth is silent, as arrogance increases troubles. I do not think that the goodly young King Egfrith of Mercia died because of his own sins; rather, I believe that vengeance for the blood shed by his father came upon the son. You know well that Offa poured out much blood to establish this son Egfrith upon the throne, not for its standing, but for its destruction.

"So warn your King Cenwulf, and warn the chieftains of my Northumbria, too, that they honour God and live purely. I am afraid that our King Eardwulf of Northumbria will lose his crown because of his insult against God in sending away his wife to ally himself openly with a mistress, so it is said. Let Cenwulf keep free of such evil. Tell your people to abide by

[6] *Epp.* IV, 170.
[7] Cf. *ibid.* 171.
[8] H. S. III, 505.

the laws of King Offa, of blessed memory. For my Northumbria is nearly dead through internal quarrels and false swearings. And, I think, the last end of these has yet to come." [9]

Similar broodings and prophecies of evil make their way in the same year from Alcuin's worried mind to King Cenwulf of Mercia himself and to Higbald, bishop of Lindisfarne.[10] Among the many forbiddings and forewarnings addressed to the latter there occurs an interesting passage:

"Let the words of God be read aloud at table in your refectory. The reader should be heard there, not the flute-player; the Fathers of the Church, not the songs of the heathen. What has Ingeld to do with Christ? Our house is not wide enough to hold both; nor was it intended for the use of those who make merry in the market-place." [11]

Alcuin here is rebuking the brethren of Lindisfarne for listening to songs that re-echoed the story of the *Beowulf,* of the great feud between the Danes and the people living near them, the Heathobards; more especially, of the Heathobard prince, Ingeld, who, incited by taunts to avenge his father's murder by the Danes rather than ensue peace by wedding a Danish princess, met his terrible defeat in attacking Heorot, the fortress of the Danes.[12]

In 798 revolt actually was raised against Eardwulf of Northumbria by the same men who had killed King Ethelred two years before, a fact which hints that Eardwulf himself had not been implicated in that murder.[13] The conspirators were put to flight in a battle, perhaps at Billington Moor in

[9] *Epp.* IV, 178ff. [10] *Ibid.* 180ff.

[11] Page 10 *supra.*

[12] Jänicke, *ZDA* XV, 1872, 314; *Beowulf,* ll. 2024ff.: ed. Klaeber, 1941, xxxivf., 202f.; *Widsith,* ll. 45ff.; R. W. Chambers, *Widsith,* 1912, 78ff.; Kemp Malone, ed. *Widsith,* 1936, 23f., 172 and *The Germanic Review* XIV, 1939, 256; Saxo Grammaticus, *Gesta Danorum,* ed. Olrok and Raeder I, 171.

[13] Sym. Dun. II, 59.

Lancashire, and Eardwulf settled back upon his throne. The next year, 799, saw vengeance worked upon the leader of Ethelred's assassins, a chieftain named Aldred. He was killed by Torhtmund, another of Northumbria's leading men,[14] and Alcuin described the slayer afterwards in a letter to King Charles: "Torhtmund, a faithful servant of King Ethelred, a man of proven loyalty, vigorous in battle, who has boldly avenged the blood of his lord." [15]

The earlier years of Alcuin's life in Tours brought news, also, of trouble in the south of England. Already in 796, before Offa, King of Mercia, had departed this life, the men of Kent had risen against his sovereignty, which held their land in firm control. The Archbishop of Canterbury and spiritual ruler at the time was Ethelhard, who had come from an abbacy at Louth in Lincolnshire and was consecrated as Primate in 793. It was one of his own clergy, Eadbert Praen, who led the revolt, under the title of "King" of Kent.[16]

Matters of the Church in Kent had also been complicated by the division we have already noted of the See of Canterbury, upon the formation, at Offa's request to Pope Hadrian, of a second Metropolitan See for the south at Lichfield in Mercia, held by Higbert, upon whom the Pope had conferred the Archbishop's pallium in 788. Doubtless this fact also vexed the minds of Kentish men. It had been King Offa who had deliberated what should be done when Archbishop Jaenbert had died four years later, in 792, and had written to Alcuin himself to ask counsel with regard to the confirming in office of Jaenbert's successor. Alcuin had answered that Gregory the Great had established two Metropolitan Sees in Britain in

[14] *Ibid.* 62. [15] *Epp.* IV, 376 (801 A.D.).
[16] Flor. Worc. I, 63; *Epp.* IV, 45ff.; H. S. III, 474ff.; *PLAC* I, 235f.

order that it should not be necessary for an Archbishop-elect to journey thence to Rome for his installing: "Your Excellency must be assured that an Archbishop is always to be confirmed in office by an Archbishop, and as now in your kingdom, given you by God, you have two Metropolitans, the survivor is to install the one newly elected." [17] Accordingly, Higbert of Lichfield was indicated as officiant for Archbishop Ethelhard.

Ethelhard was closely attached to Offa, from whom he received wide lands in Middlesex,[18] and to Cenwulf after Offa's death. In fact, so evident was his support of Mercia and of Mercia's rule in Kent that after the Kentish men rose in 796 he fled from Canterbury in fear of his life. Alcuin, after hearing this, wrote to the clergy and laymen of Canterbury, "where the most radiant torches of Britain have their resting-place, from which the light of truth has shone out through all the land." "Now," he continued, "very great peril is threatening that island and its people: pirates and robbers from without, division and strife between king and king, between king and people, within its borders. Scarcely any one—and I say it with tears—from the ancient lineage of kings is found among the English, and the more obscure the origin of your rulers, the less sure their courage." Let the men of Kent look to the pages of Gildas, wisest of the Britons, to understand why their parents lost kingdom and country; then let them see the like in themselves. And let them call back their pastor, Ethelhard. "It is not good that the seat of holy Augustine, our first Preacher, should remain empty; nor may another be ordained in Ethelhard's place." [19]

In 798 trouble in regard to the Archbishopric of Lichfield

[17] P. Lehmann, "Holländische Reisefrüchte," *SBM* 1920, 13 *Abh.* 29ff.; Levison, 244ff.
[18] Birch I, 369ff.; Stenton, 223f.
[19] *Epp.* IV, 191f.; H. S. III, 509ff.

spread abroad in Mercia itself, and its King Cenwulf sent a letter to ask counsel of Pope Leo the third: "Our bishops and learned men are saying, beloved Father, that this division of the See of Canterbury was contrary to the canons and apostolic statutes established by Pope Gregory; that he appointed two Metropolitan Sees in Britain, Canterbury and London, of which London, by direction of Augustine, was replaced by York, and so it has seemed good to our race. Then, as you know, it was, first, King Offa who, because of his hostility toward Jaenbert and the people of Canterbury, set to work to turn aside honour from its See and to divide it in two; and your predecessor, Pope Hadrian, at Offa's request, did what no one had before taken in hand when he gave an Archbishop's pallium to the bishop of the Mercians. We blame neither of these. Yet we beg of you to inquire into this matter with your wise men and to write to me what seems good to you, lest the seamless tunic of Christ suffer division of schism among us."[20]

The Pope's answer gave as reason for Hadrian's action that presented by Offa, the immense territory covered by the See of Canterbury and by the realms under control of Mercia, "as well as very many other causes and expediencies." The letter touched also on other points put forward by Cenwulf. "You have asked me," wrote Leo, "whether London might not be the seat of the southern Archbishopric, as Gregory purposed? This I can by no means allow; the Metropolitan honour belongs now to Canterbury.[21] With regard to the letter sent to us by Ethelhard, we answered it by excommunicating that apostate clerk who had assumed the throne. If this clerk continues in his impious action, inform us swiftly, that we may send word to all chieftains and people of Britain that they drive him out from his ill-gotten reign."[22]

[20] Birch, 396ff.; H. S. III, 521ff.
[21] See Stenton, 224f.
[22] *Epp.* IV, 187f.; H. S. III, 523ff.

The Pope's thoughts were soon abruptly turned in other directions. But Cenwulf settled the revolt of Kent by invading its land in this same year, 798, and bringing its people back to his own obedience, not, however, to desire for his lordship over them. He ravaged their fields far and wide "in hideous plundering" (so the report ran) "almost to extermination; he captured Eadbert Praen, tore out his eyes, cut off his hands, and carried him in bonds back to Mercia." [23]

Ethelhard returned to his cathedral of Canterbury, where he received a long letter from Alcuin. "I have heard," Alcuin wrote, "that at the advice of your priests you left your See for a time on account of the wicked invasion of the kingdom. You have asked me what I thought of this. Should the pastor flee when the wolf comes? You yourself know why you left—whether through fear of death or hideousness of tortures or curse of idolatry. But, whatever the cause, I think you should do penance, that both you and your people should fast, offer Masses and alms; you, because you forsook your seat, they, because they condoned your fault. For you gave the devil cause to rejoice."

With regard to the southern province, Alcuin also gave his judgment to Ethelhard: "I hold it good, with the sanction of all the pastors of Christ and of your fellow-bishop of York, that the unity of the Church, broken not by sound reason, I believe, but by greed of power, should be healed and mended, and that the primacy should once again be limited to its first seat, at Canterbury. Yet the holy Father" (Higbert) "should be allowed to use the Archbishop's pallium for the rest of his days. I have written this, not of my own impulse, but because you did ask me. So do not hold me rash or presuming." [24]

Lichfield, however, remained a Metropolitan See until 803.

[23] Sym. Dun. II, 59; *A-SC ann.* 796. Will. of Malmesbury (*De Gest. Reg.* I, 94f.) tells of kindly treatment; Flor. Worc. (I, 63) omits the barbarities.

[24] *Epp.* IV, 189ff.; H. S. III, 518ff. (dated 798).

2

The news of sin and bloodshed was not confined for Alcuin to messengers from England. Tidings from the East were equally grave. There, in Constantinople, the tension between the ambitious Empress Irene and her son and co-ruler, Constantine the sixth, in 796 was reaching its climax. In September of that year they had moved their Court for a while to Brusa in Asia Minor,[25] much frequented then, as now, for its hot mineral waters. There Constantine heard that a son had been born of his union with his "Empress," Theodote. At once in his joy he rushed back to Constantinople; and Irene, left alone with officers of the army and the Imperial Guard, used her opportunity busily. By flattery, by promises, by presents, she won them to assurance that they were ready for action. Constantine, they vowed, should be deposed, and she should rule alone; it only remained to draw matters carefully toward this end. Chief among her agents was again the Patrician Stauracius, who, with many other friends of the Empress, accompanied Constantine in March, 797, on a campaign against the Arabs and by lies and treachery brought it to a miserable failure.

On July 17 the attack thus plotted was launched. As the Emperor, after leaving the Hippodrome, was passing through the suburb of Saint Mamus, he was suddenly surrounded by soldiers of the Imperial Guard. Just in time he broke away, reached the State galley moored on the shore of the Bosphorus and crossed to Pylae, on the Gulf of Nicomedia,[26] hoping to reach the Anatolic district (*theme*) in Asia Minor. Word of this escape threw Irene into consternation. The people, she feared, would rally to her son's defence. Should she in this case sue for his pardon and for her own safety? Sterner counsels finally won her mind, and she gave her friends of the army a

[25] Brousse, Turkey; Theophanes, 471f. [26] Ismid.

definite choice—either they would seize the Emperor and deliver him to her will, or she would tell him of their share in the plot against him. They chose the former, carried their captive to the Great Palace in Constantinople, and left him to await his destiny in the Purple Chamber in which he had been born some twenty-seven years before. He did not wait long. Early in the afternoon of this same day of August, 797,[27] hirelings of the Empress burst into the room to put out his eyes, maiming him so savagely that they left him as dead, "without hope of healing." Thereupon, the chronicler reports, "the sun was darkened for seventeen days and gave forth no radiance, so that ships on the sea lost their course. All men declared it came about through the blinding of the Emperor." [28] Other tradition asserts that Constantine still lived on.[29]

"Thus Irene, his mother, came to the power." As sole "Emperor" she ruled the East for five years, while her fortune flowed to high tide, turned, and swiftly ebbed. The Church received the full flood of her devotion. Monasteries were built, nunneries were endowed, monks were recalled from exile, among them the well-known abbot, Plato, whose monastery at Saccudion in Bithynia she enriched, and his nephew, Theodore, known to fame as abbot of the Studion in Constantinople. His denunciation of Constantine the sixth for his forsaking of Maria for Theodote—"Adulterer, even as a second Herod"—is equalled by his exultation over the virtuous Irene: "All have clapped their hands, noble Lady, dear to Christ, crying, 'Blessed be God for you, who make angels and righteous men to rejoice.' " [30] The people, also, acclaimed her with resounding applause for her remission of taxes, in her capital city, at

[27] Theophanes, 472. [28] But cf. Ostrogorsky, 124.

[29] Zonaras III: *Corp. scr. hist. byz.* 304; Cedrenus II: *ibid.* 31; Gibbon, ed. Bury V, 191; Ostrogorsky, 124f.

[30] G. A. Schneider, *Der hl. Theodor von Studion*, 1900, 26; Alice Gardner, *Theodore of Studium*, 1905, 64f.; Baynes and Moss, *Byzantium*, 1948, 107.

Abydos, and at the headland of the Hieron overlooking the Bosphorus.[31] History pictures her, on Easter Monday, 799, proceeding from the Church of the Holy Apostles in a golden chariot with four white horses and with four of her Patricians as drivers, while right and left she casts largesse of money to the crowd.[32]

But she was at last the prey of her favourites among her statesmen, not only of Stauracius, but also of one, Aetius, who had earned her gratitude by quelling the princes, her brothers-in-law, when they rose against her, and by sending them into exile at Athens. The two politicians quarrelled violently one with another; and although neither, as eunuch, could hold the throne, each plotted constantly to seize it for one of his own kin. Then sickness came upon her; and hardly had she struggled back to life when, early in 800, she was forced to issue measures of discipline against Stauracius. Nonetheless, he continued to plot, even to the day he died, coughing blood as he lay, surrounded by his doctors and secretaries and "monks that were no monks," all vowing to the last that Stauracius would live to be Emperor himself. Two days after his death Irene learned of his latest treachery against her rule and speedily gave orders for the punishment of its supporters.

Thus gradually, as the year 800 wore on, the Empire of the East, under an Empress sick and aging in years, was sinking more and more, in contrast with the rising hope of the Frankish kingdom in the West.[33]

When Alcuin, thirdly, turned his thoughts from England and from Constantinople to Rome, centre of his Catholic life, no happier story met him here. The Book of the Popes and the Frankish Annals paint for us a vivid picture of the sufferings

[31] Theodore, *Epist.* I, No. 7: *PG* XCIX, col. 932; Theophanes, 475.
[32] Theophanes, 474.
[33] Diehl, *Byz. Portraits,* 100.

of Pope Leo the third.[34] This present ruler of the Holy See was Roman by birth, had lived all his life in close connection with the Lateran, had held office in Papal administration, and was well loved for his kindliness and generosity. Shortly after his election he had sent to King Charles the keys of the shrine of Saint Peter and the standard of the city of Rome, with a letter asking that Charles send to Rome one of his leading men to receive oath of homage from the Roman people. Angilbert, abbot of St. Riquier, was sent on this mission, bearing with him as gifts to the various members of the Papal Palace much spoil of the conquered Avars.[35]

The letter of Charles to Leo rejoices "in your unanimous election, in the obedience of your humility and in the faithfulness of your promise to us," before going on to mark the functions of King and Pope in the manner already noted.[36] We have seen the reverence and loyalty with which Alcuin greeted this new Head of the Church.[37] Alcuin's counsels were so generally given to high and lowly alike that admonitions sent by him to Leo need not unduly concern us here.[38] But the tone of the King's instructions to his envoy Angilbert was markedly strong: "Advise our Apostolic Father diligently in regard to all honour in his own life, and especially on observance of the canons, on the loyal governing of the Church of God, so far as your opportunity and his consent allow. And tell him again and again how brief and passing is his own present office, how long-lasting the reward given to him who labours well." [39]

In 798 the Pope conferred upon Salzburg the honour of Archbishopric, the first Metropolitan See of Bavaria; and Arno

[34] *Lib. Pont.* II, i; *ARF ann.* 799; Abel-Simson II, 111ff.

[35] *ARF ann.* 796.

[36] *Epp.* IV, 136ff.; p. 87 *supra.*

[37] Page 140 *supra.*

[38] *Epp.* IV, 138f.

[39] *Ibid.* 135f.; cf. Halphen, *Charlemagne,* 122; Glotz I, ii, 449: "Léon III prenait figure d'évêque franc."

was in Rome to receive the pallium.[40] Alcuin, seizing the occasion, begged repeatedly to be kept informed concerning Leo and all that was happening in Rome.[41] This Arno did, and Alcuin wrote back: "I am so glad to hear of the well-being of the Pope and of the happenings in Rome," and in another letter: "You have told me of the religious and just living of our Apostolic Ruler." Then: "You have also told me with what spirit he bears unjust attacks from the sons of discord. I admit it will give me great joy and encouragement to think that the Father of the churches is busy serving God with faithful heart, free from guile." [42] The next year, however, found Alcuin writing to Arno in perplexity: "The letter you wrote some time ago has reached me, containing complaints in regard to the Pope's conduct, with word of the danger you ran at Rome because of the Roman people. Since I did not want it to fall into another's hands, I allowed only Candidus to read it, and then I put it in the fire to avoid any hint of scandal." [43]

Nothing definite or convincing emerges from these records. We do know, however, that a strong faction at Rome, doubtless urged on by political ambition and jealousy, was bitterly opposed to Leo's election, and that it was led by two kinsmen of the late Pope Hadrian. Their names were Paschalis and Campulus; both held important office in the Papal Chancery. Matters came to a climax on April 25, 799, when the Pope was to observe by solemn procession and the Greater Litany that day of intercession for the early harvest which in Christian Rome had replaced the old pagan ceremony of the *Robigalia,* the prayer to the gods to turn rust and blight from the fields. Leo had left the Lateran and was on his way to meet the gen-

[40] J. W. Nos. 2495f., 2498, 2503; *Epp.* V, 59f.; Nottarp (see ch. I, note 30 *supra*) 67.

[41] *Epp.* IV, 235f., cf. 254.

[42] *Ibid.* 245, 258.

[43] *Ibid.* 309. For Candidus (Witto) see p. 151 *supra.* He had returned from England to work with Alcuin on the continent.

eral congregation of Roman clergy and people, gathered at the church of Saint Laurence in Lucina, when from the shadow of the monastery of Saint Stephen and Saint Silvester a band of armed men, under the two ringleaders themselves, rushed upon him, threw him from his horse to the ground, brutally beat and tore his face, and left him lying helpless in the street. All the crowd fled for safety on hearing of this horror; the story flew around that the assailants had torn out the Pope's eyes and cut out his tongue. Later on these returned, to find him still on the ground. They dragged him, first, to the neighbouring monastery, then to the Greek cloister of Saint Erasmus on the Coelian Hill, where they kept him closely guarded from possible rescue.

"But Almighty God," rejoices the Papal biographer of Leo, "marvellously destroyed their iniquitous attempts, working with the prayers of blessed Peter." The Pope's wounds began to heal, and through the aid of his chamberlain Albinus and other friends he was let down by a rope from the walls of the monastery and escorted safely to Saint Peter's.[44] The conspirators could only take revenge by pillaging the house of Albinus, while the people, once more gathering courage, burst into psalms of triumph. Fortunately it happened that two envoys from King Charles were in Rome at this moment: Wirund, abbot of Stablo, and Winichis, Duke of Spoletium. They received the Pope in all reverence, and Winichis at once set out with him to Spoletium's fortified capital. Here Leo remained until his recovery was assured, and then, with a train of bishops, priests, and nobles, he proceeded across the Alps. Once more a Pope of Rome was on his way to seek help from the King of the Franks, who was also, however, the ruler of Lombard Italy.

[44] *Ann. Laur. min. ann.* 799; *Lib. Pont.* II, 4f.; Abel-Simson II, 163ff.

The Saxon war was still in progress, although it was approaching its final stages. Summer after summer, of 796, 797, 798, 799, saw Charles on campaign, while in great numbers Franks were settled on Saxon land and Saxons transported into Frankish territory.[45] He was now, in 799, encamped in Saxony, at Paderborn, and from there he sent, first his archchaplain, Hildebold, Archbishop of Cologne, and next his son, Pepin, King of Italy, to greet his guest with fitting ceremony. Then he himself welcomed the Pope in magnificent marking of respect.[46]

Word of events of so deep concern to Rome moved Alcuin to the quick. He was weary of constant reports of killing, of banishing, of levying of fines among the ever-conquered, ever-to-be-conquered Saxons. Their "treachery," as he judged it, in rising to battle against their plighted word of homage, roused his keen condemnation. Yet, might not charity succeed where wrath had failed? And what, after all, mattered even Saxony, one remote part of the Church's charge, in comparison with Rome, and the Apostolic Father himself?

In 798 we find him writing to his King: "Your letter bids me compose some melody of verse to mitigate the roar of arms and the harsh notes of trumpets." . . . "May God make you victor over all your enemies and bring you swiftly home with honour and praise." In 799: "If possible, let peace be made with that unspeakable people. Leave threats for a little while, lest they harden their hearts and flee from you. Be content to hold fast what you have, lest in pursuing the lesser gain, you lose the greater." . . . "Would that at last Divine grace might set you free from that unmentionable Saxon people—to travel, to govern, to do justice, to renew the churches, to correct the people, to defend the oppressed, to draw up laws. . . ." [47] He

[45] *ARF* ed. Kurze, 98ff.; *Ann. Lauresh. ann.* 799; Halphen, *Etudes,* 208; von Schwerin, ed. *Leges Saxonum,* 45ff.

[46] J. W. No. 2500; *Lib. Pont.* II, 6; *ARF ann.* 799; *PLAC* I, 374ff.

[47] *Epp.* IV, 242, 245, 289, 293.

wrote in even stronger terms in 799 to Arno, who, as Archbishop of Salzburg, was charged with crusade for the conversion of the lately-subdued Avars: "Just as you said, this neglect of the Huns" (he means "the Avars") "is our ruin, while we keep on toiling among that accursed race of Saxons, despised of God, and neglecting those who, as I see it, would bring us greater reward from God and greater glory among men." [48]

To Charles also went his cry of horror over the iniquity wrought on the Pope: "Has not uttermost wickedness come to light in the See of Rome, where, of old, religion shone forth in greatest radiance? Men, blinded in their hearts, have blinded their own Head. . . . No! never must care for that Head be forgotten! Better that the feet should suffer than the Head. . . ." Then comes his joy in the hospitality of Charles: "Your delightful letter tells me what you have done in regard to the Apostolic Ruler, rejoicing to come to your most gracious presence. Thank you for all your goodness . . ."; "Spare your subjects, now Christian, and defend the churches of Christ, that the blessing of the King on High may make you strong over the pagans. . . . You must consider very carefully and wisely what is to be done about those men" (the conspirators in Rome), "and how our holy Pastor may be enabled to serve God without fear in his See." [49]

But now there comes a significant note into the desires of Alcuin for his King. Its immediate source may be given in his own words to Charles, written in June, 799: "Up to this time there have been three persons of highest standing in the world. The first was that Apostolic Eminence who rules as Vicar the See of blessed Peter—and what has been done to its holder in

[48] *Ibid.* 309; cf. 344.

[49] *Ibid.* 288f.; cf. 286 (to Arno), 292, 294f.; *PLAC* I, 296f. (LXXV); Seppelt, 187; Glotz I, ii, 475: "Une lettre d'Alcuin le" (Charles) "détourna de toute mesure de rigueur à l'égard du Souverain Pontife."

these times, your courtesy has told me. The second is the Imperial dignity and secular power of the Second Rome" (Constantinople)—"and its governor has been cast down, by his own fellow-citizens, as is being told everywhere. The third is that royal dignity in which the will of our Lord Jesus Christ has made you ruler of the Christian people—you, surpassing in power these other aforesaid dignities, outshining them in wisdom, standing even higher than they in the glory of your Kingship. See, all hope of the churches of Christ rests upon you alone. To you it falls to avenge crimes, to guide the wandering, to comfort the distressed, to lift up the good." [50]

These words represent, however, no sudden thought. For years the wave which was soon to break in Imperial honour for King Charles had been rising, fed by various streams, and all flowing through Alcuin's mind. First, there were the tragedies of Constantinople and of Rome. A woman held the throne in the East. Who was to punish the assailants of the Pope and hold in check such criminals in the future? Who could henceforward ensure the peace of the Church and the wider knowledge of the Faith? In England Alcuin could not forget the evils of Northumbria and of Mercia. Moreover, the first raids of the North had made a deep impression on his thought, and he held in general little hope for the future of his native land. On the continental side, the Avars had been conquered by Charles, the Saxons were coming toward the end of their long struggle against his rule; Charles was Lord over Germany and France and Italy; the Spanish March acknowledged his suzerainty; his sons were Kings of Italy and of

[50] *Epp.* IV, 288; Kleinclausz, *Alcuin,* 252; Dawson, 217ff.; Carlyle, *Hist of med. Polit. Theory* I, 224; Heldmann, 88ff. For Alcuin as conceiving of Charles as *Rex et Sacerdos* see Lilienfein, *Die Anschauungen von Staat und Kirche im Reich der Karolinger,* 1902, 30ff., 44f.; for him as dreaming of a return under Charles to a Christian Golden Age in a current conception traceable to Byzantium, see Kampers, *HJ* XLV, 1925, 501ff., 504. Cf. also Voigt, *Staat und Kirche,* 358ff., 419; Ketterer, 108ff., 134f., 178; Fichtenau, 64ff.

Aquitaine. Alcuin saw the subject barbarians far and near bowing their heads in baptismal rite; he saw Charles leading crusade in Council against heresy; he looked to him, as did all, for the support and the increase of the Catholic Church, for the secular administration of order and peace throughout the world of his time.[51] Secondly, from England Alcuin had brought with him the Anglo-Saxon conception of the "imperium" of a ruler whose power extended over lands outside his own special dominion; no one, in this sense, now so merited by actual control the title of "Emperor," "holder of Imperial dignity," as did this King of the Franks.[52] Thirdly, Alcuin's work in liturgical writings had influenced him in the same direction. "The Carolingian Kings and even more the Carolingian and German Emperors were, through the Church, attached to the tradition of the ancient Roman Empire. . . . It is obvious that the liturgical association of the ancient Empire with the Empire to come preceded the actual renovation of the Western Christian Empire by Charlemagne." [53] Wherever Alcuin went, he heard the name of his King held up before God in the prayers of sacramentaries and missals.

"The immensity of your faithfulness makes my littleness impatient for you," he writes to Charles; "it makes me dare ex-

[51] Cf. Tellenbach, *HJ* 1949, 129ff., for a conception by Charles of political and religious *imperialismus*; and Halphen, *Charlemagne*, 124ff., for a conception by Alcuin of "empire chrétien" under him. For the growth of the power of King Charles over State and Church in relation to the Papacy see Knabe, 30ff.

[52] Löwe, *Forsch. z. Kirch-und Geistesgesch.* XIII, 1937, 147f.; Stengel, *DAGM* III, 1939, 26; cf. M. Deanesly, *EHR* LVIII, 1943, 134, note 3; Levison, 123ff. The growth of "supremacy" among Anglo-Saxon kings is illustrated by Stenton, *EHR* XXIII, 1918, 43.

[53] Against this conception see Heldmann, 31ff., 46; for it, Hirsch, *MOG* XLIV, 1930, 4ff., 12f.; Tellenbach, *SBH* XXV, 1934–1935, 25f., 30f., 34f., 52ff.; Biehl, *Görres. Gesell., Sektion f. Rechts-und Staatswiss.* LXXV, 1937, 41f., 56; Ladner, *Speculum* XVII, 1942, 198; Ohnsorge, 16. Against the "Hellenistic-Roman model" and for "the image of the Kings of the Old Testament" here see Kantorowicz, 62f.

ceedingly. May He in whose hands are kings and the laws of kingdoms, Himself multiply your crowns, protect and overshadow them." . . . "Blessed be the power and reign of yourself, your son, and your sons' sons for all time in the world, most illustrious ruler and defender of the Church of Christ." "With many following your well-known zeal and aim, perhaps a new Athens might be raised up in Frankland, nay, a far better Athens. She, under Plato, shone with the light of the seven arts. This Athens of yours would be enriched also by the sevenfold fullness of the Holy Spirit." "Great as your power as King, so greatly do you excel all in the fervour of holy religion. Happy the people who rejoice in such a Prince." "This is your special gift from God, that with equal devotion you work to purge and defend the churches of Christ from the teaching of traitors within, and to protect them without from the ravagings of the heathen. So is your power armed with two swords, on the right and on the left." "Needful it is for all to uphold you, blessed as you are, by prayers and intercessions, that through your goodly workings the Christian Imperium may be protected, the Catholic Faith defended, and the rule of justice become known to all."

Det tibi perpetuam clemens in saecla salutem
Et decus imperii, David amate, Deus.[54]

[54] *Epp.* IV, 224, 279, 281f., 292. Alcuin was strongly opposed to power of the people, as his words to Charles show: "The people, by Divine ruling, is to be led, not to be followed, and for witness persons of high standing are to be preferred. The saying, 'The voice of the people is the voice of God,' is not to be listened to, since the seething of the crowd is always near to madness": *ibid.* 199; cf. Bastgen, *HJ* XXXII, 1911, 823. For the "two swords" cf. Caspar, *ZKG* LIV, 217f.: "Für die doppelte Rolle des Königtums—Verteidigung der Kirche nach aussen, Reinerhaltung nach innen—fand Alcuin zuerst das biblische Gleichnis von den zwei Schwertern, das nachmals in der mittelalterlichen Theorie in sehr verschiedener Ausdeutung eine grosse Rolle spielen sollte"; see also Lecler, *Recherches de Science religieuse,* XXI, 1931, 304f.; Cappuyns, *BTAM* I, 1932, 516.

Twice within recent months Charles had invited Alcuin to leave his monastery at Tours and to stay a while at the royal Court. From his camp in Saxon territory, where the King was spending the winter of 797–798, had come one suggestion, given in answer to Alcuin's longing to see him, but Alcuin had replied that he wanted to enjoy a visit in peace, not in the land of contention and war. As Virgil had written, so "must he, Alcuin, keep the nets at home, while Charles pursued the wild boars." [55] Again, in the summer of 799, Alcuin pleaded the frailties of old age in answer to an invitation of Charles that he accompany him to Rome: "I would have been so eager to go, if I only could manage it." Already in 799, soon after the attack upon the Pope, Charles was planning this journey to Rome. Partly in jest, partly in mild vexation, he reproached Alcuin with preferring the "smoke-begrimed roofs of Tours to the golden citadels of Rome." To which the abbot of St. Martin's again retorted, in all courtesy, that violence was worse for the eyes than smoke. Was not Rome poisoned by strife of conflicting brethren? [56]

Doubtless Charles had thought of escorting in person the Pope back to his See at Rome. The King's presence there seemed desirable for investigation of the grievous charges which had followed Leo across the Alps to Paderborn. The "sons of the devil" in Rome had sent messengers to King Charles, declaring the Pope guilty of serious offence. Their echoing was heard both in the royal Court and by Alcuin at Tours. In August of this year, 799, Alcuin wrote to Arno: "I understand that there are many who are contending against the Pope, trying to depose him by crafty rumour, to accuse him of adultery and perjury. They are saying, I hear, that he must clear himself from these charges by a solemn oath. If he does

[55] *Epp.* IV, 234f. (*Eclogues* III, l. 75).
[56] *Epp.* IV, 293, 295f.

not do so, they are secretly plotting that he shall lay down his holy Office and live in retirement at some monastery.[57]

"Now," Alcuin went on, "this certainly must not be, either that he should consent to bind himself by any oath or that he should lose his See. I would answer for him if I were at his side: 'He who is without sin among you let him first cast a stone'. . . .

"I have read in canon law that the Apostolic See is appointed to judge, not to be judged. . . . [58] What pastor in the Church of Christ can be immune, if he who is Head of the churches shall be cast down? In his Lord shall he stand or fall. And he shall stand, for the Lord is powerful to hold him upright.

"Please, dear son, labour for him, for the authority of the Holy See, for the sound and safe standing of the Catholic Faith."

The Pope lingered at Paderborn until the late autumn. Then, attended by two Archbishops, Hildebold of Cologne and Arno of Salzburg, he returned to Italy and entered Rome on the eve of St. Andrew's Day, November 29, 799, amid rejoicing and celebration, spiritual and secular.[59] It would be interesting to know in detail the conversations that had passed in Paderborn between the Pope and his royal host and the leading Frankish nobles.

Some days later the envoys of King Charles, two Archbishops, four bishops, including Atto of Freising and Jesse of Amiens, one bishop-elect and three counts, ten in all, sat in the great hall that had been built by Leo himself in the Lateran. There, beneath the mosaic that pictured Saint Peter giving the pallium to Leo on one hand and the standard of Rome to King

[57] *Epp.* IV, 297; *Lib. Pont.* II, 6.

[58] Mansi I, 1257.

[59] *Lib. Pont.* II, 6; *Ann. Juvav., Lauresh., Maxim. ann.* 799. References in Alcuin's letters (*Epp.* IV, 309, 311) show Arno's presence in Rome.

Charles on the other, they heard the accusations brought against this same Pope by Paschalis and Campulus and their adherents. After more than a week of trial, the Holy Father was declared innocent. His accusers "had nothing to say," and the Court referred them for judgment to King Charles himself.[60]

In spite of increasing troubles of old age, of arthritis and attacks of fever, Alcuin not only ruled his monastery of Saint Martin at Tours but also visited those other religious houses entrusted to his care by Charles. We hear of journeys in 798 to Baralle, near Arras, to Saint Lupus of Troyes, to Saint Peter of Ferrières; in 799 he spent some time at his cell of Saint-Josse near Etaples. He found time and energy, also, for other business—at Aachen, at St. Amand, monastery of Arno, and at Choisy-au-Bac; in 799 he had the joy, hitherto delayed by his ill-health, of talking with his chief woman friend, Gisela, in her abbey at Chelles near Paris.[61]

In April of the following year, 800, King Charles kept Easter at St. Riquier, near Abbeville, as guest of Angilbert. Alcuin, also, was there, and was asked by his host to rewrite a *Life* of its patron, Saint Richarius (Riquier), then in use at the abbey. This he eventually did, the more readily since he was vexed to find that so wonderful a Saint was represented by "so small a *Life*" and "horrified" that material available, telling of the Saint's miracles, was being used in all its crude style for the edification of the uneducated.[62]

[60] *Lib. Pont.* II, 6f. They were condemned to death by Charles at Rome, but spared for exile at the Pope's prayer: *ARF ann.* 801; Ketterer, 72.

[61] *Epp.* IV, 245f., 248f., 267, 275, 291f.

[62] It was sent to Angilbert in Alcuin's later years at Tours, dedicated to Charles: *Epp.* IV, 465f. For its text see *SRM* IV, 389ff., and cf. Levison, 161, note 2; Kleinclausz, *Alcuin*, 223.

The King then travelled to Rouen, and at last arrived to make a long-hoped-for "retreat of prayer" at Saint Martin's.[63] With him came his Queen, Liutgard, and his sons Charles, Pepin, and Louis. But the stay which began so hopefully ended in trouble. Liutgard, for whose recovery from sickness the King had come to pray at this holy place of Frankland, grew steadily worse and died on the fourth of June. She was buried near the Saint's tomb, and Alcuin in a letter to Charles poured out sympathy for him and prayer for the departed Queen, perhaps the best loved of the four whom Charles had brought to his court.[64]

Long and earnestly the King must have talked with Alcuin at this time in Tours. At his request Charles confirmed monastic rights and privileges for Saint Martin's and its daughter and auxiliary houses, among them a small congregation of monks which had recently settled at Cormery, near Tours. For this foundation he had asked his friend, Benedict of Aniane, to send him monks trained by Benedict himself, and Benedict had sent twenty from his country of "Gothia"—Septimania, in the region of Frankland bordering upon Spain. Now, however, others were coming from the neighbourhood of Tours to increase this number.[65] When Charles left, Alcuin went with him, it would seem, on the way through Orléans and Paris back to Aachen; [66] for we shall find that he was very busy there for a week in this same June.

At last, in the autumn of this year, 800, the King judged it time to visit Italy. He stayed some days in Ravenna, then sent his son Pepin to pillage the land of Beneventum, where the young Duke Grimoald was rising in revolt, and arrived himself in Rome on the 24th of November. The Pope had come

[63] *ARF ann.* 800; *Epp.* IV, 266f.; *Ann. Lauresh. ann.* 800.

[64] *Epp.* IV, 325f.

[65] Ardo, *Vita Bened.: SS XV*, i, 210; *Epp.* IV, 309; B.M.L. 159ff., Nos. 354, 355, 358.

[66] *ARF ann.* 800; *Epp.* IV, 343, note 2.

to meet him as far as Mentana (Nomentum), about twelve miles outside the city, and had dined with the King on the evening before.

After the ceremony of welcome had been duly and lavishly observed, Charles addressed himself to the business for which he had come, the investigating once again of the charges laid against Pope Leo. A great assembly was held on December 1 in Saint Peter's, at which he put forward all this matter of accusation. Of our mediaeval sources one, the Frankish annals, records that no one was then found willing to maintain it. Another, the Papal biographer, states that all the archbishops, bishops, and abbots at the hearing answered in unison: "We do not dare to judge the Apostolic See, which is the head of all the Churches of God. We ourselves are judged by it and its Vicar; it itself is judged by none, as has been the custom from time of old." Then the Pope, the narrative goes on, said: "I follow in the steps of the Popes, my predecessors, and am ready to purge myself of these false charges which have burst into evil flame against me." [67] Three weeks later, on the 23rd of December, in the presence of a vast congregation assembled in the same Church, Leo rose, holding the Book of the Gospels in his hand, mounted the pulpit, and declared before God and His angels and Saint Peter that he was innocent of all part in those crimes alleged against him. This oath, he attested, he gave of his own free will, compelled by none.[68]

Three of Alcuin's friends were present in Rome to support the Pope in this crisis. Theodulf, bishop of Orléans, was there in this December to receive from the Holy See the pallium of Archbishop. The following year Alcuin wrote to congratulate him on this honour and added: "Our son Candidus, your faithful servant, says many good things concerning you, how frankly you witnessed to the truth in the public assembly."

[67] *Lib. Pont.* II, 7; *Ann. Lauresh. ann.* 800; *PLAC* I, 257ff. (XLV).
[68] *Ann. Lauriss. min. ann.* 800; Jaffé, *Mon. Car.* 378f.; *Epp.* V, 63f.

Candidus, or Witto, Alcuin's student, was spending part of his time at Saint Martin's with his abbot and master, part in the Frankish court at Aachen or on various journeyings, part with Arno at Salzburg. When Alcuin had written to Charles that he could not go with him to Rome, the King had asked him to send in his place some of his monks from Saint Martin's. Alcuin had answered that, no doubt, his sons could labour instead of him, but they certainly could not carry out his own personal responsibilities and functions—any more than Joab, who had borne the burden of the fight, could himself crown David as King! It may be, however, that he had sent Candidus, who was one of the multitude in Saint Peter's on these eventful days.[69] Another letter, written by Alcuin to Riculf, Archbishop of Mainz, tells of a like report: "Now you stood by the Apostolic Ruler, as I had begged of you." [70] The same day two monks arrived from the Patriarch of Jerusalem, bearing to Charles the keys of the Holy Sepulchre and of Calvary, with the standard of that holy City.[71]

The sequel is known to all. Two days afterward the King entered Saint Peter's for Mass on Christmas morning and knelt in prayer before the Apostle's shrine. When he rose from his knees, the Pope placed on his head a crown of gold, and all the people shouted, "To Charles Augustus, crowned by God, great and peace-making Emperor of the Romans, life and victory!" Then the Litany of Praises was sung, crying to the Lord Christ and His angels and saints to aid this Lord of the Franks, the Lombards, and the Romans.[72]

[69] *Epp.* IV, 295, 368. On Candidus cf. Sickel, *Alcuinstudien* I, 81ff.; *PLAC* I, 255ff. (XLIV).

[70] *Epp.* IV, 353.

[71] *ARF ann.* 800. For Alcuin's delight, perhaps over-great, in this honour see *Epp.* IV, 358; cf. Runciman, *EHR* L, 1935, 611; Halphen, *Charlemagne,* 128.

[72] *Lib. Pont.* II, 7, 37f.

The crowning of King Charles as Emperor of the West has brought forth a flood of discussion.[73] Did the Pope act on the spur of the moment, for the deliverance of the Papacy and of Rome from present crisis? Or was his crowning of the Frankish King the culmination of a long and deliberate designing for the benefit of the Papal See and the Western world? Had Leo and his counsellors in Rome desired the transferring of the Imperial power from East to West, the absorption of Constantinople and its rule in a new and single world-Empire, centred in Charles and the West? Did Charles secretly approve the Pope's act? Or was he averse to becoming Emperor, in title, in responsibility? Or had it been his determined aim to win this Empire for himself by his own power, through his own hand to transfer Imperial sovereignty to himself and to centre it in Aachen for the glory of the Christian Faith and his own Frankish people? Was he then taken by surprise on this Christmas morning, and was he so deeply affronted by the Pope's action that, according to the famous words of Einhard, "the King himself declared he would never have entered the church, even on so high a Feast-day, had he known the Pope's purpose in advance?" Did he resent an act that might well cause enmity between Frankland and Constantinople? Did the shouts of the Roman people confirm the Pope's deed for Charles, however reluctant, as for the world, and was he indeed compelled to accept, at least to some extent, the Imperial title and responsibility forced upon him after this manner? After all, if

[73] Einhard, *Vita Karol.* c. 28; *Ann. Lauresh., Maximin. ann.* 801. Among modern discussions see that by Ohnsorge, 15ff., and cf. *CMH* II, 620ff. (Seeliger); Hartmann II, 2, 348ff.; Amann, 160ff.; Seppelt, 191ff.; Bryce, *Holy Roman Empire,* 1904, 50ff.; Halphen, *Charlemagne,* 129ff., and *Les Barbares,* 257ff.; Arquillière, *L'Eglise au M.A.* 91ff., and *L'Augustinisme politique,* 105ff.; Heldmann, 1ff.; Ketterer, 81ff.; Levillain, *RHEF* XVIII, 1932, 5ff.; Bonnaud Delamare, 167f.; Haller II, i, 18ff.; Glotz I, ii, 476ff.; Geoffrey Barraclough, *The Mediaeval Empire, Idea and Reality,* 1950, 8ff.; 9, note 1.

the Pope was innocent and his accusers were guilty of treason, their punishing called for Imperial jurisdiction. What of the Lady Irene? Did she in her heart resent this crowning of the King of the Franks as an insult to herself and her Imperial dignity? Or did she perforce acquiesce? Or might we even believe that its suggesting came from her herself?

And what of Alcuin, whose share in the preparation for this event has also been disputed? Here, however, we may think the student's task somewhat easier. Alcuin was concerned with Church rather than with State politics as such. His letters to the King seem to show clearly that this climax held for him a culminating hope and delight, for Church and State and all his world.[74] Early in 801 he wrote to Abbess Gisela, sister of Charles: "I give thanks for the exaltation of my most excellent Lord David, for the wellbeing of the Pope, and for the embassy from that Holy City in which Our Saviour deigned to redeem the world with His blood." [75] Above all, he witnessed to his joy in a burst of thanksgiving written for "David, Father of his Fatherland": "Blessed be the Lord God, and blessed His

[74] Kleinclausz, *L'Empire carol.* 185ff., 197f., and *Alcuin*, 245ff., 248, note 21, 255f., 261f. (but cf. Halphen, *Charlemagne*, 123ff.; *Etudes*, 227f.). See especially Ganshof, in *BHR* IX, 1947, 15ff.; in *Speculum* XXIV, 1949, 524: "It was, I believe, owing to Alcuin that he" (Charlemagne) "went to Rome with the idea of putting order into the affairs of the Church; it was under the same influence that he accepted there the imperial dignity"; and in *Glasgow Univ. Publications* LXXIX, 1949, 1ff. (an admirable exposition of the problem of the coronation of Charles as Emperor): "In the eyes of Alcuin it appeared a necessity for the sake of the Church that there should be an emperor, successor of the Christian Roman emperors, who would end the scandals and above all prevent new ones" (16f.). Cf. also *Zeitschrift für schweizerische Gesch.* XXVIII, 1948, 445f.; Glotz I, ii, 477; Levillain, *RHEF* XVIII, 12. It must be admitted, however, that in letters to king and archbishop in England Alcuin prescribed, and bade, a "Gelasian" division of spiritual and secular powers and spheres of function which was very different from the union of those powers which he saw, and by force of circumstances was content to see, concentrated in Charles.

[75] *Epp.* IV, 358; cf. (to Arno) 361.

everlasting mercy upon His servants, for whose prosperity and salvation He has led you forth with triumph and brought you home in peace, has kept, honoured, and exalted you, and has everywhere made justice and righteousness to shine before your face."[76]

3

Apart from this concern for the Church, its welfare and its enemies, Alcuin looked out from Tours in these earlier years of his rule at Saint Martin's upon other crises of the Catholic world. Once more the Adoptionist tares, weeded out at the Council of Frankfurt in 794, were growing up among the wheat; and some years later he wrote to those monks of Septimania who were being nurtured in religion by Benedict of Aniane that they watch with all their might against the "new sects of Spanish error." The menace appears more clearly in a letter sent by him about the same time to Paulinus, Patriarch of Aquileia: "That ancient serpent from the briars of the Spanish countryside is trying to raise its head again."[77] In March, 798, he sent to King Charles for criticism loose sheets of a treatise he was writing against this heresy; in June he warned Arno in a brief letter: "All Spain is still going astray in Adoptionism."[78] Some months afterward Charles heard from him again: "A treatise has lately reached me from that infelicitous Felix. I glanced over a few pages of it through curiosity, and I found worse heresies—no, blasphemies—than ever before in his writings. He declared that Christ Jesus was

[76] *Ibid.* 372; Halphen, *Charlemagne,* 131; Levison, 123; Rüngeler, 50ff.; Kleinclausz, *Charlemagne,* 306ff.; Höchstetter, *Karl der Grosse,* 1934, 50f. Against Alcuin's influence in the crowning of Charles as Imperator see Heldmann, 20f., 61ff., 334f., and W. Ohr, *Die Kaiserkrönung Karls des Gr.,* 1904, 85ff.

[77] *Epp.* IV, 211, 221.

[78] *Ibid.* 233f., 236. The treatise was his *Adversus Felicis haeresin;* see Hauck II, 314ff.

neither true Son of God nor even true God, only by name.[79] That in itself is enough to damn him. Answer must be made, with great care and many workers. I cannot make it alone. So, please, find men equipped for so difficult, so necessary a task. Rise, chosen of God, soldier of Christ, and defend the bride of your Lord, her whom God has given it you to rule and keep in safety." A copy of the writing of Felix accompanied this letter.

In July Alcuin rejoiced that the King was carefully considering the arguments of Felix. Might copies of these be sent to the Pope, to Paulinus, to Ricbod, Archbishop of Trier, and to Theodulf, bishop of Orléans, "that each may answer them for himself?" "I am working hard at the matter," he assured the King, "only I need time and quiet with my students here at Saint Martin's to think over the teachings of the Fathers in regard to this heretic and his treatise." He wrote, too, to beg Theodulf's aid in the defence of Catholic truth.[80]

This treatise of Felix, bishop of Urgel, had been sent by Felix to Alcuin in answer to his courteous letter, written some years before.[81] In it Felix had revealed that it was Beatus of Liébana who had first risen to attack the Adoptionist heresy. And so Alcuin eagerly seized his pen to pour out to Beatus his joy, his congratulation, and his horror at Felix, "who is steadily descending to greater evils." If Beatus chanced to come across Alcuin's book, *Against the heresy of Felix*, that writing which Alcuin had sent in sheets to King Charles, would he very kindly examine it, too? "For it is better to be corrected by a friend than to be censored by an enemy." [82]

[79] *nuncupativus: Epp.* IV, 241. This *libellus* of Felix, now lost, can be reconstructed in part from fragments given in the *Adv. Felic. haer.*

[80] *Epp.* IV, 243f., 258f. The writing of Felix was also condemned at a Council held in Rome, October, 798, under Pope Leo III: *Conc. aevi Karol.* I, 202ff.

[81] Page 179 *supra.*

[82] Levison, 314ff. (text and history).

The next year, 799, Charles at last sent back this book to Alcuin, who was worrying by this time as to its fate and who was somewhat disappointed that the King left him to do the necessary revising. "Another's judgment in any work is usually better than the author's," he remarked. It was published before December, full of ammunition drawn from the Bible and from "the spicy cells of the Fathers." [83]

Not only the pen and the soul of Felix were in danger, however. There was still that fierce old gentleman, Elipand, bishop of Toledo, to be warned against spreading his own poisonous doctrine. About this time Alcuin sent him a long letter of sound counsel, composed with studied courtesy toward both Elipand and his fellow-sinner. "Felix has written to me," it said. "He is a man of religious life and marked goodness of character, if only he would preach Catholic truth. Do not trust goodness that appears on the surface; no one who breaks the unity of the Church can please God. You, holy Bishop, are a city placed upon a mountain, and it cannot be hid. Its wall must not be pierced at any place by treacherous tunnels; it must be surrounded on all sides by the mighty ramparts of the Faith. It is not for me to enter into high debate with you, but rather to make you humble prayer that you, as a standard-bearer for the people committed to your charge, follow earnestly the doctrine of the Apostles. If, of your charity, you will read this letter of mine, I shall be eager to write to you again. In the meantime, would you remember me in your prayers?" [84]

Such a communication, even if filled with argument against the teaching of its recipient, held no offence to a well-poised mind. But Elipand was not well-poised. It reached him in July, and some months later Alcuin received his answer, in-

[83] *PL* CI, coll. 87ff.; *Epp.* IV, 282, and note 3, 284. Alcuin also sent this refutation of Felix to the monks in Septimania by the hand of Benedict of Aniane.

[84] *Epp.* IV, 268ff.

scribed: "To the most reverend brother Albinus, deacon: no minister of Christ, but disciple of the stinking, ill-named Beatus: a new Arius risen in Austria in the time of its glorious Prince: opposed to the doctrines of the holy Fathers Ambrose, Augustine, Isidore, Jerome: To him, if he shall turn from the error of his way, Eternal Salvation from the Lord; and if he will not, Eternal Damnation."

From this cheerful beginning the rest of the letter may be imagined. Elipand left no word of abuse untold, and Alcuin was bidden to beware lest he in turn become like "the basilisk that came forth from the root of the serpent," like "Nicolaus, whose deeds the Lord hates," like "the fool who speaks foolish things." He is, indeed, "the enemy and the avenger" whom the Lord shall destroy, and he is known to possess twenty thousand slaves and to be swollen with this world's wealth. He had better recall to mind the lesson of the rich man and Lazarus. There follow many arguments for the Adoptionist creed, arguments which rested on what appeared to Elipand to be entirely logical interpretation of Biblical, liturgical, and patristic evidence.[85]

In the same month of October, 799, Elipand also wrote to Felix, enclosing a copy of this letter of his to "that pitchy heretic, that son of hell, Albinus." He had been devoutly glad to receive word from Felix, especially in those hard times which made life a burden. "You must know," he ends, "that I am decrepit with old age, eighty-two, last July the 25th. Pray for me, as I constantly do for you, that God may bring us together in the land of the living." [86]

It was time, the King decided, to meet this dragon of heresy face to face, and Alcuin should be the Saint George for its

[85] *Ibid.* 301ff.; Isaiah XIV, 29, XXXII, 6; Rev. II, 6; Psalms VIII, 2. For the name Albinus see c. I *supra,* note 31.

[86] *Epp.* IV, 307f.

destruction. Accordingly, the next year Charles sent Laidrad, bishop of Lyons, to the Spanish March with a compelling invitation for Felix, that he appear before a Council in Aachen to defend his belief. Alcuin expected that this great event would come about in May, and he longed for the support of his friends Arno of Salzburg and Paulinus of Aquileia.[87]

But it was not until the middle of June, 800, "the thirty-second year of the glorious King," when Charles and Alcuin had travelled from Tours to Aachen by way of Orléans and Paris, that the debate was opened at the royal Palace there.[88] For six days Alcuin and Felix hurled at one another the words of Scripture and of the Fathers of the Church, while the scholars assembled around them held their breath to see what would happen, on this side and on that.[89] The outcome of the contest may best be described in the words of Felix himself, written shortly after its end to the clergy of his see of Urgel: "I was conducted to the presence of our glorious King Charles and received from him, as the reverend Lord Bishop Laidrad promised me at Urgel, permission to put forward before him and the bishops whom the King had brought together the opinions which I had, as I thought, gathered from sacred books concerning the adoption after the flesh of the Son of God. I was not induced by violence to appear there, but for judgment upon my declarations and for their confirmation, should they not be rejected.

[87] *Ibid.* 320, 322.

[88] The date of this Council of Aachen has been variously estimated. For 800, now generally accepted, see *ARF ann.* 800; Levison, 156, 317; Halphen, *Charlemagne,* 217; Amann, 149; Hauck II, 317; Kleinclausz, *Alcuin,* 231; Dümmler, *Epp.* IV, 343, note 2; 344, note 8; B.M.L. 161, No. 358a; Jaffé, *Mon. Alc.* 558, note I, 520, note 4; Alcuin, *PL* CI, col. 252 (*Adv. Elip.* I, 16). For 799, see Grössler, 27f.; Abel-Simson II, 159; Gaskoin, 259ff.; *DTC* I, i, col. 407 (Quilliet). For 798 see Hefele-Leclercq III, 2, 1096ff.

[89] *Alc. Vita,* 190.

"So, then, it was done, and my beliefs were cut from me, not by violence, as I have said, but by reason and truth. Partly this came about through the authority of Bishop Cyril, of Pope Gregory, of Leo and of others hitherto unknown to me; partly through a Synod lately held in Saint Peter's, Rome, by request of our Lord Charles, in which Pope Leo and fifty-seven bishops, with many priests and deacons, gave judgment against the treatise I recently addressed to the venerable Alcuin, abbot of Tours.

"Therefore I was convicted, and with heartfelt belief and profession of my own mouth, I have returned by Divine grace to the One Body throughout the world. This is my confession of faith which I make in penitence, beseeching you to pray the Lord to have mercy upon me, through whom even until this day strife is stirred up within the Church of God." [90]

The rest of the unhappy prelate's story may be told in a few words. There was no thought of his returning to Urgel; indeed, he had described himself in the letter given above as "formerly a bishop." King Charles had intended to hand him over to Riculf, Archbishop of Mainz, "for holding and chastising"; but at the plea of Alcuin he was committed to Laidrad in order that his penitence might be well tested, together with one of his priests whom Alcuin judged "worse than his master." With Laidrad he stayed a brief while at Saint Martin's, Tours, before Alcuin returned there, and declared he felt no resentment against the man who had defeated him. "He loves me much," Alcuin wrote; "all the feeling he had against me has turned to affection." [91]

It would be pleasant to end on that note. But after Felix died at Lyons in 818, having spent eighteen years in the keep-

[90] *Epp.* IV, 329f. For the Council of Aachen, see *Conc. aevi Kar.* I, 220ff.; on the Synod at Rome, Hauck II, 317; *Conc.* I, 202ff.

[91] *Epp.* IV, 344f., 346.

ing of Bishop Laidrad and of his successor, Agobard, the latter, so he declared, found among the possessions of Felix a paper which seemed to show that he had once more reverted to his old and bad ideas.[92]

To complete the work of rooting out evil doctrine, Charles sent Laidrad again into the Spanish March, together with Benedict, abbot of Aniane, and Nefridius, bishop of Narbonne.[93] Benedict had already fought hard against the Adoptionists in Septimania and was, moreover, of great repute as a teacher of the monastic life. Not only did he send monks of his training to Alcuin at his desire, but, also at their petition, to two of Alcuin's friends: to Laidrad, for the renewing of the monastery of l'Île-Barbe, on an island in the river Saône near Lyons, and to Theodulf, bishop of Orléans, for enlivening discipline in his ancient house of Saint Maximin at Micy. To Alcuin himself, as abbot of Tours, Benedict became so close a friend that "a whole book was made of Alcuin's letters to him." [94]

The three, Laidrad, Benedict, and Nefridius, came and conquered, according to Alcuin's words of triumph, written to Arno in this same year, 800: "My friend, I must tell you that my son, Bishop Laidrad, by gift of God, has made great advance in those hearts and is making it, day by day. Men from that country, good and truthful men, have told me that as many as twenty thousand have been converted, bishops, priests, monks and layfolk, men and women, lamenting their former error and giving thanks to God daily for their learning of the truth." [95]

[92] *PL* CIV, col. 33.
[93] *Epp.* IV, 345, 331, 342f.
[94] Ardo, *Vita Bened. Anian.*: *SS* XV, i, 209f.; Theodulf, *PLAC* I, 520ff. (XXX); Watkin Williams, *Monastic Studies*, 91f. Alcuin's letters to Benedict are nearly all lost: Kleinclausz, *Alcuin*, 10, note 13.
[95] *Epp.* IV, 346.

The mass of evidence with which Alcuin had besieged heresy at Aachen was arranged by him in another work, known as *Seven Books against Felix*. He apologises for its length, its rambling periods, and its lack of orderly sequence, on the ground that he had to answer questions as they had been thrown at him by his opponent, in person and in writing, and that the questions were so many and so disconnected. Its tone is remarkably sharp for Alcuin, and seems to reflect the excitement of verbal dispute: "What do you say now, you heretic? Is this enough evidence, or must you have more? Do you need a sign from Heaven, as the Jews of old?" [96] Once again, Alcuin sought criticism and *imprimatur* from his friends: from the King, to whom he sent a list of the sources he had used, with explanation for his inclusion of Origen, always suspect to the orthodox, and from his monastic friends on the borders of Spain.[97] "Five loaves and two fishes," he called its seven parts, in the hope that they would bring food to the hungry in desert places.[98]

The venerable Elipand was still obdurate in error. That "poisonous letter" of his could not go unanswered, if only for conscience' sake, and Alcuin had already taken out his pen, to write *Four Books against Elipand*. These he had sent as "a solace for their journey" to those three friends of his, Laidrad, Nefridius, and Benedict, setting out to contend against Adoptionist teachings in Spanish Frankland. They were composed, not so much for the sake of the old bishop of Toledo, who might well be dead before they reached him, but for the sake of those humbler men led astray by "Spanish error." Alcuin added: "Elipand also rebuked me for possessing a multitude of riches, as many as twenty thousand slaves. He did not know how one should live in the world. It is one thing to possess the world;

[96] *PL* CI, coll. 126f., 144f., 173, 203.
[97] *Epp.* IV, 335ff., 340.
[98] *Ibid.* 336.

it is another thing to be possessed by it. One man has riches and has them not; another has them not, and yet has them. I have never acquired a man as my slave; rather, I have longed to be servant of all who wait upon the Lord Christ." Would his friends please read and judge this work before he ventured to publish it? [99]

To the end Alcuin wrote with respect for this aged heretic. Doubtless, however, Elipand did not appreciate his charitable words, making excuse for him: "Perhaps, good Father, the busy cares of your pastoral office and the worry given you by impious people in Spain prevented you from thinking out your argument carefully in your writing. Perhaps you were brought to believe things clearly false and heretical through following in your old age what younger men wrote or told you." [100] Apparently the old bishop died impenitent.

Before we leave the history of this contention in matters spiritual, we shall do well to recall the part played in it by Paulinus, Patriarch of Aquileia. It was he who had drawn up the document which set forth Catholic doctrine for the clergy of northern Italy at the Council of Frankfurt, and in 800 he wrote at the command of King Charles *Three Books against Felix of Urgel,* which Alcuin praised highly in a letter to Arno.[101]

Finally, through the working of Paulinus and of Alcuin, it would seem, and as a result of the battle against Adoptionism, the practice of singing the Creed at Mass spread in the churches of Frankland. The Church of Rome did not chant the Creed during the Mass; the custom came originally from the East, passed into the Church in Spain during the sixth

[99] *Ibid.* 330ff., 333f.; *PL* CI, coll. 243ff. Cf. *Epp.* IV, 89, note 3: *Admones me . . . regem Carolum non corrumpere.*

[100] *PL* CI, col 270.

[101] *Epp.* IV, 346; cf. his poem *Regula Fidei: PLAC* I, 126ff.; Paulinus, *Conc. aevi Kar.* I, 180f.

century, thence to Ireland, to Alcuin's own Church of Northumbria in England, and to Frankland. At the end of the eighth century King Charles made this singing of the Creed part of the liturgical rite of the Mass in his own chapel at Aachen. In course of time the practice was followed by churches throughout Frankland and at Rome. This sequence, Northumbria to Frankland, when combined with Alcuin's prominent part both in the quelling of heresy and in the course of liturgical development, surely points to him and to his labours. It may well be that here, too, the Catholic Church throughout the world still feels his influence.[102]

4

Among all these varied occupations, Alcuin still, as ever, found time at Tours for letters. To Charles the King he wrote constantly, pleading that "your friend Flaccus may now at your own time be read by you, as once you used to listen to his voice." He writes from Tours about his teaching of the boys and young men in its monastic School, their training in Scripture, in the liberal arts, especially in grammar and astronomy: "I am made many things to many that I may train many for the advance of the Church and the glory of your realm."

But, he complains, the books are wanting in Tours which he and his master, Aelbert, had collected with devoted labour in York. Would Charles, therefore, approve of his sending some of his students to bring into Frankland "the flowers of Britain, that not only in York there may be a garden enclosed, filled with the fruits of wisdom?" "Exhort, Lord King," he goes on, "the young men in your Palace to learn with all diligence and daily effort, even as I, here in Tours, shall not

[102] Capelle, *RTAM* I, 1929, 10ff.; VI, 1934, 249ff.; Dix, 486ff.; Levison, 159; cf. Alcuin to Paulinus of Aquileia, c. 798: *Epp.* IV, 220.

cease to work in my own field. In the morning, with the zeal of youth, I sowed the seed in Britain. Now, as evening draws on and my blood grows cold, I still sow in Frankland, and always, here as there, I long for the springing to harvest by gift of grace." [103]

Many discussions by letter passed between the royal Court and Alcuin's abbey, on details of the stars and planets, of the Zodiac, of the lunar cycle and the astronomical calendar.[104] Alcuin will reckon the year from Christmas, not from September, and complains of the views of the young scholars who now debate and teach in the Palace School: "Of course I am ignorant! I did not know that you now had an Egyptian School in your Court; when I went away I left Latin students there. *I* was not so foolish as to begin the year with the coming on of darkness, as the Egyptians did, but with the growing light, according to the Roman custom." [105]

It is possible to see here a touch of querulousness, of the sensitive mind that misses its former joy of familiar friendship among the merry crowd at Aachen. A like note appears in Alcuin's acceptance of criticism from his royal friend: "You said it was not worth while to repeat what is already known. Well, then, I don't know what the countryman Flaccus can say to the wise David that he won't know. If we can't bring forward things heard long ago, we shall have to think up new rules of grammar when we talk about letters, syllables, and

[103] *Epp.* IV, 185, 176ff. The "garden enclosed" is to yield its fruit to Charles: a strange flight of Alcuin's imagination, as Rand remarked: *Survey* I, 39.

[104] *Epp.* IV, 185ff., 231f., 243, 250ff.; 279f., 282. Alcuin refers to a writing of his own on the *saltus lunae: ibid.* 234. On the extant writings *De Saltu Lunae* and *De Bissexto,* formerly attributed by error to Alcuin, see Charles W. Jones, *Bede, De Temporibus, MAA* XLI, 1943, 97, note 2; 110; 375f.

[105] *Epp.* IV, 231f.; Bede, *De Temp. Rat.* c. XXXVI: Jones, *ibid.* 250; Poole, *Studies in Chronology,* 1934, 10, note 2; Bresslau, *AU* VI, 1918, 22f.

words which we use every day. But, all the same, I do want you to correct me; my faults are my own." [106] Absence from the keen air of the Court's intellectual give-and-take, as Alcuin had known it in the company of Paulinus, of Theodulf, of Angilbert and countless others, brings out repeatedly this thought of the "countrified": "Here I am, struggling day by day with the uncultured minds of Tours. I do make some progress, though it isn't much." [107] And so he turns away from "the rustics" to refresh his mind by letters to Charles on mathematics: "You know well what delight there is in arithmetic, how necessary it is for understanding the Bible. How few care now about such things! Worse still, they run down those who are keen to learn." Answers are sent in careful detail to the questions of Charles on points Biblical, ethical, legal, and grammatical. Sad lament goes to the King on the dreadful boorishness of the brethren at Tours in regard to the punctuation of manuscripts. The meaning of the words "Septuagesima, Sexagesima, Quinquagesima" is discussed between the two as though no miles divided them, one of many questions put to Abbot Alcuin by his students and sent on to Charles, "although I know how much ignorance they must reveal. . . . But, then, these boys pester me with their little problems like flies in summertime at our windows!" Allegory explains Scripture at great length.[108] At another time Alcuin sends a gift, editions of the spurious letters supposed to have passed between Saint Paul and Seneca and between Alexander the Great and the Indian philosopher, Dindimus, king of the Brahmans. These

[106] *Epp.* IV, 232f.

[107] For the influence of this *rusticitas* upon Alcuin's letters see P. Taylor, *Romanic Review* XV, 1924, 127.

[108] *Epp.* IV, 285, 241, 239, 198ff., 224ff., 205ff. For Alcuin's occasional impatience with the ignorant cf. *PLAC* I, 251, in the little poem (XXXIV) on his "dear home":

Rustica turba tuo habitet sub tegmine nunquam:
Sit procul e tecto rustica turba tuo!

revisions, very probably made by Alcuin himself, are of interest as a link in the chain of tradition of manuscripts.[109]

So, also, messages, exhortations, sermons, passed from Alcuin's pen at Tours to the members of the royal family: to Abbess Gisela, rejoicing in her building of the Church of our Lady at Chelles, telling his pleasure in her gift to him of a cross; to other princesses, words of counsel, of affection, of instruction concerning the heresy of Adoptionism; to Prince Charles, son and heir of the King; to Adalhard, who was laggard in his correspondence and did not come to see him, a note of fanciful playing with words. To Adalhard he wrote also of his worry over that brother-abbot, Angilbert of St. Riquier, who was still indulging in worldly frivolities: "I am afraid that 'Homer' will be angry at the prohibition of theatricals and such inventions of the Devil. But all holy Scripture forbids this, and Saint Augustine (so I read) actually declared: 'The man who brings actors and mimes and dancers into his house does not realize how great a crowd of foul spirits follows them.' God forbid that the Devil hold power in a Christian home! I have written to you about this, for I long for the happiness of that dear son of mine. I want you to do for him what I know cannot come about through me." [110]

To Angilbert there were sent more pages of discussion of words. Ricbod, Archbishop of Trier, who also kept silence from letters, was rebuked and begged to send *Bede on Tobias* as a loan. Theodulf, the prelate of wit and culture so palatable to Charles, received a more frivolous petition, that played with

[109] *PLAC* I, 300 (LXXXI); cf. 295 (LXXIII) and 298 (LXXVII). For the "correspondence" of St. Paul and Seneca see C. W. Barlow, *Papers of the Amer. Acad. in Rome* X, 1938, 94ff.; for that of Alexander and Dindimus, F. Pfister, *Kleine Texte zum Alexanderroman,* 1910, 10ff.; for the supposed "Categories of Augustine," Hauréau, *Hist. Phil. scolast.* I, 1872, 94, and cf. Alcuin, *Versus de Sanctis,* l. 1549. See also Manitius, 248, 279; E. Liénard, *RBPH* XX, 1941, 589ff.

[110] *Epp.* IV, 249, 266, 337ff., 315f., 290ff.

the language of the *Song of Songs* and of the Gospels in an epicurean spirit: "If you have not three loaves of bread, I know you have at Orléans seven firkins of wine for the governor of the feast at Tours. But please see to it that you do not send new wine in old bottles! Happy is he who speaks to an understanding ear." [111]

More seriously, Alcuin wrote to Paulinus of Aquileia on "that cold North wind that blows against the wall of the Church in Spain, working to change the Catholic ceremonies of baptism," or "that secret doubt which some have conceived, whether the souls of Apostles and Martyrs really do gain entrance to Heaven before the Day of Judgment." To an English priest, Odvin, and to the monks in Septimania he also carefully explained the rites of baptism, according to the Roman Order so greatly desired by King Charles. He warned the community in Septimania, moreover, against other Spanish error, through the use of salt in bread in the Sacrifice of the Eucharist, and bade them relax the Lenten rigour on Holy Saturday: "For God does not care so much what we eat as He cares how we obey, in refusing what is really forbidden and using with due moderation what is allowed." [112] These same monks, as well as those of Murbach and those living under obedience to Archbishop Arno in Salzburg, were urged to follow faithfully discipline and study in Religion: "O how happy

[111] *Ibid.* 260ff., 318f.

[112] *Ibid.* 221, 202f., 210ff.; cf. *PLAC* I, 244 (XXIV). The letter to Odvin was frequently used in later days: Andrieu, *Les Ordines Romani du haut M. A.* I, 1931, 340. On Alcuin's battle for the Roman ritual of triple, as opposed to the Spanish custom of single, immersion, see Kleinclausz, *Alcuin,* 95ff.; cf. Cabrol, *DACL* s.v. *Alcuin,* col. 1089; Férotin, *Mon. Eccles. Lit.* V, 32f., note 3. Woolley, *Alcuin Club Tracts* X, 1913, 18f., comments on the early mention by Alcuin (*Epp.* IV, 211) of unleavened bread in the Eucharist. Wilmart, *Analecta Reginensia, Studi e Testi* 59, 1933, 153ff., points out the hand of Alcuin in "un florilège carolingien sur le symbolisme des cérémonies du baptême" (*Reg. lat.* 69).

is the life of monks!" Alcuin wrote to Salzburg; "It finds favour with God, love among the angels and honour among men." "But I myself," he lamented to Septimania, "distracted by the storms of the world, have toiled with vain effort in many places, and now in God's pity am cast up as a ship-wrecked man, weary and wounded, in a haven of peace. Pray for me, that I reach the meadows where grow the flowers of virtue." This, too, is not merely a reminiscence of the traditional language of the saints.[113]

Two letters, written for the layfolk of Septimania and for Alcuin's own students at Tours, press with energy the duty of confession in the ear of God's priest. They read just like a modern Catholic sermon on the difficulties and objections commonly raised by the unwilling or the uninitiated. The Goths in Septimania neither would nor did go to confession at this time, and Alcuin pleads anxiously with their reluctance. Again and again he bids all men to practise, and the clergy to preach, this "second baptism" for the remission of sin, needful for the young and the old, the sick and the well, the sinner in matters both grievous and common, the monk and the secular, man and woman, those facing danger in war or in journeying. Here again, Alcuin was trying to spread the use and discipline of his Saxon England upon the continent, and his labour increased far and wide the movement there toward sacramental penance.[114]

Above all, letters went from Tours to Arno of Salzburg, the "eagle of the Gospel" and "the dearest bird upon the Alpine

[113] *Epp.* IV, 276f., 314.

[114] *Ibid.* 216ff., 193ff. See Watkins, 666ff., 689ff.; Teetaert, *La confession aux laïques dans l'église latine* (siéc. VIII–XIV), 1926, 18: "La mérite d'avoir fixé la doctrine de la nécessité de la confession" (aux prêtres) "revient à Alcuin, qui en a fourni la première démonstration scripturaire"; cf. 31, 37, 41, 82, and E. Göller, *Römische Quartalschrift* XL, 1932, 261ff.

heights." To him Alcuin writes of his happiness in Arno's wearing of the pallium, of the responsibility this entails; he sends him *Songs for Easter,* lends him books, and bursts out so vehemently in the joy of love here and hereafter that he apologizes for this exuberance within the pages of a letter: "Please keep it to yourself. But I *must* write! Who knows, except He Who gave me all my good things, how long I *have* to write or to talk to you?" [115]

Now and again in these letters to Arno a name of interest occurs. Alcuin commends his friend to the monastery of Saint Servatius near Maastricht, which was under his own control.[116] He mourns the untimely deaths of Eric, that bold Duke of Friuli who had stormed the *Ring,* the fortress of the Avars, in 795, and of Gerold, Governor of Bavaria, brother of Queen Hildegard. Eric had been killed in 799 by Croat insurgents in Liburnia. Paulinus of Aquileia wrote for his dying a *Lament* which is worth reading. Gerold met his end the same year when riding with his men against the Avars on the Danube.[117] More tragic was the fate of John, Patriarch of Grado, an island in the Gulf of Trieste. Feeling of hostile contention was running high in Venice and the adjacent district at the end of the eighth century between supporters of the Byzantine and of the Frankish powers. The Patriarch of Grado was furthering the claim of King Charles and had grievously vexed the Byzantine Duke of Venice, who thereupon sent his son, Maurice, with a fleet to exercise vengeance. The young man did his work thoroughly. John of Grado was seized and hurled from the highest tower of his Palace, to bespatter the pavement with blood, which, so tradition told, horrified the eyes of pil-

[115] *Epp.* IV, 310f., 319ff., 286f., 278 (cf. *PLAC* I, 298), 321f., 254f.

[116] *Ibid.* 267.

[117] *Ibid.* 310; *ARF ann.* 799; Einhard, *Vita Karol.* c. 13; *PLAC* I, 131ff. and 114 (No. X: anonymous epitaph for Gerold). See especially James Bruce Ross, *Speculum* XX, 1945, 212ff.

grims for many years. Alcuin wrote in 800, not long after the deed, to advise Arno on the matter: "Put your mind prudently to work, that a better head of the Church of Grado be chosen and that this impious crime be punished. It is more dangerous to offend God than men. And so, if all homicide is punished by law, what judgment must be passed on the slaying of so high a dignity and in so wicked and cruel a manner? Not that I desire the *death* of any offender; rather, as saith the Lord, I desire that he may turn from his sin and live. No; but that wise use may be made of other kinds of penalty, perhaps of permanent exile, for the honour of priests and bishops of the Church." [118]

From this we may, perhaps, fitly come to Alcuin's words to Arno on the due keeping of the Feast of All Saints, which he himself, it would seem, was now, in 800, beginning to introduce into Frankland from his knowledge of the calendar followed in his own York.[119] "On the first of November comes the Feast of All Saints, purposed for you, reverend Father Arno, as we said. Hold it ever in mind and never cease to celebrate it year by year, remembering that if Elijah, one of the saints of the Old Testament, could by his prayer close the heavens to the teachers of falsehoods and open them to the converted,[120] how much more can all the saints in the New Testament, to whom the keys of the Kingdom were specially and openly committed? Surely they can shut Heaven to the un-

[118] *Epp.* IV, 344; Giovanni Diacono, *Fonti per la Storia d'Ital., Cron. Venez. ant.,* 1890, 99f.; Andrea Dandolo, *Chronica, RIS* (Muratori) XII, i, 1938, 126; *SS* VII, 13; F. C. Hodgson, *Early Hist. of Venice,* 1901, 68.

[119] *Epp.* IV, 321; Wilmart, *RB* XLVI, 1934, 50ff.; Levison, 160; *RPTK* I, 375, *Allerheiligenfeier* (Caspari); Hennig, *MSPI* X, 1948, 151ff.; cf. *Epp.* IV, 504 (letter of Cathwulf, c. 775 A.D.). The Feast had, indeed, been authorized under Arno in 798 at his Bavarian Synod of Riesbach: Hauck II, 459, note 2; Levison, 160, note 1.

[120] III Kings XVII, 1; XVIII, 1; St. James V, 17f.

believing and open it to the faithful, if they are honoured by those faithful in love and seemly ritual. May Christ Jesus enlighten our hearts to this end, and may the peace of God which passeth all understanding, by the pleading of all His saints, keep us to the day of eternity. So let us prepare, by fasting, prayer, Masses, and giving of alms for three days beforehand in true devotion, for this most holy solemnity."

Chapter VII

ALCUIN IN TOURS: LATER YEARS

CHAPTER VII

ALCUIN IN TOURS: LATER YEARS

I

ONE OF the most interesting, and perhaps the most widely discussed, among the occupations of the monks of Tours is the work of the scriptorium, the copying of manuscripts, which since the sixth century had become an integral part of monastic life. The subject is of special pertinence here, as Alcuin came to Frankland at a time when the history of Frankish and, indeed, of European script was steadily evolving from crudeness and confusion into that clearness, order, and symmetry for which the name of Tours in the ninth century was to be famed throughout civilized Europe.[1]

As one taught and trained in Northumbrian England, Alcuin naturally had learned much about writing in his own country. There the English had received the art of script from the Irish, who had formed their own half-uncial writing after the Roman model brought to Ireland by missionaries from Gaul. This Irish half-uncial was flourishing in the seventh century, and by that same time the Irish scribes had also developed a minuscule hand of their own.[2] Both types were passed on by them to northern England. There monks early in the eighth century were writing Anglo-Saxon half-uncials with highly skilled art, and had learned, as well, to use an

[1] For the general history of European script see bibliography under Lowe, Ullman, Maunde Thompson, Foerster.

[2] Lowe, *CLA* II, Nos. 266ff.

Anglo-Saxon minuscule in their manuscripts.[3] For some time there had been little difference, if any, between the Irish and the English hands.[4] Gradually, however, the English types had drawn away and had formed their own special characteristics.

When, therefore, missionaries from Ireland and from Anglo-Saxon England crossed the sea to work among the heathen peoples on the continent, their books and their art of writing went with them. Thus Luxeuil and Bobbio, St. Gall, Würzburg, Echternach and Fulda each filled a scriptorium with monks eager to practise and to teach their native Irish and English hands, based, indeed, on the Roman half-uncial, but wrought in these seventh and eighth centuries in many forms, which are now known as varieties of Insular script.

These, however, did not hold the field alone. The pagans of continental Europe had learned from the Roman Empire in the West the Roman cursive hand. This they had used as their base of experiment in their different countries and in this way had gradually developed various "national" scripts, known also as pre-Caroline minuscule hands. Among these "national" hands northern Italy wrote one formerly called the "Lombardic," Spain practised the "Visigothic" ("Westgothic"), and Frankland the "Merovingian."

This Merovingian writing was to play by far the most important part in European culture. It was a minuscule cursive hand, as derived from Roman minuscule cursive, and it was used in the seventh century for official documents, for the charters, edicts, and State letters of the Merovingian Kings. But it was angular and cramped, lacking in grace and clearness.[5]

[3] Lowe, *ibid.* Nos. 138f., 187ff., 194a. Of course uncials were also known, in capital letters and superscriptions.

[4] Lowe, *ibid.* xii. This was true in spite of the presence in England of uncial writings from Italy: Foerster, 125, 128.

[5] E. Maunde Thompson, 355, 498; Foerster, 152.

At the same time, the Roman half-uncial, which had long held its home in Roman Gaul, was still in use in Frankland, employed, together with the more formal uncial, for elaborate type. This half-uncial, then, was ready to aid scribes of the eighth century who were keen to devise a more set, a more artistic minuscule script than the Merovingian cursive. In the various monasteries of Frankland they strove long and hard toward this end, with varying success, in an interplay of the two elements, the cursive Merovingian and the Roman half-uncial. Two of the scripts thus produced mark stages along the way from crudeness to beauty of form: that known as the "Luxeuil" hand, and a younger relative of this, practised at Corbie in northern France and known as the *a b* type. In these hands Merovingian angularity is already giving place to characters curving, better spaced, and therefore more readable.[6]

Toward the end of the century, when Alcuin arrived at Aachen, the aim had already been in part realized by the production of the earlier "Caroline" minuscule script, pioneer of that beautifully distinct, gracefully rounded hand that has ever since been the delight of libraries. Henceforth it only remained to progress still further in the rooting out of crudities, toward the perfection both of the individual letters and of their formal setting in words. Under this enthusiastic movement the old Merovingian cursive slowly disappeared from the Frankish scriptorium.[7]

The exact place of origin of the Caroline minuscule is unknown, although many cloisters have been suggested.[8] It would seem that the monks who finally created it were well

[6] Lowe, No. 173.

[7] For various views see Foerster, 158ff., 165ff.; Ullman, 105ff.

[8] A. de Boüard, *Pal. Lat.* ed. Lindsay, IV, 1925, 71ff.; Lesne IV, 387; Lowe, in Crump-Jacob, 216ff.; Peeters, *RBPH* X, 1931, 1289ff. See, also, the argument for "asceticism" of H. Fichtenau, *Mensch und Schrift im Mittelalter*, 1946, 146ff.

versed in the legacy of Rome, especially in the more formal scripts of its ancient use, in capitals, uncials, half-uncials.[9] To Corbie belongs the honour of the first example we can date in our records; its Abbot Maurdramnus, who died in 778, saw Caroline minuscule written in the text of the Bible which bears his name and which was made by his order.[10] Already distinct, then, at this time, this minuscule was still to run a youthful course marked by confusion of varied character as it swayed between cursive and half-uncial, always tending toward the latter. Finally it was to become the ruling script of Europe, although not through lack of rivals, for other countries were also trying to create the ideal minuscule in their books and documents. But it surpassed them all, even the admirable hand known as "Beneventan," evolved in southern Italy, where it flourished through the Middle Ages.[11]

The "Caroline" minuscule, as we call it, owes its name to its adoption, for its legibility and grace, by King Charles as official script for his realms. In the year 781, which saw Charles in Rome and in Parma, inviting Alcuin to the Frankish Court, we find the script, not yet ripe but advancing toward maturity, in a Book of the Gospels which was being written as a lectionary for use at Mass. The scribe gave his name as Godesscalc, and he worked upon purple parchment in uncial characters of gold. He adorned his work, moreover, before he presented it to the King, with a page of verses in praise of Charles and his queen, Hildegard, at whose bidding this "excellent book" had been made. These verses he inscribed in the new minuscule, which evidently by this time held an honoured place at the Court.[12] Whether Godesscalc worked at

[9] Lowe, in Crump-Jacob, 216; *EHR* XLVI, 1931, 149f.
[10] Laistner, 181; Lowe, 217.
[11] Ullman, 94ff.; Loew (Lowe), *The Beneventan Script,* 1914.
[12] B. N. lat. 1203; *PLAC* I, 94f.; Steffens, *Latein. Paläographie,* 1909, 45; *Ada-Handschrift,* 85f. (Janitschek).

the Court or not we do not know, but many authorities have held that he did.[13]

Two other scripts known to us belong, by the date assigned them, to the years of Alcuin's residence at the Court of King Charles. One was that of the *Dagulf Psalter,* also inscribed in gold uncials, presented by Charles to Pope Hadrian sometime before Hadrian's death in 795. Dagulf was its scribe, and he, too, offered his work to the King in verses of this minuscule hand.[14] The other bore the newer minuscules in its body, the famous Golden Codex of the Latin Gospels, ordered by Charles and presented by a Lady Ada to the Abbey of Saint Maximin at Trier early in the ninth century. Its writing belongs to two periods, of which the earlier is dated *c.* 790–799. Verses addressed to "Ada, handmaid of God" are found at the end.[15] It is not improbable that these two sumptuous books, commanded by the King, were made in the scriptorium of the Frankish Court and its School at Aachen, and that Alcuin, as "head" of this School, watched and encouraged such making of script, as he did the work of collecting books and of reading them. It is not beyond possibility, also, that he was author of the verses inscribed on the "Ada-script" made for King Charles.

The relation of Alcuin to the history of script at Tours has been sharply disputed. Theory has ranged from giving him no place at all in it to seeing him, falsely enough, as the actual inventor of that "Caroline" minuscule which he found awaiting him in Frankland. Against his sharing actively in its prog-

[13] Cf. Lowe, in Crump-Jacob, 217; Beer I, 61.

[14] *PLAC* I, 91f., 88; Beer I, 29ff., and 43ff., 56, 61, for discussion of its provenance; Plates 17ff.

[15] See *Ada-Handschrift,* 7ff. (Menzel); Beer I, 59ff.; Rand and G. Howe, *Memoirs of Amer. Acad. in Rome* I, 1917, 20; Steffens, *Lat. Pal.* 45. The tradition of the Abbey of St. Maximin calls Ada "sister of the Emperor Charles": *PLAC* I, 287; cf. Menzel, *Ada-Handschrift,* 10, 15; Einhard, *Vita Karol.* c. 18: *unica soror nomine Gisla.*

ress it is pointed out that he was of advanced age when he reached Tours and that his letters show him there as a sick and weary man, who would gladly retire, so far as his conscience would suffer him, from secular burdens and duties.[16]

Yet undoubtedly Alcuin at Tours did all that was in him to rule his monastery; undoubtedly he was still keen to aid Charles in the advancement of spiritual learning. During these years at Saint Martin's he was busy as could be in revising the text of the Latin Vulgate at the King's request, in compiling detailed commentaries, missals, manuals of doctrine or prayer for Charles and the royal family, for students and for friends who asked his help. Moreover, the new "Caroline" script was now closely bound up with education, spiritual and secular, under Charles. Already, as we have seen, the King had ordered special care to be given to the copying of Holy Scripture, of Office-books and of missals; [17] as preface to his announcing of the *Homiliary* to be prepared by Paul the Deacon, he had sounded a trumpet call to the scholars of his realm, that they get them busily to begetting books for the continual progress of his churches, an art "almost blotted out of sight by the sloth of our ancestors." [18] His insistence upon the *Rule* of Saint Benedict at the synod of Aachen in 802 and his orders, taken from its chapters, led to renewed copying of this *Rule* and to careful revision of its text; [19] the compiling of the Frankish *Sacramentary* by Alcuin called for copies innumerable; so, also, did that revision of the Vulgate Scriptures. All these works, undertaken at royal command, led inevitably to

[16] Cf. Traube, *NA* XXVII, 1902, 281; *Vorles. und Abh.* II, 25; Menzel, *Ada-HS.* 4; Gaskoin, 198, note 1; Lowe, *EHR* XLVI, 1931, 148.

[17] Page 122 *supra.*

[18] *Cap. reg. Franc.* I, 80.

[19] *Ibid.* 105, 108f. Sometime after 787 Charles had obtained by request a copy of the *Rule* of Saint Benedict from Abbot Theodemar of Monte Cassino: *Epp.* IV, 510.

intense consideration of script, and of a script that should be easily and correctly read. Hence the ever-increasing use of the Caroline minuscule in official writings.[20]

This script had already advanced far on its way when Alcuin became abbot at Tours. We shall not strain probability if we think of him, too, as fostering the work of the scriptorium in Saint Martin's. As he encouraged his monks to read, so he would encourage them to take their own part in the general work of Frankish copying of important documents. We know that he wrote verses to hang upon the wall of a scriptorium and, it may be, that of his own monks at Tours. Let no frivolous chatter, he bade, cause to stumble the hands that write here. "Let meaning be carefully defined by punctuation, lest the reader in church read wrongly to his brethren." "It is a splendid work to write out sacred books; better this than to tend vines, to serve the spirit before the stomach." [21] We have also seen him writing to his King in 799 to lament the neglect of proper punctuation among scribes of his time—"through their boorish lack of culture, with which I struggle here daily, though I don't get very far"—and he begs Charles to train well the boys at his Court to write well and clearly official and royal Papers.[22]

Certain elements in his character and training seem, indeed, to support the thought that he was ready to encourage this Caroline minuscule hand. He was always gifted with a sense of order, of desire to organize for clearness and for efficiency. In spite of qualms of conscience, he loved, as did Charles, the ancient spirit of Rome and the logical formality which clothed

[20] Lowe, in Crump-Jacob, 218.

[21] Rand, *Survey* I, 43; *PLAC* I, 320; Beer I, 54ff., 61. Cf. W. Arndt and M. Tangl, *Schrifttafeln zur Erlern. der lat. Pal.* II, 1906, 29: Nos. 44–47. For a positive view of Alcuin's work for Caroline script see especially H. Delitsch, *Geschichte der abendl. Schreibschriftformen*, 1928, 74.

[22] *Epp.* IV, 285; cf. Hessel, *AU* VIII, 1923, 210f.

her books, in word and in letter. He had known and admired half-uncial writing in England.

In any case, script was progressing at Saint Martin's while he was abbot there. Its scriptorium grew steadily more skilled in the writing of various forms and in their proper usage in the various parts of a book. This multiple skill, this clear distinction in the use of different types, became the glory of the School of Tours. Thus its books were duly headed by square capitals, were ended in rustic capitals; their chapters began in uncials, their prefaces were written in half-uncials; the body of their text appeared in the minuscule of the Frankish Court. All was done in orderly ritual; each part held its own distinct style, each word and each letter its own distinct place.[23]

The reign of the Caroline minuscule lasted four hundred years. Then it bowed for three centuries to the Gothic script, after which time it was again revived to flourish as "revised Caroline" in the hands of the humanists of the Renaissance. Thence it passed into the printed "Roman" type which still forms the books of today. Once more, Alcuin, it may be, played his part in the culture which was to influence our modern world.

Reference has been made to a revision of the text of the Vulgate Bible undertaken at the King's request by Alcuin. In regard to this revision, evidence is not so detailed as one

[23] Rand, *Survey* I, 40f.; Rand-Howe, 51; Ullman, 113; Lesne IV, 148f.; C. H. Beeson, *Class. Philol.* XXV, 1930, 285f. The dating of MSS., as of either Alcuin's time or before or after this, has been keenly disputed. Perhaps we may cite, as written during or soon after his lifetime, Paris B. N. lat. 17227 (Gospels of Adalbald); Troyes 1742 (Alcuin: *De virtutibus et vitiis*); London B. M. Harl. 2790 (Gospels of St. Cyr of Nevers); London B. M. Harl. 2793 (Psalter). But for much interesting detail of varying theory see, in bibliography *infra,* Köhler, Rand, Foerster, Rand-Howe; Wilmart (*Speculum* VI, 1931, 573ff.; *RB* XLII, 1930, 43ff.); Lesne (IV, 153ff.). Naturally, also, Alcuin encouraged the influence of his own Anglo-Saxon script at Tours: Lowe, *EHR* XLVI, 148; Morey, *Mediaeval Art,* 1942, 199.

could wish. Certainly Charles, in his general desire for order and truth in the texts, liturgical and legal, current among his subjects, here again turned his mind toward gaining the same necessities for them in their version of the Scriptures. Biblical texts, indeed, were in a deplorable state in his realms, through ignorance and carelessness of copyists under the Merovingian Kings.[24] Versions now differed radically from one another and from the readings in the Liturgy as put forward by Alcuin; errors of grammar abounded, for the offence of the learned and the leading astray of the simple. It was high time that some one should set to work at rooting out the weeds that had overgrown the fair pasture of Saint Jerome's Latin.[25]

In the "General Letter" issued to authorize the *Homiliary* of Paul the Deacon, Charles declared that: "By the grace of God, we have scrupulously corrected, some time since, the books of the Old and the New Testament, depraved through ignorance of scribes." There is no proof, however, that he was referring here to Alcuin's work in particular.[26] Of this work we learn through a letter sent by Alcuin to Abbess Gisela and her niece Rotrud at Chelles shortly before Easter in the year 800. He has been busy, he writes, obeying the King's command to emend the text of both Testaments.[27] In 800 or 801—the year is disputed—he wrote to Charles that he had long been purposing to offer him a gift worthy of his splen-

[24] Berger, 328f.; Gaskoin, 239ff.; Kleinclausz, *Alcuin,* 216. For interest and work of Charles in revision of Scripture see *PLAC* I, 89f.; Thegan, *Vita Hlud.* c. 7: *SS* II, 592; for the view that Alcuin's revision was not an official one, but succeeded and spread through its own merit and the respect felt for Alcuin, Corssen, *GGA,* 1894, 867.

[25] Berger, xvii; Kleinclausz, *Alcuin,* 213ff. Alcuin, however, did not judge it his task to restore St. Jerome's version *per se;* rather, to make a text in conformity (1) with grammar, (2) with the best MS. evidence he could find: Sparks, *The Bible in its Ancient and English Versions,* ed. H. Wheeler Robinson, 1940, 118f.

[26] Page 198 *supra;* de Clercq, 181, note 3; Ganshof, *BHR* IX, 1947, 2, note 1.

[27] *Epp.* IV, 323.

dour. What could be more fitting than these books of Scripture, bound in a volume of text diligently revised? This, then, he is now sending by the hand of his "most dear son, Nathanael." [28] Another letter bids this "Nathanael," as Alcuin called his former student Fridugis, now "faithfully serving" the King at Court, present this offering to Charles on Christmas Day, "with all the blessings to be read therein." [29]

As sources needed for this work of revision Alcuin drew, naturally, upon Anglo-Saxon and Irish manuscripts which he had known in northern England, together with the Italian readings also current there. It was this unique heritage which had, in fact, made him the man of the King's choice.[30]

In addition to this Bible, magnificently written and bound, which was Alcuin's Christmas gift to Charles, verses written by him himself tell of other copies, presumably of the same "Alcuinian" text: one made for Gerfrid, bishop of Laon, and another, now known as the *Codex Vallicellianus.*[31] Alcuin's actual text is given in no manuscript now extant. Various authorities have seen in various codices the nearest approach we can find to this original: in the Codex 75 of Saint Gall,[32] in the *Codex Vallicellianus,*[33] in the Bamberg Bible, or in that of Zürich.[34]

[28] *Ibid.* 418f.

[29] *Ibid.* 419f. On Dümmler's dating of *Epp.* IV, Nos. 261f. see Kleinclausz, *Alcuin,* 215, note 70; cf. *PLAC* I, 294, ii; Jaffé, *Mon. Alc.* 699; Ganshof, 14f.; Berger, 190f.

[30] Rand, *HTR* XXIV, 1931, 382ff.; Chapman, *Notes on the early hist. of the Vulgate Gospels,* 1908, 49; Glunz, *Hist. of the Vulgate in England,* 1933, 29ff.

[31] *PLAC* I, Nos. LXV, LXVI, i; cf. LXVIIf.

[32] Köhler, *Die Schule von Tours* I, 59, 84ff., 313ff., 364; Lesne IV, 147, 150; cf. de Bruyne, *GGA* CXCIII, 1931, 352.

[33] Berger, XVf., 193, 197ff., 240.

[34] *Ada-Handschrift,* 36, 38, 59 (Corssen), 74 (Janitschek); Rand, *The Earliest Book of Tours,* 97ff.; *HTR* XVII, 1924, 239ff.; XXIV, 1931, 336ff., 364, 377f., 388f.; Rand-Howe, 21ff.; Rand, *Survey* I, 49, 50, note 1; cf. Steffens, 46f.

A more learned edition of the Biblical text was made in the time of Charles by that friend of Alcuin and favoured courtier of the King, Theodulf, bishop of Orléans, who amplified it by a multitude of variant readings. Its erudition still exists in manuscripts, but its influence was little compared with that of Alcuin's Bible.[35] Alcuin's text inevitably suffered countless changes in the course of time through errors of transcription; but part of its original lived on and still holds its own thread in the weaving of the Vulgate of today.[36]

Only a little less interesting to him than the study of the text of the Bible was the effort to interpret and to explain its meaning and doctrine for the enlightenment of all who would read. To his friends Gisela and Rotrud at Chelles, encouraged by their fervent petition, he sent in two installments his *Commentary on the Gospel of Saint John.*[37] This Gospel had always deeply moved him; indeed, his biographer tells a story of his student days in York when he was suddenly rapt into vision while reading, in class before Aelbert, of the Beloved Disciple on the first Holy Thursday. Long afterward he prized it above the other Gospels for its dwelling upon the Divinity of the Lord Christ.[38]

In 800 we find him writing from Frankland to his former student Calvinus, now a priest and a monk of the cell of Saint Stephen in the northern English Province, under Archbishop Eanbald the second: "Saint Stephen's cell will give you all you need, I think, for a good life, and there is no reason why you should wander about through countries of different sorts

[35] Delisle, *Les Bibles de Théodulfe, Bibl. de l'Ecole des Chartes* XL, 1879, 1ff.; Berger, xvii; Cuissard, 193.

[36] Gaskoin, 243.

[37] *PL* C, coll. 743ff., in 7 books; *Alc. Vita,* 195.

[38] *Alc. Vita,* 188f.; *Epp.* IV, 355. Of course, Alcuin regarded the Beloved Disciple as the author of St. John's Gospel.

to hear of the disloyalties of other men, to get angry at their sins, and so to lose that wonderful peace of mind . . . Write the Gospel in your heart, chant it very often, as you do the Psalms, especially the Gospel of Saint John and its deep mysteries. I am working hard at it myself, making a brief Commentary from the writings of the Fathers—a work very necessary and one that would give you delight, if ever I can finish it." [39]

In Lent of this same year he sent off to Chelles the first part of the work for the meditation of his friends in "these holy days." Their gratitude and their earnest prayer for more of the same spurred him on to finish: "We do have, indeed," they wrote, "the writings of learned Augustine on this Gospel. But in some places he is far too deep and goes into far too much detail for our humble minds to grasp! Saint Jerome dedicated to women treatises on Prophetic obscurities and wrote very many letters from Bethlehem to his women learners in Rome. Tours is *much* nearer to Chelles! Please do not let your light be hid under a bushel, or in the depths of a quiet armchair. . . ." [40]

They were delighted to receive the remaining part, early in 801.[41] For thirty years, Alcuin told them, he had wanted to write on this Gospel, but he had lacked stimulus until they had urged him. His sources had been Augustine, Ambrose, the Homilies of Pope Gregory the Great, and of Bede, from whom he had borrowed much detail.[42]

As in all his writings, so here Alcuin held himself a channel by which the teaching of the Fathers of the Church should

[39] *Epp.* IV, 347, 349.

[40] *Ibid.* 322ff.

[41] *Epp.* IV, 357f.

[42] *Ibid.* 358, 357. A. E. Schönbach (*SBW* CXLVI, 1903, No. 4, 43ff.) gives a detailed account of this Commentary, and rejects (67ff.) one on St. Matthew's Gospel. Hauck (II, 144, note 6) assigns to Alcuin a short treatise: *Interpretationes nominum Hebraicorum progenitorum domini nostri Jesu Christi* (*PL* C, coll. 725ff.).

reach the men and women of his time. Nothing could be, should be, devised or added by himself to these words of authority, save of exhortation toward their study. "What better purpose shall we ordinary men," he had written to Felix of Urgel from Aachen, "be able to devise, in these loveless days of the world's last age, than that we should follow with all energy of faith and truth the doctrine of the apostles and evangelists, not inventing new terms, not bringing forth anything unfamiliar, not singing vain praise for our own name through any new doctrine whatsoever." [43] And he added now for Gisela and Rotrud some explanation of his thought as interpreter of the Bible: "I think that perhaps some middle point can be found between my refusal to write for you and your prayer to me, between silence on my part, which would disappoint you, and rashness, which would deceive your hopes. Just as doctors concoct medicines for their patients from many kinds of drugs and yet do not boast that they themselves create the herbs they use, but only collect their ingredients and mix them into one healing draught, so with me. I, likewise, do not think that I should gather my flowers from any one field of patristic learning. No, I must search over the meadows of many Fathers, stooping humbly to pick what I need, without danger of disgrace and failure." [44]

Other Commentaries written by Alcuin, according to the evidence of his biographer, dealt with Genesis, Psalms, Proverbs, Ecclesiastes, and the Song of Songs, from the Old Testament; with the Epistles to the Ephesians, to Titus, to Philemon, and to the Hebrews, from the New.[45]

[43] *Epp.* IV, 61; Hauck II, 142ff. For the spirit underlying Alcuin's *deflorationes* cf. Picavet, *Essais,* 341.

[44] *Epp.* IV, 356f.

[45] *Alc. Vita,* 195. On the *Song of Songs* cf. *PLAC* I, 299 (LXXVIII), trans. H. Mumford Jones: P. S. Allen, *The Romanesque Lyric,* 1928, 229.

The book on Genesis was written amid "distractions of secular business and the troubles of divers journeys" for his student, the priest Sigulf, in the form of a dialogue in which Alcuin drew upon Jerome and Gregory the Great in answer to the enquiries of his young friend.[46] For the comment on the Seven Penitential Psalms, sent to Arno of Salzburg sometime after 798, no special source has been found; for Psalm 118 and the fifteen "Psalms of Degrees," 119–133, also discussed at Arno's request, Saint Augustine was the guide.[47] Here are developed long ponderings over numbers in mystic interpretation. Why seven Penitential Psalms? Why fifteen Gradual Psalms? Why is Psalm 118 divided into twenty-two periods, and why does each have eight verses? But from these tedious meditations Alcuin rises to the joy of the songs themselves. "As the angels live in Heaven, so live men on earth who rejoice in the praises of God, in the pure heart of psalmody. No mortal man can fully declare the virtue of the Psalms. In them are the confessions of sinners, the tears of the penitent, sorrow of heart. Here is foretold all the dispensation of our redemption, the wondrous delights of heaven's mirth. Here shall you find the Incarnation, the Passion, the Resurrection and the Ascension of the Word of God." [48]

The work on Proverbs is not now known. That on Ecclesiastes, drawn from Jerome, reached in 801 or 802 the three

[46] *PL* C, coll. 515ff. Hauck (II, 143, note 3), Jaffé (*Mon. Alc.* 273, note 1) and Dümmler (*Epp.* IV, 122, note 3) assign this to Alcuin's years with the Court. But the earlier years at Tours, 796–801, were also full of interruptions: Gaskoin, 135, note 1. The sources were Jerome, *Quaest. in Genesim, PL* XXIII, coll. 935ff., and Gregory, *Moralia, PL* LXXV, coll. 509ff. For the translation of this work, attributed to Aelfric, see G. E. MacLean, *Anglia* VI, 1883, 425ff.; VII, 1884, 1ff.; C. L. White, *Yale Stud. in English* II, 1898, 131ff.; *CHEL* I, 134 (Westlake); M. M. Dubois, *Ælfric*, 1943, 92.

[47] *PL* C, coll. 570ff.; *Epp.* IV, 389ff., 417; *Opera*, ed. Froben I, 342ff.

[48] *Epp.* IV, 391 and note 1.

young men, once students of his, for whom Alcuin compiled it, the priests Onias and Candidus (Witto), and Nathanael (Fridugis), not in priest's ordering, but distinguished as archdeacon.[49] All three were at the Court of Charles, and Alcuin writes that he has laboured thus on the "subject of 'Vanity of vanities, saith the Preacher, all is vanity' " for his sons "who have flown from his care into the open skies of secular business." The temptations of the wicked world often troubled Alcuin's thought for those he had instructed. Once again about this time he begged Fridugis "not to suffer the ringed doves that fly through the chambers of the Palace to come to his windows." [50]

The Song of Solomon attracted him, as it attracted so many mediaeval writers, for its mystical possibilities, and he naturally went for its interpreting to Bede. More of his own devising, probably, from its apologetic preface, "Please discuss this only among friends, it isn't meant for the very learned," was the complicated letter in which he "explained" for his student "Daphnis" the number "sixty" of the queens and the "eight hundred" of the concubines of Solomon, as mystically referring to the rule of Holy Church.[51]

[49] *PL* C, coll. 667ff.; *Epp.* IV, 406f., 351, 412; Jerome, *PL* XXIII, coll. 1009ff., cf. col. 1061; *PLAC* I, 297f.

[50] *Epp.* IV, 392; Isaiah LX, 8. Cf. Alcuin's verses to "Corydon," a young student who has yielded to the temptations of the Court: *PLAC* I, 249f.; Ebert, *ZDA* XXII, 1878, 329ff.; Manitius, 549.

[51] *Epp.* IV, 200f.; *PLAC* I, 299 (LXXVIII). For the commentaries on other books of the N.T. see *PL* C, coll. 1009ff.; Manitius, 277; Vernet, *DTC,* col. 690; that on Ephesians is not extant. The attribution to Alcuin of a commentary (also consisting of excerpts) on Revelation, in 5 books (Werner, 155; Hauck II, 144), printed in *PL* C, coll. 1087ff., is doubtful; see Wilmart, *Auteurs spirituels et textes dévots du M.A. latin,* 1932, 52, note 6; Kleinclausz, *Alcuin,* 206, note 24. The title does not appear in the list of *Alc. Vita,* 194f. As Kleinclausz remarks, it is not possible to fix exactly the date of these works; probably they were written at Tours. For Alcuin's use of Bede see Ogilvy, *MAA,* 1936, 107f. His work on Hebrews shows the influence of Chrysostom: Hauck II, 144.

From time to time Alcuin turned from this interpretation of Scripture to the teaching of the Church's doctrine, not only in his letters, but in formal treatises.[52] Two dominant notes sound here throughout his instruction, as a necessary accompaniment in all his pages.[53] First: if one would know God, above all he must hold the true, the Catholic, Faith, and assuredly for this end the wisdom of the Fathers of the Church, in theology, in philosophy, in dialectic, was given to men by God. Upon this learning Alcuin held his stand. At the same time he declared that none can enter into the Catholic Faith save by the light of justice and of love. He could not rest content with a concept of theology *per se,* in many complexities and nice distinctions, as guide to Heaven. The Catholic creed in his view must live and bear sound fruit, in love for God through worship and adoration and in love for man through thoughts, words, acts, if the believer is to win happiness in the Beatific Vision of the hereafter.

The second note follows from the first. Neither justice nor love, nor, indeed, the knowledge of God, can dwell in the heart that is poisoned by sin. It is, therefore, of the fundamental essence of life for the pilgrim to Eternity that his soul be cleansed by forgiveness through the gift of redemption from God. The Atonement to Alcuin was not only an article of his professed creed; it was an integral part of the life he longed to live and honestly tried to live, day by day.

It may rightly be said that Alcuin, constant reader of Augustine, thus shared in the belief and practice of all true Catholics. Yet, in trying to picture him as man, as teacher, and as writer, as one who was to cast his influence far into

[52] The letters deal with Baptism (*Epp.* IV, Nos. 134, 137); the Eucharist (Nos. 28, 137); Penance (Nos. 55, 131, 138); the Religious life in Community (Nos. 1, 54, 168, 187, 219, 223, 250, 271f., 278, 280, 282, 286f.); the hermit life (No. 22); the active and the contemplative lives (Nos. 86, 213); prayer for the dead (Nos. 77, 105f.).

[53] Hauck II, 145f.

the Middle Ages, it is important to give these points definite mention. The times were at hand when Churchmen were often to judge of Christian standing by profession of creed, by exact knowledge of theology, alone. Indeed, this already was evident in Alcuin's own writings.[54] Moreover, he unconsciously aided in making this knowledge of patristic teaching the supreme test, by that very scrupulosity which forbade him even to think or to declare anything for which he could not quote exact chapter and verse from a Father of consecrated honour in the Church's roll. But his own character fought against this theological spirit, now rising to vigour. His life was consistently marked, in his bearing toward other men, by an eager hunger for a personal relationship which should aid, in the Lord's cause, all whom he might touch; in his thought of himself, by the constant cry for mercy at Heaven's hand, by fear of judgment to come. A story told by his biographer, very probably true, illustrates the latter. His friend, Benedict of Aniane, one day asked him what prayer he especially made his own? And Alcuin answered: "This do I ask of Christ: 'Lord, give me to know my sins, to make true confession, to carry out fitting penance; and do Thou give to me forgiveness.' " That was all he held needful in his prayer, for that was in itself the attainment of joy. But Benedict had to remind the Lord of the rest: "Let us add, Father," he said, "one thing more: 'And after forgiveness, grant me to enter Heaven.' " "Oh, yes, certainly, revered son," was the courteous reply.[55]

Alcuin considered that his chief writing on doctrine was the *Handbook on the Faith of the Holy Trinity,* sent to his King and Emperor Charles in 802, at the time of the Synod held in Aachen that year. He included with it a letter clearly showing that it was intended as an official guide to orthodox belief, developed by aid of Augustine's dialectic, for use in

[54] *Ibid.* 146.
[55] *Alc. Vita,* 192; Hauck II, 147ff.

the Caroline Court and realms. As such it was to be formally presented to the Synod.[56]

To Fridugis and to Arno he also sent answers to problems concerning the same dogma of faith; to Charles he wrote in detail on the redemption of Man.[57] Scholars have disagreed on the question whether he wrote a treatise on the *Filioque* doctrine. This doctrine was certainly professed by him, and maintained in the *Caroline Books* and other witness of King Charles.[58]

In his *On Virtues and Vices*, written for his friend Wido, he gives a practical application, for a layman, of the ascetic theology of the Church and her scholars. Wido, "an ideal

[56] *PL* CI, coll. 13ff.; *Epp.* IV, 414ff.; *Alc. Vita,* 194; *PLAC* I, 300 (LXXXII). See A. J. Macdonald, *Authority and Reason in the early M.A.,* 1933, 25ff., 67f., for an interesting discussion of Alcuin's use of dialectics: "So convinced a believer in authority and tradition . . . he helped to begin a new tradition—the rational interpretation of theology." Macdonald illustrates this by *Epp.* IV, 466ff., 337ff. Hauck (II, 146) holds Alcuin's *On the Holy Trinity* "der Anfang der mittelalterlichen Theologie"; cf. Grabmann, *Gesch. der schol. Meth.* I, 1909, 195.

[57] *Epp.* IV, 447f., 426f., 466ff.

[58] For the *Libellus de Processione Spiritus Sancti* see *PL* CI, coll. 63ff.; for Alcuin's authorship, Jugie, *Theologia Dogmatica* II, 1933, 505; Kleinclausz, *Alcuin,* 204, note 17; against it, Dümmler, *Epp.* IV, 2, 482, 490f.; Hauck II, 347, note 3. Werminghoff calls the work anonymous (*Conc. aevi Kar.* I, 235). Amann (182) rejects for Alcuin the work printed in Migne, but attributes to him (99) a writing on the subject and gives a detailed account of the *Filioque* controversy between the Franks, the East, and the Papacy (173ff.). See also *DTC* s.v. *Filioque* (Palmieri); Every, *The Byz. Patriarchate,* 1947, 114f. Cf., for Alcuin: *De fide S. Trin., PL* CI, coll. 16, c. 5; 20, c. 11; 22, c. 14; for Charles: *Epp.* V, 65f.; for the *Caroline Books: Lib. Car.* III, 3, ed. Bastgen, *Conc.* II, *Suppl.* 110. The dispute at this time centred around the manner and method of expressing a doctrine held in substance by all parties. *The Confessio Fidei* (*PL* CI, coll. 1027ff.) is not by Alcuin; see Möller-Hahn, 368, and Wilmart, *Auteurs spirituels et textes dévots du M.A. latin,* 1932, 56, note 3, and 198. Wilmart assigns this work, erroneously ascribed to Alcuin by Mabillon, to Jean de Fécamp. On the question *de pretio salutis humanae cui daretur* (discussed in the Palace School, as Alcuin remarked), and on the Greek suggestion, refuted by him, *huius pretii acceptricem esse mortem* (*Epp.* IV, 466ff.), see Rivière, *RSR* XIII, 1933, 354ff.; Cappuyns, *BTAM* III, 1937, 20.

man, an uncorrupt judge and a faithful emissary of the King," as Alcuin described him, was Count of the Breton March and had conquered all Brittany for Charles in 799. The date of this book is probably that year or shortly afterward. "Mindful of your urgent petition and of my promise as your spiritual Father," Alcuin explained, "to write for you, as a man on military service, a brief book of counsel and inspiration, I send this now, not composed in great eloquence, but certainly with all Christian love. I have divided it into short chapters, because you are so busy. Keep it by your side, that by its light you may examine yourself, may learn what to shun, what to practise, on your way toward perfection through the changes and chances of this earth. Don't worry about your layman's life in the world, as though that would keep you from entering Heaven. Neither sex nor age nor rank matters there. A man does not win or lose honour within its gates just because he was lay or cleric, rich or poor, young or old, slave or lord, at his departing hence; each one shall be glorified for his merit in goodly work." [59] And so Wido, in brief daily readings, is told to follow faith, hope, and charity, peace, patience and humility; to make confession with contrition, to give alms, to deal honestly, to flee the eight deadly sins. We can see the writer following in the steps of Cassian and of Aldhelm, extracting his matter from the sermons of Augustine, as he prepares this guide to the good life.[60]

Alcuin passed from moral to abstract philosophy in a letter, *On the Nature of the Soul,* composed about the same time,

[59] *PL* CI, coll. 613ff., 638; *Epp.* IV, 402, 464f.; *Alc. Vita,* 195; *ARF ann.* 799.

[60] Hauck II, 147, note 1. He gives 799 as date of the work; Dümmler (*Epp.* IV, 464) gives c. 801–804. For witness of the book's influence see George T. Flom, who has edited an Old Norwegian translation, said to have been made early in the 13th century: Codex *AM 619 Quarto, Univ. Illinois Studies in Lang. and Lit.* XIV, 1929, No. 4, 465ff.; cf. C. R. Unger, *Gammel Norsk Homiliebog,* 1864, 1ff. (Latin and O. N. texts) and G. Indrebø, *Gamal Norsk Homiliebok,* 1931, 1ff.

also at request, for Gundrada, cousin of King Charles and sister of Abbot Adalhard of Corbie. We have already met her as student under Alcuin in the Palace School, and now again he calls her by the name, "Eulalia," he had given her there. She is still at Court. To her his discourse is also brief, and in this difficult subject he is conscious of a lack of books. He bids her read Augustine to Jerome, if she can get hold of this treatise: "I read it in England, but it is not here, at Tours, neither is Jerome's brief but most acute letter in answer." Several other writings by Augustine are also recommended to her: "If they are to be found in the Emperor's library, hunt them up and read them, and for the love we share send them on to me." From discussing the soul the letter proceeds to the praise of wisdom, "which will not be found in the lies of Virgil, but in abundance within the truth of the Gospel." "Eulalia," apparently, was not very well-known to Alcuin, but he had heard repeatedly of her reputation for study and learning. He ends his instruction with some elegiac verses, the metre of which the Emperor Charles will explain to her. "How wonderful," he goes on, "that in all the distractions of his Court and realm, the Emperor has found time and energy for the secret mysteries of philosophy, which our idlers rarely want to learn." "Eulalia" need not write to Tours to inquire into "the causes of things" while she is living in that wise and revered Presence! [61]

Lastly, Alcuin turned from theology, from philosophy, and from counsel for their practice in daily life, to the compiling of books of devotion. In addition to his revision of the Missal

[61] *Epp.* IV, 473ff.; *PLAC* I, 302f. On Alcuin as student of Augustine see Gilson, *La Philosophie au M.A.*, 191f. Cf. also Hauréau, *Hist. de la Phil. scol.* I, 126: "Alcuin n'est pas un philosophe . . . il est un grammarien," and Picavet, *Essais*, 6: "père de la scolastique française et allemande"; see also Gilson-Böhner, *Gesch. d. christ. Phil.*, 1937, 245; Hessen, *Patrist. und schol. Philos.*, 1922, 50. For an analysis of Alcuin's *De animae ratione* see Seydl, 35ff.; Schneider, *PJ* XXXIV, 1921, 358ff.; Kreutle, *ibid.* XXXI, 1918, 347f.

for official use throughout the dominions of Charles, he now compiled from various sources a Sacramentary for particular use. Of this, with proper differences, three editions are mentioned by him: one in use in his own abbey of Saint Martin at Tours, one sent to that of Fulda, and a third to the monks of Saint Vedast (St. Vaast) at Arras. A letter, dated in 801 or 802, accompanied his gift to the community of Fulda. It gave friendly exhortation, as from one who also relied on the prayers of Saint Boniface, "our Father"; then it continued: "I have sent you a Missal, holy priests, that you may have Masses for each day, to use as you will—of the Holy Trinity, of Wisdom, of Penitence, of Love, of the Holy Angels, of All Saints; for your own sins, for friends living and departed; of Blessed Mary, Mother of God, Ever-Virgin, of your own Saint Boniface."

The list given in his letter to the monks of Saint Vedast is not so long. In this he states: "I have sent you some Masses from our own Missal for use in daily rite and custom of the Church." Among these was a Mass of Saint Vedast, with a promise to keep his word to write a homily on the Saint for their pulpit.

This action of Alcuin marked at least a step in the path which led to the Catholic practice of the votive Mass of the Holy Trinity on Sunday (later, on Monday), of the Holy Angels on Tuesday, of the Holy Cross on Friday, of our Lady on Saturday.[62]

[62] *Epp.* IV, 405f., 455; Pamelius, *Liturg. Lat.* II, 517ff.; *PL* CI, coll. 445ff.; Cabrol, *RHE* XIX, 1923, 511ff.; *DACL* s.v. *Alcuin,* coll. 1078ff.; Levison, 158; Delisle, *Mémoires, Acad. des Inscr.* XXXII, i, 1886, 117, 247, 286; Leroquais I, 73, 113, 245. On the discrepancy between lists of Masses given by Alcuin in his letters, and the text of Migne, cited above, and on the problem of this text, see Hauck II, 141, note 6; for various theories in regard to the "Masses of Saint Augustine" (*PL* CI, coll. 446ff.), see W. Henry, *DACL,* s.v. *Augustin, Messes de Saint.* Cf., also, Micrologus, *De eccles. observ.* c. 60: *PL* CLI, col. 1020 (although he attributes far too much to Alcuin: Hauck II, 141). For the church of St. Vedast see Alcuin, *PLAC* I, 308ff., and, for his hymn in honour of this Saint, *ibid.* 313.

From Tours, also, and from Alcuin's compiling hand, there came to King Charles,[63] at his request, a manual of brief devotions for the Hours, suited for a layman's busy life.[64] Alcuin called this an "abbreviated" book, a "breviary," as he had previously described his short Commentary on the Preacher.[65] From this use of the word here, to describe a shortened handbook of prayers, sprang the name of the Catholic "Breviary." [66] In this royal *vade mecum* once again Alcuin's sources were liturgical, in that they gave to prayers for private use the moving dignity and beauty of the Church's rites.[67]

2

In the meantime life went on under his administration in the Abbey of Saint Martin at Tours, a responsibility that appealed directly to his heart and mind. Again and again in his letters to monks of various communities he dwelt upon the excellence of their calling: "A soldier fights better in company of battle formation than alone by himself on the plain, and by the plain I mean the open range of the world." "He who keeps vigil for the praises of God lives on earth as the angels and saints in heaven, save that they live ever thus, and human weakness only at appointed times." [68]

The aim of the monk's life, as Alcuin summed it up, is to do the will of God, and thus to work for the salvation of his

[63] Not, as Hauck suggests (II, 149, note 3), for the younger Charles.

[64] The compilations *De Psalmorum usu* (*PL* CI, coll. 465ff.) and *Officia per Ferias* (*ibid*. coll. 509ff.), although containing some writing by Alcuin, were made after his death; see Wilmart, *RB* XLVIII, 1936, 262ff. For the admonitio *Alcuini ad Carolum Magnum* see Wilmart, *Prec. Libelli IV aevi Kar.* I, 33ff.; cf. the *Confessio, ibid.* 21ff., and 163ff.

[65] *Epp.* IV, 407, 462.

[66] Bäumer, *Hist. du Bréviaire,* trans. Biron, II, 1905, 38, 425f.

[67] Cabrol, *DACL* s.v. *Alcuin,* col. 1084.

[68] *Epp.* IV, 430, 435.

own soul. But in this are bound up many commands, many forbiddings. The monk must keep the vow he has offered to God. He must remain faithful to his monastery, love and honour his abbot, ever be found reading in his own place in choir, not merely listening to words but giving to them all his thought. He is an individual soul; let that soul be free from all that is impure, greedy, self-indulgent, lazy. He is one of a community; love, obedience, humility, are the basic essentials of its character. The numerous exhortations of Alcuin to members of Religious Orders are supported by the official instructions given by Charles to his emissaries, that those dedicated under ecclesiastic rule do not wander abroad, be not given to evil money-making, plunder, sport or theft, to fornication, quarrelling, blasphemy, drunkenness, revelry or manslaughter.[69]

Further, so Alcuin wrote to his monastic friends: Let there be no discontent or murmuring of the brethren at one another or at the Father Abbot. Let all work as one, in fellowship, not only of secular but of spiritual possessions; let no time be wasted, as the monastic day passes from Mass and Office to work of the mind and of the hands. Let study be given to sacred writings, and secular; knowledge drawn from secular books is a weapon for good in the hands of the Church militant. It is no good to have libraries unless there be men to read and to understand. Nor does fame of glorious tradition avail an Abbey if its monks fall away from its former strictness of life. Of course, Alcuin warns, the novice must not expect perfection as he enters Religion. There are bad monks as well as good, just as failure was found among the angels, and sin in the Garden of Paradise. Let the monk, too, be found on his knees in Penance; better to feel shame before one

[69] *Ibid.* 444f., 438, 405, 276, 441, 98, 363, 430f., 434f.; *Cap. reg. Franc.* I, 92ff., 95f.

man here on earth than to meet the jeers of the Devil face to face on the Judgment Day.[70]

Various Father Abbots receive their exhortation individually. It is they who on that Day of Judgment will be called to account for the souls of their sons, at the peril of losing their own if they be found lacking. The progress of his monks in the spiritual life is to their Abbot his reward. Patience and forbearance he must have, if he will keep them in perseverance. It is he who must journey hither and thither that his monks may live, soul and body, and keep the Rule he has taught them. His heavy duty it is to reconcile their minds to necessary changes, to weld the community by prudent and wise selection of its members, as a bee plucking pollen from many flowers, into the compact honey of true Religion. Let the angels, as they visit his House of prayer at the appointed Hours, find him the first at the Work of God, leading his community in intercession for the people of Christ. Not a ring of gold on his finger, not a mantle of silk, shall be his treasure, but the church he shares with his brethren, and the stole of a holy life for the healing and nurture of all within its gates. Jealous he must be for his community's good fame, for Religion finds more critics than followers, and from the keynote of his own faithfulness will spring the chorus of its harmony.[71]

Toward this ideal of his own prescription Alcuin worked hard in these last years at Tours. His biographer, writing some twenty years after his death, urged men who would be monks to follow Benedict of Aniane, and those who desired the life of canons to follow Alcuin, for Alcuin's life, he declared, was

[70] *Epp.* IV, 314, 276, 445, 18, 438.

[71] *Ibid.* 277, 366f., 405, 431, 441, 445. The "Monastic Precepts" of *PLAC* I, 275ff., once assigned to Columban, are now generally attributed to Alcuin, who drew upon the verses of Cato; see Boas, 1ff.; Streib, *Münch. Mus. f. Philol. des Mittelalt. und der Renaiss.* II, 1914, 343ff.; Cappuyns, *BTAM* III, 1939, 377f.

"not inferior to the monastic." [72] We hear, from the same witness, of Alcuin's fasting, of his constant and regular prayer and intercession, of his recitation of Hours by night and by day, of his Mass, with different intentions for different days of the week, according to the use which he himself had compiled, of his strict observance of Sundays and holy-days. We are told, moreover, that he begged Charles to release him from his duties at Tours, as well as at his other monasteries at Ferrières and at Troyes, and to let him retire "to live the life of a Benedictine monk" at Fulda, and that he gave up this purpose only at the will of the Emperor.[73]

Undoubtedly, therefore, Alcuin looked upon the monastic life with intense reverence, even with longing in his own heart. Here, it is true, he never lost sight of the ideal, although, in prescribing for human life, he ruled his thought by practical considerations. "You have asked me, dear son," he wrote to one of his students who was lying near death from sickness, "which of the two lives brings one nearer Heaven; whether it is better to await one's last breath in the seat of a canon or in the holiness of a monk? I answer that God is everywhere and that He regards a man's deserving rather than his place on earth. If you have laboured for Him in the stole rather than in the cowl, why at the hour of death should you cast away the mark of your own particular toil and seek that of another sort? It may be that if by God's mercy you recover from this sickness, you will decide to fight the Christian battle under a monk's cowl; prayer and intercession of brethren in a monastery seem to promise solace and quiet for your body's need. But, all your life long, set your will and thought toward the greater profiting of God's holy Church." [74]

For others, then, he was always ambitious; he knew both

[72] *Alc. Vita,* 185 (prol.), 191. [73] *Ibid.* 191, 195f.

[74] *Epp.* IV, 99. The date is uncertain.

his own weaknesses and his own responsibilities, and lived accordingly. He was never addicted to abstinence, in the more extreme sense of the word, in excess of the Church's norm. He denied himself dishes he specially liked, but he drank the wine his friends offered, and enjoyed it. So Theodulf of Orléans describes him at Aachen, "gladly sitting at the board, it may be quaffing his cup that he may teach the better!" "Old wine *is* superior, and I am so glad you know this, dear brother," he wrote to that same Theodulf, "a great Bishop and Father of vineyards." [75]

Among his clergy, his students and boys at Tours, and there was "a great multitude," [76] we know the names of a few: Sigulf, Adalbert, Aldric, Raganard, Waldramn, Hildegar, Hatto, Raban, Amalar.

Sigulf, "Vetulus" as Alcuin called him, was his best-loved follower from the days in York onward. At Tours he was Alcuin's chaplain and said a private Mass for him every Sunday at daybreak before the conventual Mass.[77] Once, we are told, Sigulf called two young men, students in the community, to read Virgil with him, "in secret, lest the Father should hear of it." But Alcuin did hear, and rebuked him for his folly. So the story goes, although very probably it springs from the monastic narrator's sense of what was fitting. Alcuin's heart always contended with his conscience when it came to the *Aeneid*.[78]

[75] *PLAC* I, 488, ll. 191ff.; *Epp.* IV, 319; cf. page 159 *supra*. Of course, also, Alcuin wrote against *tristitia* and *acedia* as two of the great sins: *PL* CI, col. 635.

[76] *Epp.* IV, 416; cf. *Libri Confrat. S. Galli, MGH,* ed. Piper, 13ff.: a list of some 200 brethren, made soon after Alcuin's death.

[77] *Alc. Vita,* 196.

[78] *Alc. Vita,* 193; Poole, *Illust. of the hist. of med. thought,* 1920, 21. Cf. Hauck, II, 131 and note 3; 140, note 5: "Carmina sacra mit Hilfe der plectra Maronis." But Alcuin's conscience does seem to have won much from his heart during his latter years; cf. Kleinclausz, *Alcuin,* 185; Lohmeyer, *Vergil im deutschen Geistesleben bis auf Notker* III, 1930, 45ff., 92, 139, 141; Bäsecke, *DVLG* XXIII, 1949, 145f.

The two young novices were Adalbert and Aldric, and Sigulf was teaching them under Alcuin, either at Saint Martin's or at the abbey of Ferrières. He succeeded Alcuin as abbot of Ferrières, and in his turn resigned his rule there to this same Adalbert, content to obey as a humble monk one of his own spiritual sons.[79] Adalbert had passed from his training at Tours to study things sacred and secular under Arno of Salzburg, where his knowledge of languages, especially of German, his native tongue, made him of special value. Alcuin wrote of him to Arno: "Be good to my 'Black Scholar,' *Magus meus niger*"—a name given for his raven hair and his quick mind—"for he will be useful in the house of God. He was very willing and humble when he was with us, in the service of the Church and in study of books. See that he shares his learning with many others." He became chaplain to Arno, then went to Ferrières and ruled until 821.[80]

Aldric followed him in this abbacy. He came of a Frankish family well-known at the Court of Charles and was excellently educated as a lad in both "the liberal arts and spiritual disciplines." Then desire for monastic life drove him to learn under Alcuin at Saint Martin's, and under Arno at Salzburg, where we find him, first as deacon, then as chaplain to the Archbishop. Under Sigulf and Adalbert he was one of the community at Ferrières, governed it from 821 until 829, and then was Archbishop of Sens until his death in 836.[81]

Raganard and Waldramn are but names, although Raganard serves to give us another glimpse of Alcuin as abbot. Raganard's excessive zeal for secret watching in prayer at night and for fasting brought on not only a sharp attack of

[79] *Alc. Vita,* 191; Servatus Lupus, ed. Levillain, II, 206; I, 6; *PL* CV, col. 803.

[80] *Epp.* IV, 253f., 320f., 322, 416, 418, 422; *PLAC* I, 249, l. 4; 269, l. 1. Adalbert seems to have ruled under Alcuin a monastic school at Berg: *PLAC* I, 249, l. 9; K. Voigt, *Die karol. Klosterpolitik,* 59.

[81] *Aldrici Vita: PL* CV, coll. 799ff.; *Epp.* IV, 418, 422.

fever but a still sharper rebuke from the Father, to whom, he imagined, the Lord alone could have revealed his carefully hidden devotions.[82]

Hatto and Raban came from the monastery of Fulda. Raban, Alcuin's most famous pupil, was sent to him about 802 by its Abbot Ratgar, "to learn the liberal arts, the science of metric and Holy Scripture," but was under him only for a short time. Alcuin called him "Maurus," after the disciple of Saint Benedict of Monte Cassino, and wrote to him under that name.[83] On him we shall dwell a little later, and also on Hildegar and on Amalar of Metz.[84]

Many were the happy hours that the Master spent with these and with others who came to Tours for the good fame of his learning. "How sweet was life," he wrote to one of them, "while we sat quietly among the rolls of the wise, among abundance of books, among the judgments of the reverend Fathers! We lacked nothing which was needed for the life of religion and of learning . . . Follow, my son, whatever of goodly custom you saw among us, that God may bless you thereby; flee anything you marked here of error and impious way, lest you be caught with us in our sins. Do not forget the daily round of Hours, of the rites of holy Mass, or the Vigils of the Saints as you knew them in our Chapel."[85]

And many were the hours of peace which Alcuin spent in his study at Saint Martin's. We have tarried some time with his letters, with his formal writings; it may be worth while to spend a moment on his verses, the delight of his leisure at home. In comparison with other Carolingian writers, with

[82] *Alc. Vita,* 191f.

[83] *Cat. abb. Fuld.: SS* XIII, 272; *Epp.* V, 403, 489; *PLAC* II, 159f., cf. I, 264; *Epp.* IV, 223f. On the date of Raban's coming to Tours see Hauck II, 157, note 3, against Dümmler, *NA* XVIII, 1893, 67.

[84] Pages 287f., 310 *infra.*

[85] *Epp.* IV, 439f., cf. 359.

Theodulf, with Walafrid Strabo, with Gottschalk, his merit in verse fades away.[86] Yet Theodulf in his courtly words called Alcuin "the glory of our poets," and Theodulf's friend, Modoin, bishop of Autun under Louis the Pious and himself known as "Naso" in the Court of Charles, sang Alcuin's praise in his own pastoral hexameters:

> Had Flaccus not been skilled to pipe his songs,
> Not his had been the prizes of this life! [87]

In the multitude of Latin verses which he poured out for his friends and his sons in the Spirit there is that same intense desire, that same hunger for affection, which is seen throughout his letters. The "poems" are, indeed, very often letters in verse—to the King and Emperor, Charles, to members of the royal family, to the Pope, to all for whom he cared—written, as the letters in prose, to share their joy or their sorrow, to encourage or to warn. There are dedications: for his own writings, for churches and their altars and chapels, for monasteries and their different parts—dormitory, library, refectory, burial-ground; there are epitaphs and hymns, prayer for travellers and grace for meals.[88]

There are, also, verses that tell of his own physical and spiritual feeling and need. Like all Englishmen, Alcuin loved the spring, its quickening warmth and colour and light. For his young friends in York he writes some lines: "The cuckoo

[86] It is the spirit of Alcuin rather than his merit as poet that attracts the reader; cf. Raby, *SLP* I, 185ff. For rhythms perhaps constructed by him see Strecker, *PLAC* IV, 3, 903ff.; Raby, *SLP* I, 182; *CLP*, 160, note 2; for the "dreadful picture-acrostic," *SLP* I, 187; Dümmler, *PLAC* I, 224ff. On Alcuin and Anglo-Saxon verse cf. Ogilvy, *Mod. Lang. Notes* XLVI, 1931, 444f.

[87] *PLAC* I, 486, l. 131; 387, ll. 87f. On Modoin's verse see Raby, *SLP* I, 202ff.; Lohmeyer, 144f.; Manitius, 549ff. Cf. Ebert, *ZDA* XXII, 1878, 330, on Naso = Corydon; *PLAC* I, 250 (XXXII, ll. 33f.).

[88] Levison, 162, note 2, for source material used by Alcuin; for hymns, Dreves, *Anal. Hymn. L*, 1907, 152ff.

now is crying on the bough, the earth is bright with flowers. It is Spring! And Father Alcuin sends you his greeting across the sea, that blessing be upon you, and evil far away. . . ." [89] Like all in Europe, he knew the early signs of its coming in the dark, cold days of the rain and the wind, and so perhaps it was he who pictured in Latin hexameters the "Strife between Spring and Winter." [90] The shepherds have come down from the high pasture lands to sing praise to the cuckoo, herald of their joy. Yet Old Man Winter is loath to yield his rule to Spring, the new-born Child of the Year, and the two contend in song for the prize of the season's life. Does not the cuckoo, Spring tells, bring growing light and budding meadows, birds building nests, ships once more free to voyage, warmth of the sun and bees among the honey? Who cares for sluggish Winter, sleep beside the fire, feasting and carefree idleness? Better to be quick with life, even though life bring toil and battle, than dead in sloth!

And thus the shepherds will it. Let the cuckoo come, their friend:

[89] *PLAC* I, 273. For the cuckoo, the swallow, and the nightingale in 8th and 9th century verse see Raby, *SLP* I, 183ff., 208, 235, 250f.; page 154 *supra*. Alcuin also received from the "Eboracensis ecclesiae scolastici" verses on Saint Ninian; ed. Strecker, *PLAC* IV, 3, 943ff.; *Epp.* IV, 431; Levison, 161, and *Antiquity* XIV, 1940, 282ff. He was a friend of Ethelbert, bishop of Whithorn, 777–789, and of Hexham, 789–797: *Epp.* IV, 27, 72f.

[90] Alcuin's authorship of this poem has been denied on the ground that its writer was echoing Horace (l. 50); see P. von Winterfeld, *RM* LX, 1905, 35ff.: "Sie kommt aus Karls Kreise, aber Alcvin der Pedant . . . ist nicht der Dichter. Das mag vielleicht doch ein Ire gewesen sein." Waddell, however (*Med. Lat. Lyr.* 310), suggests that Alcuin may have learned something of Horace from the Irish Colcu and Joseph; cf. Dümmler, *Alchvinstudien,* 505f.; Hauck II, 137, note 7. Dümmler (*PLAC* I, 270ff.) and Waddell (82ff.) assign the poem to Alcuin. H. Walther, *Das Streitgedicht in der lat. Lit. des Mittelalters,* 1920, 36, and Raby, *SLP* I, 208f. leave the question definitely undecided. Traube, *Karol. Dicht.* 76, is against Alcuin here on metrical evidence. Miss Waddell's translation should be read: 83ff.

Dear Love awaits thee, guest most dear to all;
All things await thee, sea and earth and sky.
Hail, our dear glory, through the ages, hail!

From his little cell Alcuin looked out upon the growing loveliness of the spring in France and knew that this beauty of earth was not his for long. We should like to think that it was he who thus sang his farewell:

O my cell, dear home of mine, beloved,
For evermore, dear cell of mine, goodbye!
Around you as a guard the whispering trees
Stand, heavy with their blossom on the bough.
Again, when I am gone, the fields around
Will spring with healing herbs anew,
The river will flow past its primrose banks,
The angler wait in joy to cast his line.
Fragrant in cloistered peace your orchards here,
Your lilies clustering white among the rose;
Your birds, of every sort, their Matins tell,
Their symphony, for Him Who maketh all.
In you, my cell, once rang your Master's words,
That taught of Holy Wisdom from his books,
In you, the chanting of the Hours' fixed times
Renewed God's praise in peace of heart and voice.[91]

All things change, and the little room will soon know a stranger within its walls. Night is settling over the day, winter follows the flowers of spring, storm is stirring the tranquil sea. The nightingale has flown from the thorn outside the

[91] *PLAC* I, 243, No. XXIII, ll. 1–16; in Alcuin's Latin "truly beautiful lines, but the rest is commonplace": Laistner, 281. This poem has been assigned to Fridugis, a "Lament for Alcuin"; see Waddell, 96f., 310; so also Jack Lindsay, *Medieval Latin Poets,* 1934, 48f. It is given to Alcuin, however, by Dümmler, *PLAC* I, 243f., and by Allen, *Rom. Lyric,* 353, 240 (translation by H. Mumford Jones). Cf. Alcuin: *O mea cara domus: PLAC* I, 250f. Another suggestion sees in it a reference to Alcuin's cell at York (Foligno, *Latin Thought during the M.A.,* 1929, 82), another (Kleinclausz, *Alcuin,* 174), to his cell at Cormery; another (H. O. Taylor II, 163) sees in it the artificial verse of a city dweller imitating classic poetry.

cell. Throughout this world's dark night her voice, so great for one so small, trilled to give glory to God, and new heart to one that watched alone in prayer. Teach us, O happy bird of song, to find more sweet His praise than the lusts of this body's flesh on earth! [92]

Sometimes among the greetings and hopes for his friends we find Alcuin's verses of prayer for himself. Such is this brief litany: [93]

Have mercy, Lord, have mercy, Christ! Let
Thy mercy be upon me, as mine upon other men,
That I may believe in Thee,
That I may learn Thee,
That I may love Thee,
That I may hope in Thee,
That my soul may live in Thee,
That my soul may be glad in Thee,
That my life may avail in Thee!
Have mercy, Saviour Christ, my health, my strength,
Have mercy, Spirit of Counsel, my comfort, mine enlightening!
Have mercy, Lord God, Trinity and Unity!
Thee I praise, Thee I adore, Thee I confess,
My peace, my hope, my praise, my light,
Thou, unto me beauty, unto me blessedness.
To Thee be praise and glory and thanksgiving,
Always and everywhere, unto all ages.

[92] *PLAC* I, 274f., trans. by Waddell, 88f.; Allen, *Rom. Lyric* (trans. H. Mumford Jones), 148f. For discussion of influence of the *philomela* of Eugenius of Toledo on Alcuin's nightingale see Raby, *SLP* I, 151, 184; cf. E. R. Curtius, *DVLG* XVI, 1938, 467: "real vorhandene Naturerlebnis in traditionelle und konventionelle Stilformen gegossen wurde." For Alcuin's knowledge of the verse of Eugenius cf. Manitius I, 197.

[93] *PLAC* I, 303, iii; cf. Wilmart, *Prec. Lib.* I, 123f., and see Miss Waddell's translation (*Med. Lat. Lyr.*, 91ff.) of Alcuin's *Sequence for Saint Michael: PLAC* I, 348f. (Dreves denies this to Alcuin: *Anal. Hymn.* L, 153).

Yet there were other things, less good to feel and to know, that entered into Alcuin's mind at Tours. In the first place, the life and discipline of the more than two hundred brethren at Saint Martin's at this time was not so devoted as he willed to believe it. Not only the outside world, but its own monks within differed in varying concepts of their exact status and of what was required of them in obedience to its Rule; confusion naturally flourished among men who had various ideals, various practices, of greater or less austerity. It is, therefore, not surprising that not long after Alcuin's death Saint Martin's became a Collegiate Church, of secular canons governed by a lay "abbot." [94] The same period saw, at the Councils of Aachen in 816 and 817, provision of strict regulation by Louis the Pious and Benedict of Aniane for the dispelling of the continued irregularity and looseness in Frankish religious life, both monastic and canonical.[95]

It was the desire of the King-Emperor to bring all the Regular monasteries in his realms under the Rule of Saint Benedict, as the records of Councils and Capitularies clearly show. "Were there any monks at all in Gaul," he asked officially in 811, "before this Rule was followed in its dioceses?" [96] Yet under him, by his enactment, while monks were to practise the Benedictine tradition, canons were to live according to the life proper for them, and exact understanding was to be

[94] On the history of Saint Martin's and of its abbot Fridugis, see *Gallia Christiana* XIV, 152ff.; Vaucelle, (see Ch. IV, note 70 *supra*) 63f.; Dalton, *Hist. of the Franks* I, 352, note 2; Deanesly, *Trans. Royal Hist. Soc.*, Series 4, XXIII, 1941, 43; Piper, ed. *Libri Confrat. S. Galli*, 13f.; Traube, *Vorles. und Abh.* III, 31; Pückert, 33, 255; *Folcwini Gesta abb. S. Bertini Sith.: SS* XIII, 614; de Moreau, *Hist. de l'Eglise en Belgique* I, 1945, 223f.; Hauck II, 587, note 5.

[95] *Cap. reg. Fr.* I, 343ff.; Mansi XIV, 147ff.; *Conc. aevi Kar.* I, 308ff.

[96] *Cap. reg. Fr.* I, 162; Philibert Schmitz, *Hist. de l'Ordre de S. Benoît* I, 1942, 87f.

held of the discipline needed for each manner of dedication.[97] Archbishop Arno wrote from Salzburg in 802 to beg Alcuin to examine into the two vocations, and Alcuin answered: "About the life of canons and the Regular ordering of monks, what can *we* do? I cannot get busy at all, and you are too busy with other things. Besides, how could I advise you, who have been familiar with these matters since you were a baby? . . . There should, of course, be a careful enquiry into what is proper for the three lives, of canons, of monks, and of the third kind which lies between these—higher than that of canons and lower than that of monks—a life not to be despised, since it is truly part of the household of God." [98]

Secondly, the Abbey of Saint Martin at Tours was revered above all cloisters in Frankland. Endowments of land and money had been lavished upon it by Charles and by his nobles; offerings of the devout had swelled its coffers. Slaves in multitude, as Elipand had taunted Alcuin, worked its farms and fields; its revenues were free of taxation; its shrine of Saint Martin was richly adorned.[99]

The King had hoped by his gifts and exemptions to release the brethren from secular burdens and thus to give them leisure for their vocation of prayer and sacred study.[100] They were, indeed, as free as was possible within the discipline of their own community, responsible to the abbot of their own choice, subject to their bishop only in cases of crisis and in times that called for episcopal rites and ceremonies.[101] In actual practice, nevertheless, their wealth, joined with the un-

[97] *Cap. reg. Fr.*, 105; *Conc. aevi Kar.* I, 230, for prescriptions put forward at the Council at Aachen in 802, drawn very largely from the *Collectio Dionysio-Hadriana*; Halphen, *Charlemagne*, 217.

[98] *Epp.* IV, 411, 416.

[99] *Diplom. Karol.* I, Nos. 81, 141, 167; Kleinclausz, *Alcuin*, 160ff.

[100] *Diplom. Kar.* I, No. 97, page 140.

[101] Cf. *ibid.* No. 195.

certainty of religious status and Rule which prevailed, had seriously undermined their morale, and Alcuin had found a heavy task in readiness for him at his arrival. On the other hand, his need for order, justice, and honest dealing kept him constantly busy with overseers, accounts, and correspondence.[102]

The fame, also, of the Church with its tomb of Saint Martin drew countless sightseers, pilgrims, penitents, of all sorts, conditions, and character, to its walls; and the abbot's prayer and study were constantly interrupted to attend to their wants. No doubt, it was glorious to be in charge of so sacred a place, although Tours, in Alcuin's eyes, was a contemptible little town, only high in honour for the miracles, still seen in abundance, of its holy Patron.[103] But, as he worked upon that Saint's *Life* by Sulpicius Severus in order to bring it into more concise form before his people,[104] he knew that he himself could not live in Tours as Martin had lived, in contemplation there and at Marmoutier near by.

According to his biographer, who declares that he drew his material from Sigulf himself, "Alcuin did his best to guide and rule those under obedience to him at Tours, and worked hard to discipline the unruly element he had received." One of those difficult to lead was a nephew of Arno, sent by him from Salzburg, Hildegar by name. Alcuin had been generous, but the lad was most unhappy, doing no good to himself or to anyone else. Finally he was despatched back, "lest I labour in vain and he lose his soul," Alcuin wrote to the irate uncle.

[102] As evidence of Alcuin's care see his letter of courteous indignation to Raganbert, bishop of Limoges, whose *missi* had declared novel taxation against the property and priests of St. Martin's: *Potens est sanctus Martinus apud Deum defendere res suas, si necesse est illi clamare ad Deum: Epp.* IV, 456f. The taxes imposed are listed by him in detail.

[103] Alcuin, *Vita Willibrordi: SRM* VII, 139.

[104] *PL* CI, coll. 657ff.

"Don't be angry with him," he added, "I knew he didn't want to be a monk, and you do well to let him stay in the world." [105]

At times, therefore, the Abbot of Saint Martin's thought back upon the years in York and in Aachen and sorely missed their happy associations. He greeted with joy visitors from England—with so great joy, indeed, that the brethren of Tours grew jealous. "O God!" they muttered, "deliver this monastery from these Britishers, who come swarming round this countryman of theirs, like bees returning to the Mother-bee!" [106]

It may be, also, that the Irishmen, Clement, Dungal of Saint Denis, and Dicuil, the geographer, grammarian, computist, were already entering upon debate, intellectual and spiritual, with Charles at the Palace Court, in that play of minds which Alcuin so long had delighted in as his.[107] Not that he himself shared the keen dislike of the Irish which was felt by Theodulf and others at the Court, probably inspired by resentment at Irish quickness of wit and love of dialectic. His letters prove the contrary. To monks in Ireland he wrote, from Aachen or from Tours, of his happiness that "the Lord Jesus in this age of decay and world's end has such men, to praise His holy Name and preach His Truth and follow His Wisdom, as I hear your famous island still possesses today. . . . In days of old, learned masters came from Ireland to Britain, Gaul, Italy, and wrought much profit among the churches of Christ." [108]

Yet the Irish, with all their Catholic devotion, did love

[105] *Epp.* IV, 257 (dated by Jaffé 797), 253, 320.

[106] *Alc. Vita,* 193.

[107] For this Dungal see Traube, "O Roma nobilis," 332ff.; Kenney, 538ff.; *Epp.* IV, 568ff.; *PLAC* I, 393ff.; Manitius, 370ff. For Dicuil see Manitius, 647ff.; Kenney, 545ff. Cf. Gougaud, *Christianity in Celtic lands,* trans. Joynt, 1932, 300f.

[108] *Epp.* IV, 437; cf. 445f.; Gougaud, 130, 299.

secular Latin poetry, did love debate and inquiry, scientific and literary. To Alcuin, with his intense respect for authority, this seemed at times to call for caution, if not a deeper restraint; perhaps a knowledge that the Irishman Clement was now leading the Palace School gave him from time to time a dismay which he tried to conquer.[109] There was nothing that he could do about it. Times were changing; the "Egyptianizing" young men were filling the Court with their argument; the Emperor delighted in it and would be impatient of old-fashioned reluctance to follow in its course; old Entellus must yield to the more modern ways of Dares, his junior, the lamb to the lion, the poor hare to the wild boar! The playfulness of the words written to Charles does not conceal a trace of bitterness.[110]

Conjecture, however, has seen in such a mention of "the Spanish Dares" a reference to Theodulf of Orléans.[111] There is no proof of this, and we have seen that the two men corresponded in gay and friendly manner. In 801 Alcuin wrote to congratulate Theodulf warmly upon his elevation to the Archbishopric of Orléans.[112] His own sober and serious spirit differed immensely, it is true, from the quick, urbane and sophisticated mind which had so attracted King Charles toward his Spanish courtier; and there may have been some temptation of envy.

At any rate, perhaps unexpectedly, a storm now blew up, compared with which the clouds of Alcuin's days at Tours

[109] Kleinclausz, *Alcuin,* 272f.; Gougaud, 166. On Clement see Manitius, 456f.; Kenney, 538; Poole, *Illustrations,* 20f. Crawford (105f.), writing on the Library at York in Alcuin's time, remarks: "No apocryphal work occurs, nor any writer whose opinions rendered him suspect. To provide such works was the privilege of the Irish, whose fondness for so dangerous a text as Martianus Capella was notorious."

[110] *Epp.* IV, 231, 234f.; Hauréau, *Singularités,* 22ff.; Monnier, *Alcuin,* 96f.

[111] *Epp.* IV, 266, note 6.

[112] *Ibid.* 368; page 278.

were as nothing. We learn of it from a long letter sent off by him post-haste, late in 801 or in 802, telling his former students Candidus and Fridugis, still in service in the Court of Charles, all that had happened.[113]

One of the clerics of the see of Orléans had escaped from severe punishment, inflicted for serious crime, and had fled to sanctuary in Saint Martin's Church. In Alcuin's opinion, he was sincerely penitent; he had confessed his guilt to a priest at Saint Martin's, and was asking that he be taken for judgment to the presence of the Emperor himself. Theodulf, however, had sent officials to claim him, and he had been handed over to their keeping. As they were starting with their prisoner on the way back to Orléans, word was brought of men lying in wait to attack them on the road. Promptly fleeing home, they left their charge once more in the shelter of the Church. Again Theodulf sent men, this time fully armed, to seize the culprit; and eight of the leaders among these entered the Church on a Sunday, escorted by Joseph, Archbishop of Tours. A hot struggle ensued between them and the brethren of Saint Martin's over the fugitive, crouching between the altar and the tomb of the Saint. Rumour spread throughout Tours that the shrine was being attacked by men of Orléans, many of whom were working on farms throughout the countryside; and from all quarters the citizens of Tours, especially the poor who looked to Saint Martin's for alms, rushed to defend their most sacred possession. Fear and confusion ran riot in the streets and in the Church itself, until Alcuin's followers rescued the officials from Orléans, now in peril of their lives from the angry mob, and cleared the way for peace.

At once Archbishop Theodulf wrote to Charles to complain of this action at Tours,[114] and Alcuin now bade his young

[113] *Epp.* IV, 393ff.
[114] This letter is not extant.

friends at Court to defend what had been done by its community. At great length he dwelt on the man's penitence, on his right to seek the Emperor, on the divine quality of mercy, on the privilege of sanctuary, recognized not only by the canons of the Church but by barbarians and heathen alike. "Is the church of Christ of less honour among Christians than the temple of Jupiter among pagans? Is the house of blessed Mary, Mother of God, to be revered less than the sanctuary of evil Juno?"

These pleadings and arguments did not appeal to Charles' sense of justice, and he sent to the Abbot and congregation of Saint Martin a caustic reprimand.[115] "A letter reached me from Theodulf the day before yours," wrote the angry ruler, "complaining of dishonour done to his men, and not so much to them as to the Bishop, and that, too, in contempt of an order of our realm. This order, for the return of a certain cleric, a fugitive from Theodulf's hands, hiding in the Church of Saint Martin, was issued under our own name and authority. . . . Your letter"—this was directed against Alcuin—"seemed to us far more angry than that of Theodulf, one not written in charity, but in defence of the guilty man and in accusation of his Bishop. It is not to the point," Charles went on, "for you to bring forward Saint Paul's appeal to Caesar. Saint Paul, unlike this notorious clerk, had not been found guilty of the crime alleged against him. Let this clerk, we command, be returned to Theodulf, from whose keeping he escaped, before whom he was tried, condemned, and sent into punishment. We are exceedingly surprised, however, that it has seemed good to you all to oppose our authority and ordering. It is perfectly evident that such decrees of ours have their origin in ancient usage and in constitutional law and that no one has the right to hold them in contempt. We are

[115] *Epp.* IV, 399ff.

the more exceedingly astonished that you preferred to yield to this criminal's prayers rather than to obey our will."

Then, in a final outpouring of wrath upon the brethren of Saint Martin's: "Well do you know, you who are called the congregation of this monastery, and the servants of God—may the description be a true one!—how many charges, and how often, are brought against your manner of life, and not without cause. Sometimes you have declared yourselves monks, sometimes canons, sometimes neither. It was I who, for your sakes and for the abolishing of the community's bad reputation, chose for you a fitting master and ruler and called him from a great distance that by his counsels and rebukes he might teach you to live aright and, as one devoted to religion, might train you by the example of his own goodly conduct. But, unhappily, everything has turned out otherwise, and the Devil has found in you his ministers, so to speak, for the sowing of discord where least of all it should be sown, between two wise men, doctors of the Church. The very men who ought to correct and punish sinners, those men you force toward the sin of envy and anger. In God's mercy they will not listen to your evil promptings!

"So now, whether you are called canons or monks, you who have held our order in contempt, it is for you to appear before our court of justice, as our envoy shall direct. . . ."

Alcuin was not slow to defend his sons in the cloister at Tours. "I call God to witness," he wrote to Charles,[116] "that I have never known them such as I hear they are said to be by those who are more ready to accuse than to save. So far as may truly be seen and known, they serve God worthily in the churches, and, I speak with all sincerity, I have never seen men anywhere working more perfectly in daily life for your health and for the firm standing of your Christian rule."

[116] *Ibid.* 401ff.

Neither he himself, he declared, nor any of his clergy had had any share, had any knowledge of the uprising in Saint Martin's Church. The officer in charge of the prisoner was, first of all, in fault for his carelessness in allowing him to escape. Then the citizens of Tours, naturally jealous for their sacred treasure, the tomb of Martin, had hastened to defend it with more zeal than discretion, egged on by rumours, by the noise and shouting, by smouldering of hostility among the crowd in the street, some of them doubtless the worse for drink, and all of them ready to act without thinking! The sight of their own Archbishop of Tours—it really was rather foolish, even if he did think the criminal should be captured—leading these strangers from Orléans into Saint Martin's Church, had brought the contention into open flame. The street seemed to be full of men from Orléans, those, so many of them, who dwelt throughout that neighbourhood. The men of Tours ran to ring the bells; the clergy of Saint Martin's ran out to see what was going on! In the end the clergy themselves actually quieted the mob, rescuing the envoys of Theodulf from their hands and bringing them into Saint Martin's cloister, where these envoys, Alcuin sorrowfully ended, "burst out in fiery wrath against me, who had worked to help them."

Such was his plea, and it came from a sore heart: "In vain have I served so long my Lord Jesus Christ if His mercy and care have so far deserted me that I should fall into the sin of disloyalty in my old age. Truly, without a moment's hesitation do I declare, that not for all the gold in France would I have worked to raise so perilous a tumult in the Church of Christ!"

The Emperor's emissary, Teotbert, stayed nearly three weeks in Tours for official investigation of those said to be implicated, inflicting upon them various penalties. Some were flogged, some were sent to prison, some were ordered to give witness on oath, others were despatched for judgment before Charles.[117]

It is a sorry recital, yet it holds one lighter note. As Alcuin hurries off one of his young novices from the peril of Tours to the protection of his faithful Arno at Salzburg, he writes: "I have sent you this tame calf of mine; do help him all you can and snatch him from his enemies. For that venerable Bishop, I mean Theodulf, is blazing with wrath against us. The calf is a reasoning animal and will bellow out all the story into your holy ears! He is learning here with me, and, God grant, will do well in his reading and grammar at Saint Martin's. O my Eagle Arno! 'Some put their trust in chariots and some in horses; but we will glory in the Name of our God!' "[118]

3

Meanwhile the world, both East and West, was still in misery and discord. In the East, Aetius, the eunuch minister of the Empress Irene, now well content at the death of his rival, Stauracius, was doing his utmost to raise his brother Leo to the Imperial throne. Plot and sedition were busily brewing, and Aetius was already well aware of other men whose power and schemes matched his own. Then in 802—if the Greek chronicler may be believed—messengers arrived from the Emperor Charles and from Pope Leo the third, bearing a proposal of marriage between Charles and the Lady Irene.[119]

The Frankish annals, also, tell of interchange of amenities between Frankland and Constantinople,[120] in a resuming, we may suppose, of more or less courteous relations after the rupture caused by iconoclasm, by the Council of Frankfurt

[117] *Ibid.* 402.
[118] *Ibid.* 401.
[119] Theophanes, 475.
[120] *ARF ann.* 802.

and the *Caroline Books*. But only Theophanes tells of this project of marriage, and his story has naturally met with much doubt and discussion.[121] Is the story true? Did Pope Leo the third see danger for the Church in a new rising to power of Constantinople, once linked with the Frankish realm? Or was the marriage part of a Papal purpose for the transferring of Imperial power from East to West? Did Charles hope through this union to turn the iconodulic spirit of Irene toward harmony with his own cooler temperament, and to confirm Aachen as seat of Imperial power in the world by bringing her there from Constantinople? Did she herself, as her strength weakened through age and sickness, as she saw around her those many enemies among her scheming nobles, among her soldiers, as she faced, now the iconoclasts who hated her cult of images, now those who watched jealously to see that she yielded none of this cult to outside influence, as she remembered that upon her death the Isaurian line would lapse and that no successor to the throne had been appointed, as she knew among her subjects the distrust and shame that a woman "Emperor" cast upon East and West alike—did she long to have beside her a man, a partner, with whom she could share Imperial dignity, who would save her self-respect?

She was tempted by the project of this Frankish marriage, it would seem, and in this tempting found destruction. Neither Aetius nor those who cared fiercely for holy images or for their Eastern power would tolerate a master from the West, a ruler in Aachen. Revolution broke out in Constantinople. On the night of October the 31st, Nicephorus, Patrician and

[121] For discussion see Ohnsorge, 20, 25f.; Halphen, *Charlemagne*, 135; Diehl, *Byz. Portraits*, 99f.; *CMH* IV, 24; Bury, *Hermathena* VIII, 1893, 17ff.; *Later Rom. Empire* II, 490; Vasiliev I, 354f.; Bryce, 66ff.; Ostrogorsky, *Gesch.* 128, note 2; for ancient authority, Theophanes, 475; *Ann. Lauresh. ann.* 801: *SS* I, 38.

Controller of the Public Treasury,[122] seized the Imperial Palace by aid of his supporters and was proclaimed Emperor, "God acquiescing in these monstrous decisions," wrote Theophanes, "because of the multitude of our sins." Irene, who was absent from the city in her Palace of Eleutherion, at daybreak was taken under guard to Constantinople and kept closely imprisoned, while in its great Church of Saint Sophia Nicephorus was proclaimed Emperor in her stead. The day, according to Theophanes, prophesied what was to be—a day cold and dark, lowering and sullen. On the morrow, he goes on, the new ruler went to make peace with his captive, declared that his action had been forced upon him, that she was to receive all kindly and worthy care and respect. Would she please at once reveal to him the hiding-place of the Imperial treasure? The ex-Empress offered no resistance, only asked that she might live in retirement at her favourite Eleutherian Palace. But she was promptly banished, under—so Theophanes declared—the very eyes of legates of Charles from Frankland, to a convent she herself had founded upon one of the lonely Princes' Islands in the Sea of Marmora. In the deep cold of the following winter, Nicephorus transferred her for his safety to the more remote Lesbos. There she died, attended by none but her guards, on August 9, 803, and was held by Theophanes and other churchmen of Constantinople as a saint and a martyr.[123] Alcuin maintained silence; he was thinking of other things.

Britain was nearer. From it came bad news regarding his former student "Simeon," Eanbald the second, Archbishop of York. In that letter of 800, sent to Calvinus, priest of Saint Stephen's cell in northern England, Alcuin had written: "My

[122] Diehl, *CMH* IV, 24f., 731. [123] *Chronographia,* 478.

dearest son, Simeon, is enduring the same vexations from the wicked as those who lived before him. Do you aid his good will by your prayers; urge and exhort him to act bravely, never to relax. I, his unworthy Father, fed and reared him, brought him to that mature man whom you chose as your Archbishop. Tell him to stand ever on guard, for he lives among wolves and serpents. Warn him constantly not to love this present world, not to listen to flattery, not to let the crowd that attends him turn his mind to ambition or greed." [124]

Eanbald himself, as Alcuin wrote him in a letter of 801, was perhaps partly to blame. Was he not giving shelter to the enemies of King Eardwulf and protecting their property? [125] Eardwulf, that King of Northumbria for now five years whom Alcuin had censured for loose living, had marched against the Mercian King Cenwulf because of this same "harbouring of enemies." [126] "Do not run away," Alcuin now counsels the Archbishop of York. "You have seen how kings have perished, those chieftains who withstood your predecessors and the Church of Christ.[127] If men think they can rage as they will,[128] does God sleep?"

Other matters, also, gave him dissatisfaction concerning Eanbald in this year of 801. "I have sent you my 'Cuckoo,' the bird of spring,[129] with some little gifts, wine for you and your friends, a hundred pounds of tin for necessary repairs, and four grilles of lattice-work. It seems only right that your bell-tower should be roofed over, for its own beauty and for the fame of its House.

"I don't know why you asked me about the Use of your

[124] *Epp.* IV, 347f.; cf. 351. [125] *Ibid.* 377; H. S. III, 535.
[126] Sym. Dun. II, 65, *ann.* 801.
[127] Elfwald and Ethelred; pages 158, 165 *supra.*
[128] A reference to the sins of King Eardwulf; page 208 *supra.*
[129] P. 154 *supra.* If this "Cuculus" be the same, it would seem that he had repented his backsliding.

Service and your Missal. Do you not have service-books in plenty after the Roman Use? You have also enough Sacramentaries of larger size according to the ancient usage. What need of composing new books when there is sufficient of the old?" For Eanbald, it seems, had asked Alcuin to arrange a new Book of Sacraments for the use of the Church in Northumbria as he had done in Frankland for Charles.

"I could have wished," Alcuin goes on, "that you had set the example of the Roman Use among your clergy, that the rites of the Church may be in good and reverent practice among you. But, you may say, there are few to aid. To which I reply, the harder the toil of good intention, the nobler the crown of perfect joy. The aforesaid bird can tell you of my infirmity. Glory be to God, I am somewhat better. But not well as I used to be." [130]

A more troubled note appears in another letter to Calvinus and "Cuculus": "I am afraid that Simeon is suffering somewhat for aiding the properties, or even the persons, of the King's enemies. He should be content with his own possessions and not have to do with those of other men, a thing that often brings danger. He is helping a few, so he thinks. In reality, he is harming many for whom it is his business to intercede day by day, and he may hurt the flock he has to rule.

"And *why* this great multitude of soldiers in his company? He makes out that he takes them for sake of charity. But he is injuring the monasteries, who have to entertain them with him. He has many more, I hear, than his predecessors. Also he has far more soldiers of the common rank and file under him than he should. Our master, Aelbert, allowed none of his

[130] *Epp.* IV, 370; H. S. III, 508. Alcuin's words here are of interest as coming from the compiler of a Sacramentary for Frankland; cf. Bishop, 55, note 1; Morin, *RB* XXIX, 345. For use of the "Gelasian" Sacramentary in northern England of the 8th century see Bannister, *JTS* IX, 1908, 399f.; XII, 1911, 452; Frere, *Studies* I, 44f.

staff to have more than one, except the heads of his household, who were allowed two." [131]

In the southern province the old trouble still persisted. The existence of two sees, of Canterbury and of Lichfield, was still vexing Ethelhard, Archbishop of Canterbury, and in 801 he left England to consult the Pope on the matter in Rome. Alcuin hurried off a word of warning: "I tried to induce you to stay at home, for I did not want the light of Britain to go out. But God's will be done for the good of His Church, and if your will is such as I found it in your letter and you meet with your desire, I admit I am well content. But return, when once your mission is over.

"If you visit our Lord King Charles, warn your staff, especially your clergy, that they observe scrupulously their calling in regard to dress and religious prescription. Don't let them wear gold and silk in the royal Presence, but appear in humble fashion after the manner of servants of God.

"I have sent you a saddle, as you asked me, one on which I have been riding myself, of the kind which our clergy use here, and a horse to carry it. May God and His angel bless your journey." [132]

The following year, 802, saw Ethelhard at home, having received from Pope Leo the third on January 18 a letter, granting by Papal privilege to the See of Canterbury its ancient rights as Metropolitan and ruler of all the churches it had governed in times of old. The same pronouncement was sent by Leo to King Cenwulf of Mercia. Lichfield now ceased to be a third Metropolitan See in England, and henceforth Canterbury and York alone held this primacy.[133] This was formally declared as of ecclesiastical law in regard to Canterbury by the Council held under Ethelhard at Clovesho in

[131] *Epp.* IV, 378.
[132] *Ibid.* 374f.; H. S. III, 532f.
[133] H. S. III, 536ff.

803.[134] Higbert, made Archbishop of Lichfield by the Pope's action in 788, had probably before this time resigned his high office to retire into monastic life.[135]

Alcuin, naturally, wrote to Ethelhard in congratulation and to declare his joy at "the mending of the tunic of Christ, the radiance of brotherly peace and goodwill between two Primates of England." Now, he declared, must Ethelhard hold firmly his own, for the leading of a united and enlightened clergy, for peace and order, for the fulfilling of episcopal rule: "The power of a bishop is entirely different from that of a King. The bishop carries upon his lips the key of the heavenly Kingdom; the King carries a sword for vengeance upon offenders. But far higher is the power that quickens than the power that slays; life is better than death." [136]

Another letter, written by him to the same prelate, throws some light on English life at the time. "I saw many practices in England," Alcuin declares, "which ought not to be. Be on your guard against them. Men are carrying amulets as sacred things. It is better to imitate the saints in the heart than to carry bones in bags, to hold the words of the Gospel in the mind than to wear ribbons, inscribed with pagan words, round the neck. That is like the phylacteries of the Pharisees.

"And, too, those gatherings, a snare to the people, who leave their churches and go off to the mountains, not to pray but to get drunk." [137]

[134] *Ibid.* 542ff.; Birch I, 431ff.

[135] Stenton, 226.

[136] *Epp.* IV, 412f.; cf. 479ff.; *PLAC* I, 262f.

[137] *Epp.* IV, 448f. For amulets see *Indic. superstitionum,* No. 10: *Cap. reg. Fr.* 223, cf. 45, No. 6; McNeill and Gamer, 229; J. A. MacCulloch, *Medieval Faith and Fable,* 1932, 16, 152; E. A. Philippson, *Germanisches Heidentum bei den Angelsachsen,* 1929, 212f. Cf. also Alcuin's warning (*Epp.* IV, 426) to some bishop, perhaps Arno, against auguries and notes of birds, and sneezings—"omens" in which men believe through deception of the Devil.

Among Alcuin's students we have seen that Dodo and Osulf, according to report, caused him worry.[138] There was also, it seems, another young friend of his, an Englishman of high promise, who had fallen into evil ways. We do not know his name.[139]

"I begot, nurtured, fed you," Alcuin writes. "By gift of God I brought you to a perfect man, schooled in the arts, enlightened by study, of outstanding character. Thus almost all Britain sings your praise, and men know of you who do not know your face. I call Christ to witness that I aided you with all the strength within me. . . .

"What is this, my son, that I hear of you, not in some lurking whisper, but in the open laughter of many, that you are still a slave to a little boy's filthy ways? Where is your learning, where your fear of hell, your hope of heaven? . . .

"I beseech you, by the terror of that Judgment which we all must undergo, that from the very day on which you read this page, written in my love and my grief, you begin to break this chain of the Devil's suggesting and your own wicked consent. . . ." [140]

Further disquiet came in 800 and 801 from Italy, where Pepin, son of Charles, was marching in repeated expeditions to subdue Grimoald, Duke of Beneventum, that rebel against the overlordship of the Frankish Emperor.[141] Alcuin could not let this pass without word to Charles: "I am so distressed to

[138] P. 153 *supra.*

[139] Against Dodo in this connection see Dümmler, *Epp.* IV, 107, note 3; against "Cuculus," page 297 *supra* and note; against Osulf, Hauck II, 156, note 2. Osulf served under the younger Charles, and died in Lombardy: *Alc. Vita,* 191f.

[140] *Epp.* IV, 451f., cf. 452ff. See *PLAC* I, 243 (XXII). Kleinclausz (*Alcuin,* 271) inclines toward Osulf for 452ff. (No. 295; cf. Hauck *ibid.*).

[141] *ARF ann.* 800, 801; Erchempert, *SRLI* 236f.

hear of the death of your faithful friend, Megenfrid, in Beneventum. And I do beg you to do the right thing in regard to this hostile invasion of that land, lest greater loss come to those in your service. You know well, how Divine Providence fought for you there, and how it made a quick end of this wicked Grimoald's father and brother. So, if Heaven bring it about, he, too, will perish, without any loss to your men. Policy perhaps will do more than open war. 'Leave vengeance to Me', the Lord declares, 'and I will fight for you'." [142]

In any case, Alcuin was always afraid for his friends in Italy, a land of "pestilential air" and sickness, especially in the south. He knew it from his own experience, for his "Roman companion," recurrent attacks of fever, troubled him much at Tours.[143]

4

But now his trials and distractions on this earth were drawing toward their end. Already in 801 he wrote to the Emperor: "It is time for me to know my body's weakness and to work for my soul's firm stand. I will do just what you wish, for I do not trust my own judgment, and everything you have decided for me has turned out well. Five years ago I planned to leave worldly affairs, and I meant it, God knows. But you wisely sent me to serve Saint Martin's. Now my frailty and my old age depend on you for counsel." [144]

The Emperor saw fit. From this same year Alcuin no longer ruled his monasteries outside Tours; he gave over Ferrières to Sigulf, put aside secular cares, and sat quietly in his cell at Saint Martin's, waiting for the Voice that should cry: "Open to Him Who knocks, follow Him Who orders, hear Him Who

[142] *Epp.* IV, 351f., cf. 360, 362, 367f. For Megenfrid see pp. 107, 131 *supra.*

[143] *Epp.* IV, 290, 362, 367, 439. [144] *Ibid.* 373f.

judges!" It was a time of anxiety, even of trepidation, for one who had always distrusted himself and feared his departing hence. Again and again he implored his friends to remember him in their prayers to that Lord of the Four Last Things. "I have laid down the sword-belt of my soldier's labour," he wrote to Adalhard, abbot of Corbie, "longing to serve God in peace. Soon, before the tribunal of God, I shall hear declared all I have done in my life. O my son! if that hour shall find you still on earth, pray! Pray, you and your brethren, for me, that I may by mercy of Jesus Our Lord escape the dread faces of the Accusing Ones!" [145]

The Emperor called him to Aachen, but he pleaded heavy sickness: "I have strength neither for travel nor for toil. All worthiness and power have gone from me, and still go, day by day, never, I fear, to return in this life. Oh, how awful for every man is that day, how necessary for each to prepare to meet his God, while light still is his, before the darkness falls."

The darkness was the deeper to his thought, as long since his physical sight had been failing and at the end was almost gone. His letters were dictated to one or another of his friends.[146] "I am trembling from head to foot at the terror of Judgment, lest that Day find me unready," he told Arno a year or so before his death. "God grant I may see you for the healing of the wounds of this unhappy life, and for a last word of farewell and support." [147] Arno at the moment was too busy with secular concerns. Charles had appointed him one of his *missi,* his emissaries, who travelled about his realms to examine into conditions, to try and to judge litigants and offenders. "What does my sloth know about secular courts?" Alcuin retorted; "*I* never wanted to be mixed up in them!" Rebuke turned to

[145] *Ibid.* 378, 380, 382.
[146] *Ibid.* 383, 385, 387, cf. 280f.; *Alc. Vita,* cc. 11, 19, 20.
[147] *Epp.* IV, 384f., 388, 424, 421, 480.

sympathy when he realized how Arno himself disliked this distraction which so interrupted his own pastoral service. They were to meet no more, and Alcuin said his last word: "One thing in your letter I would see blotted out, never to be—this, that you could not hope to see my face again. God's will be done! If it cannot be now, may it be in eternity."

The end came on May 19, 804. He had been able to keep Lent and Easter well, but on the eve of the Ascension a stroke of paralysis left him unable to move or to speak for more than a week. Then, two days before he died, those by his bed heard him chanting the antiphon, *O clavis David*: [148]

> O Key of David and Sceptre of the House of Israel,
> Thou Who openest and no man shutteth,
> Who shuttest and no man openeth:
>
> Come and lead the captive from his house of prison,
> him who sitteth in darkness and in the shadow of death!

At dawn of the Feast of Pentecost, as Matins ended and the first Mass was beginning, his soul found release. It was the day on which he had prayed that he might die.[149]

Sigulf, his student and intimate friend, made ready his body for burial. It was laid within Saint Martin's Church, by bidding of his Archbishop Joseph. The epitaph which his clergy placed on the wall above his tomb had been written by himself. Some of its lines, here roughly rendered, are old as Archytas in their prayer:

> Stay here a moment, thou that passest by,
> Think well upon my verse;
> Thine own like fate herein thou shalt descry,
> My lot doth thine rehearse.

[148] *Ibid.* 409, 411, 422, 424. Cf. Thurston, *The Month* CVI, 1905, 622.

[149] *Alc. Vita,* 196.

What thou art now, I was, renowned to all,
As I, so sometime thou;
Once following the world's delicious call,
Dust, worms, and ashes now. . . .
Alcuin my name, wisdom I always loved,
Pray, reader, for my soul.

"Here lies Alcuin, Lord Abbot of blessed memory, who died in peace, the nineteenth of May. When this you shall have read, pray you all for him and say, 'The Lord give him eternal rest.' "[150]

Throughout his life Alcuin walked the middle path. He was neither priest nor layman. He lived according to rule, *monachus animo*; yet he was not a Regular monk. He denied himself many things; yet he did not wed the Lady Poverty. He loved peace and prayer; yet his hours were full of distractions, and of his human impulse he enjoyed them. He adored the Palace School, his relations with his King and the household of the Court; yet Charles often preferred to jest with others of less sober spirit at his table. He compiled a Sacramentary which was to serve the Church for centuries; yet he never offered for his people the Holy Sacrifice at the altar. As teacher and as Master in England and on the continent, he influenced numberless minds, and his work as organizer of education, as editor of text-books, as student of ancient classic literature, of sacred writings and their truths, was to live on through the Middle Ages. Yet he himself contributed nothing original. Instead, he drew reverently, scrupulously, from the sources of older time, and by this very drawing conserved for future generations the wisdom of the past. He was in himself no

[150] *PLAC* I, 350f.; *Alc. Vita,* 197. For a translation that rises far above its original see Waddell, *Med. Lat. Lyr.* 95. No trustworthy portrait of Alcuin in art remains to us; see Kleinclausz, *Alcuin,* 43f.

philosopher; yet he did much to make ready the way for mediaeval scholasticism. He encouraged, we may think, the growth of the Caroline minuscule; but he neither invented it nor lived to see it in perfect form. He was a poet at heart, but his verses were for the most part mediocre. His prose was simple, full of quotations, its grammar not without fault; yet he brought the Latin he had learned in England after the tradition of Bede to purify and to discipline Latin language on the continent.[151] If, in truth, he was no Bede in scholarship, neither was he a Boniface in Christian heroism and self-denial.[152] He did, indeed, give and prescribe alms for the poor. But in his dealings with men who were not directly connected with him by ties of loyalty or admiration, friendship or work, in his outlook upon the multitude of those beaten down by war, by slavery, by economic necessity, he did not rise above the level of his day. For the heathen he craved conversion, not liberty; Widukind he saw only as the enemy of the Church and King Charles. He held it better to work in the peace of Frankland than to endure with his own country and people in their hour of desperate need. He was content to see and to know in his Frankish world a power of its King over the Church which in normal circumstances he would have forbidden and refused. He accepted from Charles the endowments of abbeys in number, abounding in wealth of servants, herds, and produce, and the thought of his own easy, unascetic years troubled him when he was old. It had been sufficient for his heart and conscience to serve, at least directly, those in high places of Church and State, and this he did with all his power. To all whom he met he gave fresh life, by his spoken or his written word, by stimulation of rebuke, of warning, of praise and of admiration entirely generous; yet all his days were

[151] Cf. Pivec, *MOG* XIV, Erg.-Band, 1939, 42.
[152] Fichtenau, 95ff., 112, 160f.

clouded by self-conscious diffidence in regard to himself and his deserving. He feared to initiate, and therefore he did much to further the rigid adherence to tradition characteristic of the mediaeval mind. He needed passionately both God and man, and he was constantly afraid of losing either. He held firmly to the articles of his Faith, and hung, swaying between its joy and its terror. He was a man and a Christian of unyielding devotion, and he walked through the shadows to their end.

The School of Saint Martin lived on, great in reputation and in the names of its students and Masters.[153] Not long after Alcuin's death, as we have seen, it became, in title as in discipline, a house of canons, to which young men of the secular clergy might be admitted. In 868, when Hincmar of Reims was examining Willebert, bishop-elect of Châlons, he asked where he had been educated. "In the School of Tours," was the reply, "to which I was sent for study of the liberal arts." [154] Berengar was taught in the same school, and in time came to preside over it, to its renown in Latin culture, we are told.[155] So, also, Hildebert of Lavardin, poet and Archbishop of Tours, sat under Berengar, it is said, in his youth; [156] Bernard Silvestris led the school's learning to high estate; [157] his pupil, Matthew of Vendôme, called the city of Martin his *alma mater*; [158] Peter of Blois amused himself there in his student days by writing verses—*ludicra*.[159]

[153] For the influence of Alcuin see, in general, Manitius and Laistner; Monnier, *Alcuin*, 187ff.; Kleinclausz, *Alcuin*, 281, 289ff.; Crawford, 107ff. For the School of Tours see Lesne V, 137ff.

[154] *Gallia Christ.* X, 149; Lesne V, 138.

[155] Lesne V, 139f.

[156] Raby, *CLP*, 265; Lesne V, 140f.

[157] *DHGE* VIII, 746f.; Manitius III, 206, *Zeugnisse*.

[158] Faral, *Les arts poétiques du XIIe et du XIIIe siècle*, 1924, 1f.

[159] *Opera*, ed. Giles I, 38; Manitius III, 293f.

These, however, were the days of the future. For the time, Fridugis, who himself was installed as abbot of Saint Martin's, followed closely in the steps of his master, saw the script of Tours rise to its highest art, and discussed dialectic for the benefit of the Court of Charles, whom he thought to persuade that Darkness and Nothing, from evidence of Scripture, have material existence. Must not Nothing, from which the Lord created all things, be the original substance? [160]

But the original thought of true philosophy was yet unborn in Frankland, awaiting the voice of John the Scot.[161] In the Palace School an Irishman, it is true, was now working; the voice of Clement the Scot spoke of grammar, and sadly lacked the warm life which Alcuin's genius had given to its prosaic study.

In 814 Charles the Great died. Under his son, Louis the Pious, to whom, as one trained therein, monastic education was of more moment than to his father, the range of its discipline was narrowed by his edict that its instruction be offered only to young oblates preparing for the monk's life.[162] More and more, compilations of extracts from the Fathers of the Church became the study of those who wrote and of those who read. And study, more and more, served purely practical ends. Delight in literature, secular and pagan as well as ecclesiastical and Christian, the involuntary delight of Jerome, of Augustine, of Alcuin, faded out in this rigorous atmosphere. Walafrid Strabo, as he looks back toward the radiance of learning in the days of Charles the Great, laments: "Now, truly, studies are turning to the opposite direction, and in most

[160] Cf. Alcuin's retort to the "Greek sophist": *Dic, rogo, dic, doctor prudentissime, utrumne mors sit substantia? Epp.* IV, 470; Endres, *Beitr. z. Gesch, d. Philos. des Mittelalt.* XVII, 2–3, 1915, 3f. For Fridugis see *Epp.* IV, 552ff.; Sickel, *Acta* I, 89f.

[161] Cf. Laistner, 268; Foligno, *Latin Thought,* 88.

[162] *Cap. reg. Fr.* I, 346, No. 45; Amann, 258ff., 262.

men the light of wisdom, finding little love, begins to die away."[163]

The ninth century, then, was busily following Alcuin in plucking flowers from the fields of patristic literature and arranging them for the use of its ordinands. It still sought service from the liberal arts, still the handmaids of theology and sound doctrine. Writings by Alcuin were still copied everywhere within its monasteries and held to be high treasure. The action of Abbot Peter of Saint Mesmin of Micy was not singular, when he offered a manuscript of Alcuin during Mass of Holy Thursday at Saint Stephen's altar and warned that "anathema be upon him who should steal it from the Abbey."[164]

Thegan, biographer of Louis, sends Alcuin *On the Holy Trinity* to Hatto, bishop or noble of high standing, that he may learn of the Fathers from this *summus scolasticus*;[165] Jonas, who followed Theodulf as bishop of Orléans, warns Mathfred, his Count, in the words of Alcuin, against the eight deadly sins;[166] Freculf, bishop of Lisieux, reads Alcuin with Augustine, source for both writers, as he compiles his *History of the Ancient World*;[167] Angelomus, monk of Luxeuil, follows Alcuin in verse as he ponders on his commentary for the books of Kings;[168] Aeneas of Paris uses Alcuin *On the Trinity* as he fulminates against the Greeks on the *Filioque* doctrine;[169] Remigius of Auxerre knows Alcuin's *Genesis*;[170] Hucbald of

[163] Einhard, *Vita Karol. Prologus:* Eginhard, ed. Halphen, 106.
[164] Lesne IV, 137.
[165] Manitius, 653; *Epp.* V, 337. Possibly this was Hatto, bishop of Basle: Kleinclausz, *Alcuin,* 281.
[166] *PL* CVI, col. 247.
[167] Manitius, 666.
[168] Cf. Alcuin, *Carm.* LXXX, ii, l. 8: *PLAC* I, 300, and Angelomus on 4 Books of Kings: *PLAC* II, 677, l. 30; Manitius, 418.
[169] *PL* CXXI, coll. 718ff.
[170] *PL* CXXXI, col. 113; cf. Manitius, 507.

Saint-Amand bequeaths his copy of Alcuin to his Abbey;[171] Amalar of Metz, as he writes of antiphons for his Church, looks back to the days when he learned Saint Martin's use of chanting under Alcuin, "the most learned master of all our surrounding land."[172]

Names might be multiplied indefinitely. And so, too, with monasteries. At Ferrières the line of Alcuin's influence ran from Sigulf, his successor, to Lupus, who mourned his abbey's slender resources and outdid the Master in his insatiate hunger for knowledge: *Mihi satis apparet propter se ipsam appetenda sapientia.*[173] The monks of Saint Riquier read his verses among those of Mico and Fredigard.[174] Tradition, told by Notker the Stammerer, reported that Grimald, Abbot of Saint Gall, was taught by Alcuin.[175] Certainly Ermenric of Ellwangen drew much from him, as he poured out all he knew to Grimald under guise of gratitude for hospitality, using Alcuin, again, on rhetoric, on dialectic, *On the Holy Trinity.*[176] Notker himself waxed more eloquent than wise in his words: "Not one of Alcuin's disciples," he declared, "but has been seen a holy abbot or bishop of renown."[177] "Such a Grammar did Alcuin compose," he told his young friend Salomo, the future bishop of Constance, "that Donatus, Nicomachus, Domistheus, and our Priscian, seem as nothing in comparison! He wrote much, too, that would be good for you, fool that you are, on dialectic, faith, hope, and charity, and even dared to put his hand to

[171] Manitius, 590, 593f.; Delisle, *Cab. des MSS.* II, 451.

[172] *De ord. antiphon.* c. 58, c. 67; *De eccles. off.* IV, c. 17: *PL* CV, coll. 1303, 1307, 1198; *Epp.* V, 240f.; Mönchemeier, *Amalar von Metz,* 15f.

[173] Servatus Lupus, ed. Levillain I, 4 and 6; Laistner, 205.

[174] *PLAC* III, 326; cf. Manitius, 470.

[175] *De Carolo Magno,* ed. von Knonau, 7; J. M. Clark, *Abbey of St. Gall,* 1926, 8.

[176] *Epp.* V, 536ff., with Dümmler's notes.

[177] Monach. Sangall. (Notker Balbulus), ed. von Knonau, 7.

the Gospel of Saint John. There are all his letters to his friends also, especially to Wido. But I had better not mention them; your youthful mind thinks them arrogant. Not to me. . . ." [178]

Above all, the tradition of Alcuin was carried on at Fulda in Germany under Raban Maur, its abbot for twenty years, from 822 to 842. In him were found the same scrupulous adherence to patristic texts, the same unceasing search among these works for the compiling of commentaries and text-books and apologetics, the same lack of originality. But in him, too, was found the same necessary turning to literature for its own delight, the same quoting from pagan poetry "in the service" of the Church. Like Hincmar of Reims, so Raban looked to Alcuin for ammunition to hurl against the erring Gottschalk, who dared, in spite of all, to follow his own thought.[179] In Raban, indeed, there is not found the passionate warmth, the friendliness, the simplicity, of Alcuin, neither in his letters, nor in his verses, full of borrowings, of repetition of phrase and word. He was a great scholar, a great teacher, but he was not, one may suppose, a very human companion and correspondent. Yet he loved Alcuin—so much that it has been thought that as a student he must have known him longer than in his brief stay at Tours some three years before the Master's death.[180] As preface to that *carmen figuratum* of which he was so proud, *In Praise of the Holy Cross,* he imagines Alcuin commending to God his disciple, Raban, whom he had taught in the ways of sacred doctrine, of ethics, and of secular learning. So, too, Raban writes to Samuel, afterward bishop of Worms, seemingly a fellow-student with him under Alcuin at Tours, that

[178] *PL* CXXXI, col. 999; *Das Formelbuch des Bischofs Salomo III von Konstanz,* ed. Dümmler, 1857, 72; cf. W. Schmitz, 75ff.

[179] Hincmar, *PL* CXXV, coll. 98, 116, 277, 535, 552, 569.

[180] Dümmler, *PLAC* II, 154; *Epp.* V, 489.

they remember and duly follow the goodly teaching he once gave.[181]

He, the Master, was never canonized, never beatified, although miracles gathered around his name. To the Middle Ages he was a pillar of the schools of the Church and of her teaching, rather than a saint. Perhaps we may think of him in the words of a writer of that France to whom he gave new light: "Sans Alcuin, on peut le dire, Charlemagne eût été bien moins grand." [182] The fruit of his endeavour under Charlemagne may be described in another quotation: "It is interesting to note that while Charles sent to England for Alcuin to educate Gaul, . . . Alfred of Wessex sent to Gaul for scholars to re-educate England." [183]

[181] *PLAC* II, 159f., 189f.; *CMH* III, 520 (M. R. James). For the influence of Alcuin on Wulfstan in England see Dorothy Bethurum, *Philologica: The Malone Anniversary Studies,* 98f.: "Alcuin was one of his favorite authorities," and in *Publ. Mod. Lang. Assoc.* LVII, 1942, 920f.; cf. Dorothy Whitelock, *Trans. Royal Hist. Soc.,* Series 4, XXIV, 1942, 29f., 40, 43.

[182] Kleinclausz, *Alcuin,* 282; Monnier, *Alcuin,* 252.

[183] LaMonte, *The World of the M.A.* 160, 197; Levison, 166; Gilson, *La Philosophie au M.A.* 193ff.

DATES

Patriarchs of Constantinople

715–730: Germanus
730–754: Anastasius
754–766: Constantine
766–780: Nicetas
780–784: Paul
784–806: Tarasius

Byzantine Emperors

717–741: Leo III, the Isaurian
741–775: Constantine V
775–780: Leo IV
780–790: Constantine VI and Irene (Regent)
790–792: Constantine VI
792–797: Constantine VI, Irene
797–802: Irene
802–811: Nicephorus I

Popes of Rome

715–731: Gregory II
731–741: Gregory III
741–752: Zacharias
752–757: Stephen II
757–767: Paul I
(767–768: Constantine, anti-Pope)
768–772: Stephen III
772–795: Hadrian I
795–816: Leo III

Kings of the Lombards

712–744: Liutprand
744 : Hildeprand
744–749: Ratchis
749–756: Aistulf
757 : Ratchis
757–774: Desiderius

Kings of Northumbria

729–737: Ceolwulf
737–758: Eadbert
758 : Oswulf
759–765: Ethelwald Moll
765–774: Alchred
774–779: Ethelred I
779–788: Elfwald I
788–790: Osred II
790–796: Ethelred I
796 : Osbald
796–806: Eardwulf II

Kings of Mercia

716–757: Ethelbald
757–796: Offa
787–796: Egfrith
796–821: Cenwulf

Archbishops of Canterbury		*Archbishops of York*	
735–739:	Nothelm	732–766:	Egbert
740–758:	Cuthbert	767–780:	Aelbert
759–765:	Bregwin	780–796:	Eanbald I
766–792:	Jaenbert	796–808–:	Eanbald II
792–805:	Ethelhard		

Kings of the Franks

751–768:	Pepin the Short
768–771:	{Charles the Great {Carloman
771–814:	Charles the Great
814–840:	Louis the Pious

ABBREVIATIONS

AA.SS: *Acta sanctorum Bollandiana.*

Acta SS. O.S.B.: Mabillon, ed. *Acta sanctorum Ordini S. Benedicti*: ed. by the Monks of Solesmes, II, 1936, III, i–iv, 1939–1940.

A R F: *Annales regni Francorum qui dicuntur Annales Laurissenses Majores* (Version I) *et Einhardi* (Version II), ed. F. Kurze, *SRGS* 1895.

A - SC: *Anglo-Saxon Chronicle,* ed. J. Earle and C. Plummer I–II, 1892–1899.

——: ed. B. Thorpe I–II, *RS* XXIII, 1861.

A U: *Archiv für Urkundenforschung, Leipzig.*

B H R: *Bibliothèque d'Humanisme et Renaissance,* Geneva.

B.M.L.: J. F. Böhmer, E. Mühlbacher, J. Lechner: *Die Regesten des Kaiserreichs unter den Karolingern* I, 1908.

B R G: *Bibliotheca rerum Germanicarum*: see Jaffé, P.

B T A M: *Bulletin de Théologie ancienne et médiévale,* Louvain.

C H E L: *Cambridge History of English Literature* I, ed. A. W. Ward and A. R. Waller, 1907.

C M H: *Cambridge Medieval History* II, 1926; III, 1922; IV, 1927; V, 1929: ed. H. M. Gwatkin, J. P. Whitney, J. R. Tanner, C. W. Previté-Orton, Z. N. Brooke.

D A C L: *Dictionnaire d'Archéologie chrétienne et de Liturgie,* ed. F. Cabrol and H. Leclercq.

D A G M: Deutsches Archiv für Geschichte des Mittelalters, Weimar.

D C B: *Dictionary of Christian Biography,* ed. W. Smith and H. Wace.

D H G E: *Dictionnaire d'Histoire et de Géographie ecclésiastiques,* ed. A. Baudrillart and others.

D R: *Downside Review.*

D T C: *Dictionnaire de Théologie catholique,* ed. A. Vacant, E. Mangenot, E. Amann.

D V L G: *Deutsche Vierteljahrsschrift für Literaturwissenschaft und Geistesgeschichte,* Stuttgart.

E H R: *English Historical Review,* London.
E L: *Ephemerides Liturgicae,* Rome.
G G A: *Göttingische gelehrte Anzeigen,* Berlin.
H B S: Henry Bradshaw Society, Publications of the
H C Y: See Raine.
H E: Bede, the Venerable: *Historia Ecclesiastica gentis Anglorum,* ed. C. Plummer I–II, 1896 (*Ven. Baedae Opera historica*).
Hist. Stud.: *Historische Studien,* Berlin.
H J: *Historisches Jahrbuch,* Görres-Gesellschaft, Munich-Cologne.
H. S.: A. W. Haddan and W. Stubbs: *Councils and Ecclesiastical Documents relating to Great Britain and Ireland,* III, 1871.
H T R: *Harvard Theological Review,* New York.
H Z: *Historische Zeitschrift,* Munich.
J L: Jahrbuch für Liturgiewissenschaft, Münster.
J T S: *Journal of Theological Studies,* Oxford.
J. W.: P. Jaffé and W. Wattenbach, ed. *Regesta Pontificum Romanorum* I, 1885.
L Q: *Liturgiegeschichtliche Quellen,* Münster.
M A A: Mediaeval Academy of America, Publications of the
M G H: Monumenta Germaniae historica.
M O G: *Mitteilungen des österreichischen Instituts für Geschichtsforschung,* Innsbruck.
M S P I: *Mediaeval Studies,* Pontifical Institute of Mediaeval Studies, Toronto.
N A: *Neues Archiv der Gesellschaft für ältere deutsche Geschichtskunde,* Hanover.
P G: *Patrologia Graeca.*
P J: *Philosophisches Jahrbuch* (Görres-Gesellschaft), Fulda.
P L: *Patrologia Latina.*
P L A C: Poetae latini aevi Carolini I-II, ed. E. Dümmler; III, 1–2, i, ed. L. Traube; IV, 1, ed. P. von Winterfeld; IV, 2–3, ed. K. Strecker.
P S S: Surtees Society, Publications of the
Q F: *Quellen und Forschungen aus italienischen Archiven und Bibliotheken,* Rome.
Q S: *Quellen und Studien,* ed. K. Zeumer.

R B: *Revue Bénédictine,* Maredsous, Belgium.
R B P H: *Revue belge de Philologie et d'Histoire,* Brussels.
R H: *Revue historique,* Paris.
R H E: *Revue d'Histoire ecclésiastique,* Louvain.
R H E F: *Revue d'Histoire de l'Eglise de France,* Paris.
R I S: *Rerum italicarum Scriptores,* ed. Muratori.
R M: *Rheinisches Museum für Philologie,* Frankfurt-am-Main.
R P T K: *Realencyklopädie für protestantische Theologie und Kirche,* ed. J. J. Herzog and A. Hauck, 1896.
R S: *Rolls Series.*
R S R: *Revue des Sciences religieuses,* Strasbourg.
R T A M: *Recherches de Théologie ancienne et médiévale,* Louvain.
S B B: *Sitzungsberichte der kg. preuss. Akademie der Wissenschaften zu Berlin, philos. hist. Klasse.*
S B H: *Sitzungsberichte der Heidelberger Akademie der Wissenschaften, philos. hist. Klasse.*
S B M: *Sitzungsberichte der bayerischen Akademie der Wissenschaften,* Munich, *philos. hist. Klasse.*
S B W: *Sitzungsberichte der Wiener Akademie der Wissenschaften, philos. hist. Klasse.*
S R G S: *Scriptores rerum germanicarum in usum scholarum, M G H.*
S R L I: *Scriptores rerum langobardicarum et italicarum, M G H.*
S R M: *Scriptores rerum merovingicarum, M G H.*
S S: *Scriptores,* ed. Pertz, *M G H.*
Z D A: *Zeitschrift für deutsches Altertum und deutsche Litteratur,* Berlin-Leipzig.
Z K G: *Zeitschrift für Kirchengeschichte,* Stuttgart.

BIBLIOGRAPHY

Abel, S. and Simson, B.: *Jahrbücher des frankischen Reiches unter Karl dem Grossen* I, 1888; II, 1883.
Ada-Handschrift, Die Trierer: ed. Menzel, Corrsen, Janitschek, Schnütgen, Hettner, Lamprecht, 1889.
Addison, James Thayer: *The Medieval Missionary,* 1936.
Alcuin: *Opera,* ed. Froben, I–II, 1777; reprinted in *PL* C-CI; ed. (in part) P. Jaffé, *Monumenta Alcuiniana, BRG* VI, 1873.
——: *Carmina,* ed. E. Dümmler, *PLAC* I, 160ff.; IV, 903 (K. Strecker).
——: *Versus de Sanctis, PLAC* I, 169ff.; Jaffé, *Mon. Alc.* 80ff.; J. Raine, *HCY* I, 349ff.
——: *Epistulae,* ed. E. Dümmler, *MGH Epp.* IV, 1ff.
——: *De Orthographia,* ed. H. Keil, *Grammatici Latini* VII, 295ff.
——: *De Rhetorica,* ed. C. Halm, *Rhetores latini minores,* 1863, 525ff.
——: *Disputatio Pippini cum Albino,* ed. W. Wilmanns, *ZDA* XIV, 1869, 530ff.
——: *Life of St. Martin of Tours* (an abridgment of that by Sulpicius Severus), *PL* CI, coll. 657ff.
——: *Life of St. Richarius* (Riquier), revision of, ed. *Acta SS. O.S.B.* II, 1936, 187ff.; B. Krusch, *SRM* IV, 381ff.; cf. VII, 438ff. (source for Alcuin).
——: *Life of St. Vedast* (Vaast), revision of, ed. B. Krusch, *SRM* III, 414ff.; VII, 819f.
——: *Homily on St. Vedast, AA.SS.* Febr. I, 1658, 800.
——: *Life of St. Willibrord,* ed. *AA.SS.* Nov. III, 1910, 435ff. (Poncelet); W. Levison, *SRM* VII, 81ff.; P. Jaffé, *Mon. Alc.* 35ff.; trans. A. Grieve, *Willibrord,* 1923, 99ff.; *PLAC* I, 207ff.
——: *Homily for St. Willibrord's Feast,* ed. Levison, *SRM* VII, 138ff.
Alcuini Vita: auctor anonymus (compiled 823 x 829), ed. W. Arndt, *SS* XV, i, 182ff.; *AA.SS.* Maii IV, 1685, 335ff.

Amann, Emile: *L'Époque carolingienne:* Fliche-Martin VI, 1947.
Angilbert: *Carmina,* ed. E. Dümmler, *PLAC* I, 355ff.
Arquillière, H. X.: *L'Eglise au Moyen Age,* 1939.
——: *L'Augustinisme politique,* 1934.
Baedae Continuatio: ed. C. Plummer, *Ven. Baedae Opera historica* I, 361ff.
Beer, Rudolf: *Monumenta Palaeographica Vindobonensia* I, 1910.
Beissel, Stephan: *Geschichte der Evangelienbücher in der ersten Hälfte des Mittelalters, Stimmen aus Maria-Laach,* 1906.
Berger, Samuel: *Histoire de la Vulgate pendant les premiers siècles du Moyen Age,* 1893.
Berlière, Ursmer: *L'ordre monastique des origines au XIIe siècle,* 1924.
——: *L'ascèse bénédictine des origines à la fin du XIIe siècle,* 1927.
Birch, Walter de Gray: *Cartularium Saxonicum* I, 1885.
Bishop, Edmund: *Liturgica Historica,* 1918 (Bishop).
——: "The Liturgical Reforms of Charlemagne," *DR* XXXVII, 1919, 1ff.
——: see also Kuypers.
Boas, M.: *Alcuin und Cato,* 1937.
Bonnaud Delamare, Roger: *L'idée de paix à l'époque carolingienne,* 1939.
Bouquet, Martin: *Recueil des Historiens des Gaules et de la France* V, 1869.
Brown, Carleton F.; "Cynewulf and Alcuin," *Mod. Lang. Assoc. of America, Publications* XVIII, 1903, 308ff.
Browne, George F.: *Alcuin of York,* 1908.
Cabrol, Ferdinand: *Les Origines liturgiques,* 1906.
——: "Les écrits liturgiques d'Alcuin," *RHE* XIX, 1923, 507ff.
——: "Alcuin," *DACL* I, i, coll. 1072ff.
——: "Gélasien (Le Sacramentaire)," *ibid.* VI, i, coll. 747ff.
——: "Grégorien (Le Sacramentaire)," *ibid.* VI, ii, coll. 1776ff.
Calmette, J.: *Charlemagne,* 1945.
Capelle, B.: "L'origine antiadoptianiste de notre texte du Symbole de la Messe," *RTAM* I, 1929, 7ff.
——: "Alcuin et l'histoire du Symbole de la Messe," *ibid.* VI, 1934, 249ff.

Capitularia regum Francorum I: ed. A. Boretius, *MGH Leg. Sect. II*, 1883.
Caspar, Erich: "Das Papsttum unter fränkischer Herrschaft," *ZKG* LIV, 1935, 132ff.
Chambers, R. W.: *England before the Norman Conquest*, 1926.
Clercq, C. de.: *La législation religieuse franque, de Clovis à Charlemagne*, 1936.
Codex Carolinus: ed. W. Gundlach, *MGH Epp.* III, 469ff.; P. Jaffé, *Mon. Car.* 1ff.
Concilia aevi Karolini I: ed. A. Werminghoff, *MGH Leg. Sect.* III, *Concilia* II, 1–2, 1906, 1908; *Supplementum* (*Libri Carolini*) ed. H. Bastgen, 1924.
Crawford, S. J.: *Anglo-Saxon influence on western Christendom, 600–800*, 1933.
Cuissard, Ch.: *Théodulfe, évêque d'Orléans*, 1892.
Dahlmann, F. C. and Waitz, G.: *Quellenkunde der deutschen Geschichte*, ed. H. Haering, 1931, 321ff.
Dawson, Christopher: *The Making of Europe*, 1939.
Deanesly, Margaret: "Medieval Schools to c. 1300," *CMH* V, 765ff.
Diplomata Karolinorum: *Die Urkunden der Karolinger* I, ed. Mühlbacher, Dopsch, Lechner, Tangl, 1906.
Dix, Gregory: *The Shape of the Liturgy*, 1945.
Drane, Augusta T. (Mother Francis Raphael): *Christian Schools and Scholars*, ed. W. Gumbley, 1924.
Dümmler, Ernst: *Alchvinstudien*, *SBB* 1891, 495ff.
——: "Zur Lebensgeschichte Alchvins," *NA* XVIII, 1893, 51ff.
Earle and Plummer: see *A-SC*.
Egbert, *Dialogue; Penitential*: H. S. III, 403ff.
Einhard, *Vita Karoli Magni*: ed. L. Halphen, 1938; ed. Pertz, Waitz, Holder-Egger, *SRGS* 1911; ed. Jaffé, *Mon Car. BRG* IV, 487ff.
Epp. (*Epistolae*): *MGH* III (*Merowingici et Karolini aevi* I), ed. Dümmler, Gundlach, Arndt, 1892; IV (*Karol. aevi* II), ed. Dümmler, 1895; V (*Karol. aevi* III), ed. Dümmler, Hampe, de Hirsch, Gereuth, 1899; VI (*Karol. aevi* IV), ed. Perels and Dümmler, 1925; VII (*Karol. aevi* V), ed. Kehr, 1928.
Fichtenau, Heinrich: *Das karolingische Imperium*, 1949.
Fliche, A. and Martin, V.: ed. *Histoire de l'Eglise* V–VI, 1947.

Florence of Worcester, *Chronicon ex chronicis*: ed. B. Thorpe, I–II, Eng. Hist. Soc. 23–24, 1848–1849.
Foerster, Hans: *Abriss der lateinischen Paläographie,* 1949.
Frere, Walter: *Studies in the early Roman Liturgy* I, 1930, III, 1935, *Alcuin Club Collections* XXVIII, XXXII.
Freudgen, Joseph: *Alkuins pädagogische Schriften,* 1889 (German trans.).
Frey, Joseph: *De Alcuini arte grammatica Commentatio,* 1886.
Ganshof, F. L.: *Pages d'Histoire,* 1944, 37ff.
——: "La Révision de la Bible par Alcuin"; *BHR*: *Travaux et Documents* IX, 1947, 7ff.
——: *The Imperial Coronation of Charlemagne*: *Theories and Facts, Glasgow Univ. Publications* LXXIX, 1949.
Gaskoin, C. J. B.: *Alcuin,* 1904.
Gebhardt, B.: *Handbuch der deutschen Geschichte* I, ed. R. Holtzmann, 1930, 131ff. (W. Levison).
Ghellinck, J. de: *Littérature latine au Moyen Age, depuis les origines jusqu'à la fin de la Renaissance carolingienne,* 1939.
Gilson, Etienne: *La Philosophie au Moyen Age des origines patristiques à la fin du XIVe siècle,* 1944 (dedicated to Alcuin).
Glotz, Gustave: ed. *Histoire Générale*: *Histoire du Moyen Age I,* i (395–768): F. Lot, C. Pfister, F. L. Ganshof, 1940; I, ii (768–888): F. Lot, F. L. Ganshof, 1941.
Haller, Johannes: *Das Papsttum, Idee und Wirklichkeit* I, 1934; II, i, 1937.
Halphen, Louis: *Etudes critiques sur l'histoire de Charlemagne,* 1921.
——: ed. and trans. *Eginhard*: *Vie de Charlemagne,* 1938.
——: *Les Barbares, des grandes invasions aux conquêtes turques du XIe siècle,* 1940.
——: *Charlemagne et l'Empire carolingien,* 1947.
Hamelin, F.: *Essai sur la vie et les ouvrages d'Alcuin,* 1873.
Hartmann, L. M.: *Geschichte Italiens im Mittelalter* II, 2, 1903; III, 1, 1908.
Hauck, Albert: *Kirchengeschichte Deutschlands* I–II, 3–4 ed., 1904–1912 (5. Aufl. unveränderte, 1935).
Hefele, C. J. and Leclercq, H.: *Histoire des Conciles* III, 2, 1910.
Heldmann, Karl: *Das Kaisertum Karls des Grossen, QS* VI, 2, 1928.

Hinks, Roger: *Carolingian Art*, 1935.
Hodgkin, R. H.: *A History of the Anglo-Saxons I–II*, 1939.
Hodgkin, Thomas: *Italy and her Invaders* VI, 1916; VII–VIII, 1899.
Howell, Wilbur S.: *The Rhetoric of Alcuin and Charlemagne*, 1941.
Jaffé, Philipp: ed. *Bibliotheca rerum Germanicarum*. III, *Monumenta Moguntina*, 1866; IV, *Monumenta Carolina*, 1867; VI, *Monumenta Alcuiniana*, ed. W. Wattenbach–E. Dümmler, 1873.
Kantorowicz, Ernst H.: *Laudes Regiae*, University of California Publications in History 33, 1946.
Kemble, J. M.: *Codex Diplomaticus aevi Saxonici* I, 1839.
Kenney, J. F.: *The Sources for the early history of Ireland* I, *Ecclesiastical*, Columbia University, 1929.
Ker, W. P.: *The Dark Ages*, 1904.
Ketterer, J. A.: *Karl der Grosse und die Kirche*, 1898.
Kleinclausz, Arthur: *L'Empire carolingien*, 1902.
——: *Charlemagne*, 1934.
——: *Alcuin*, 1948.
Knabe, Lotte: *Die gelasianische Zweigewaltentheorie bis zum Ende des Investiturstreits: Hist. Stud.* 292, 1936.
Köhler, Wilhelm: "Turonische Handschriften aus der Zeit Alkuins": *Festgabe für H. Degering*, 1926, 172ff.
——: *Die karolingischen Miniaturen I, Die Schule von Tours* I–II, 1930–1933.
——: Review of Rand: *GGA* CXCIII, 1931, 321ff.
König, A.: *Geistesleben und Unterrichtswesen zur Zeit Karls des Grossen*, 1902.
Kowalski-Fahrun, H.: "Alkuin und der ahd. Isidor," *Beiträge zur Gesch. der deutsch. Sprache und Lit.*, Halle, XLVII, 1923, 312ff.
Kurth, Godefroid: *Les Origines de la civilisation moderne* II, 1898.
Kuypers, A. B.: ed. *The Book of Cerne* (with "Liturgical Note" by Edmund Bishop), 1902.
Laistner, M. L. W.: *Thought and Letters in Western Europe A.D. 500–900*, 1931.
Lavisse, Ernest: ed. *Histoire de France* II, 1 (C. Bayet, C. Pfister, A. Kleinclausz), 1903.

Leach, A. F.: *The Schools of medieval England,* 1915.
Leclercq, H.: "Ecriture," *DACL* IV, 2, coll. 1930ff.
——: "Gallicane (Liturgie)," *ibid.* VI, i, coll. 473ff.
——: "Gellone (Sacramentaire de)," *ibid.* coll. 777ff.
——: "Images, Culte et Querelle des," *ibid.* VII, i, coll. 232ff.
Lehmann, P.: "Holländische Reisefrüchte" III, *SBM* 1920, 13 *Abh.* 29ff.
——: *Fuldaer Studien, SBM* 1927, 2 *Abh.* 4ff.
Leroquais, Victor: *Les Sacramentaires et les Missels Manuscrits des Bibliothèques publiques de France* I–III, Planches, 1924.
Lesne, Emile: *Histoire de la propriété ecclésiastique en France* IV, 1938; V, 1940; VI, 1943.
Levison, Wilhelm: *England and the Continent in the eighth century,* 1946 (Levison).
——: *Aus rheinischer und fränkischer Frühzeit,* 1948.
Liber Pontificalis: ed. Louis Duchesne, I–II, 1886–1892.
Libri Carolini: ed. Hubert Bastgen, *MGH Concilia II, Supplementum,* 1924, 1ff.
Lietzmann, Hans: *Das Sacramentarium Gregorianum nach dem Aachener Urexemplar, LQ* III, 1921.
——: "Handschriftliches zu Alkuins Ausgabe und Sacramentarium," *JL* V, 1925, 68ff.
Lindsay, Wallace M.: ed. *Palaeographia Latina* IV, 1925; V, 1927.
Long, Omera F.: "The attitude of Alcuin toward Vergil," *Studies in honor of Basil L. Gildersleeve,* 1902, 377ff.
Lorenz, Friedrich: *Alcuins Leben,* 1829; trans. Jane M. Slee, 1837.
Lot, F.: *Naissance de la France,* 1948.
Lowe, E. A.: ed. *Codices latini antiquiores II, Great Britain and Ireland,* 1935 (*CLA*).
——: "Handwriting," *The Legacy of the Middle Ages,* ed. C. G. Crump and E. F. Jacob, 1926, 197ff.
McNeill, John T. and Gamer, Helena M.: *Medieval Handbooks of Penance,* Columbia University, 1938.
Maitre, Léon: *Les écoles épiscopales et monastiques en Occident avant les Universités* (768–1180), 1924.
Manitius, Max: *Geschichte der lateinischen Literatur des Mittelalters* I, 1911 (Manitius); III (with Paul Lehmann), 1931.

Mann, Horace K.: *The Lives of the Popes in the early Middle Ages* I, 2, 1903; II, 1906.
Mansi, J. D.: ed. *Sacrorum Conciliorum nova et amplissima Collectio* XI, 1765; XII, 1766; XIII, 1767.
Maycock, A. L.: "Bede and Alcuin," *Hibbert Journal* XXXIII, 1934–1935, 402ff.
Möller-Hahn: *Alkuin, RPTK.*
Monachus Sangallensis (Notkerus Balbulus): *De Carolo Magno*, ed. G. Meyer von Knonau, 1920.
Moncelle, P.: *Alcuin, DHGE.*
Monnier, Francis: *Alcuin*, 1853; *Alcuin et Charlemagne*, 1863.
Morin, Germain: "L'homéliaire d'Alcuin retrouvé," *RB* IX, 1892, 491ff.
——: "Une rédaction inédite de la Préface au Supplément du *Comes* d'Alcuin," *RB* XXIX, 1912, 341ff.
Moss, H. St. L. B.: *The Birth of the Middle Ages*, 1935.
Mullinger, J. B.: *The Schools of Charles the Great*, 1877.
Netzer, H.: *L'introduction de la messe romaine en France sous les Carolingiens*, 1910.
Nicephorus: *Opuscula historica*, ed. C. de Boor, 1880.
Oakley, Thomas P.: *English Penitential Discipline and Anglo-Saxon Law in their joint influence*, Columbia University, 1923.
Ogilvy, J. D. A.: *Books known to Anglo-Latin writers from Aldhelm to Alcuin (670–804), MAA* 1936.
Ohnsorge, Werner: *Das Zweikaiserproblem im früheren Mittelalter*, 1947.
Oman, Charles: *England before the Norman Conquest*, 9th ed. 1949.
Ostrogorsky, Georg: *Geschichte des byzantinischen Staates*, 1940.
Page, Rolph B.: *The Letters of Alcuin*, 1909.
Picavet, François: *Essais sur l'histoire générale et comparée des théologies et des philosophies médiévales*, 1913.
Pirenne, Henri: *Mahomet et Charlemagne*, ed. J. Pirenne and F. Vercauteren, 1937; Eng. trans. B. Miall, 1939.
——: *A History of Europe*, trans. Miall, 1939.
Plummer, ed. Bede: see *H E.*
Probst, Ferdinand: *Die ältesten römischen Sacramentarien und Ordines*, 1892.
——: *Die abendländische Messe vom fünften bis zum achten Jahrhundert*, 1896.

Pückert, Wilhelm: *Aniane und Gellone,* 1899.
Puniet, Pierre de: "Le Sacramentaire romain de Gellone," *EL* New Series VIII–XI, 1934–1937.
——: *Le Pontifical romain* I–II, 1930–1931, trans. M. V. Harcourt, 1932.
Raby, F. J. E.: *A History of Christian-Latin Poetry,* 1927 (*CLP*).
——: *A History of Secular Latin Poetry in the Middle Ages* I–II, 1934 (*SLP*).
Raine, James: ed. *Historians of the Church of York* I, *RS* LXXI, 1879.
Rand, Edward K.: *A Survey of the Manuscripts of Tours* I–II (*Studies in the Script of Tours* I), *MAA* 1929.
——: *The Earliest Book of Tours* (*Studies in the Script of Tours* II), with Leslie Webber Jones, *MAA* 1934.
——: "A preliminary study of Alcuin's Bible," *HTR* XXIV, 1931, 323ff.
——: Review of Köhler, *GGA* CXCIII, 1931, 336ff.
——: and G. Howe: *Memoirs of the American Academy in Rome* I, 1917, 19ff.
Rösler, Margarete: "Erziehung in England vor der normannischen Eroberung," *Englische Studien* XLVIII, 1914, 1ff.
Roger, Maurice: *L'enseignement des lettres classiques d'Ausone à Alcuin,* 1905.
Rüngeler, Josef: *Das Bild Karls des Grossen in der zeitgenössischen Annalistik und in der Gedichts—und Briefliteratur,* 1937.
Sanford, Eva M.: "Alcuin and the Classics," *Class. Journal* XX, 1925, 526ff.
Sayles, G. O.: *The medieval Foundations of England,* 1948.
Schmitz, Wilhelm: *Alcuins Ars Grammatica,* 1908.
Schnürer, Gustav: *Kirche und Kultur im Mittelalter* I, 2nd ed. 1927.
Schubert, Hans von: *Geschichte der christlichen Kirche im Frühmittelalter,* 1921.
Seppelt, F. X.: *Geschichte des Papsttums* II: *Das Papsttum im Frühmittelalter,* 1934.
Seydl, Ernest: "Alkuins Psychologie," *Jahrbuch f. Philosophie und spekulative Theologie,* Paderborn, XXV, 1911, 34ff.
Sickel, Th.: *Alcuinstudien* I, *SBW* LXXIX, 1875, 461ff.

Sinclair, J. S.: "The development of the Roman Rite during the Dark Ages," *Theology* XXXII, 1936, 142ff.

Stenton, F. M.: *Anglo-Saxon England,* 1947.

Storia di Roma (Istituto di Studi Romani): IX, O. Bertolini, 1941; X, P. Brezzi, 1947.

Strecker, K.: "Drei Rhythmen Alkuins," *NA* XLIII, 1922, 386ff.

Stubbs, William: *Alcuin; Offa, DCB.*

Symeon Dunelmensis: *Opera,* ed. T. Arnold, I–II, *RS* LXXV, 1882–1885.

——: *Opera et Collectanea,* ed. Hodgson Hinde, I, *PSS* LI, 1868.

Taylor, Henry Osborn: *The Mediaeval Mind* I–II, 1925.

Thalhofer, V. and Eisenhofer, L.: *Handbuch der katholischen Liturgik* I–II, 1912.

Theodulf of Orléans: *Carmina, PLAC* I, 437ff.

Theophanes: *Chronographia* I, ed. C. de Boor, 1883.

Thompson, A. Hamilton: *English Monasteries,* 1923.

——: ed. *York Minster Historical Tracts,* 1927.

——: ed. *Bede: His Life, times, and writings,* 1935.

Thompson, E. Maunde: *An Introduction to Greek and Latin Palaeography,* 1912.

Thompson, James W.: ed. *The Medieval Library,* 1939.

Traube, Ludwig: *Vorlesungen und Abhandlungen,* ed. F. Boll, II, 1911; III, 1920.

——: *Karolingische Dichtungen,* 1888.

——: "O Roma nobilis," *Abh. d. k. bayer. Akad. der Wiss.* I Cl. XIX, Bd II. *Abth.* 1891.

Ueberweg, Friedrich: *Grundriss der Geschichte der Philosophie* II: *Die patristische und scholastische Philosophie,* ed. B. Geyer, 1928.

Ullman, B. L.: *Ancient writing and its influence,* 1932.

Vasiliev, A. A.: *Histoire de l'Empire byzantin,* traduit du russe par P. Brodin et A. Bourguina, I (324–1081), 1932.

Vernet, F.: *Alcuin, DTC.*

Viard, Paul: *Histoire de la dîme ecclésiastique,* 1909.

Voigt, Karl: *Die karolingische Klosterpolitik,* 1917.

——: *Staat und Kirche von Konstantin dem Grossen bis zum Ende der Karolingerzeit,* 1936.

Waddell, Helen: *The Wandering Scholars,* 1932.

Waddell, Helen: *Mediaeval Latin Lyrics,* 1933, 1948.
——: *Poetry in the Dark Ages,* 1948.
Ward, Maisie: ed. *The English Way* ("Alcuin," Douglas Woodruff, 44ff.), 1933.
Watkins, O. D.: *A History of Penance* I–II, 1920.
Wattenbach, W.: *Deutschlands Geschichtsquellen im Mittelalter* I, revised E. Dümmler, 1904, 167ff.
Wells, Benjamin W.: "Alcuin the Teacher," *The Constructive Quarterly* VII, 1919, 531ff.
Werner, Karl: *Alcuin und sein Jahrhundert,* 1881.
West, Andrew: *Alcuin and the rise of the Christian Schools,* 1892.
Wiedemann, Heinrich: *Karl der Grosse, Widukind, und die Sachsenbekehrung,* 1949.
William of Malmesbury: *De gestis Pontificum Anglorum,* ed. N. Hamilton, *RS* LII, 1870.
——: *De gestis Regum Anglorum,* ed. W. Stubbs, *RS* XC, 1887–1889.
Wilmart, André: "Manuscrits de Tours copiés et décorés vers le temps d'Alcuin," *RB* XLII, 1930, 43ff.
——: "Un témoin Anglo-Saxon du calendrier métrique d'York," *ibid.* XLVI, 1934, 50ff.
——: "Le lectionnaire d'Alcuin," *EL* New Series XI, 1937, 136ff.
——: *Precum Libelli quattuor aevi Karolini* 1: *EL* 1940.
——: and Edmund Bishop: "La réforme liturgique de Charlemagne," *ibid.* V, 1931, 186ff.
Wilmot-Buxton, Ethel M.: *Alcuin,* 1922.
Wilson, Henry A.: ed. *The Gelasian Sacramentary,* 1894.
——: ed. *The Gregorian Sacramentary under Charles the Great, HBS* XLIX, 1915.
Wright, Thomas: *Biographia Britannica Literaria, Anglo-Saxon Period,* 1842.
Wulf, Maurice de: *History of mediaeval Philosophy* I, trans. E. C. Messenger, 1935.
Zeumer, K.: ed. *Formulae Merowingici et Karolini aevi, MGH Legum sectio* V, 1886.

ADDITIONAL BIBLIOGRAPHY, 1965

Amiet, Robert: "Le prologue Hucusque et la table des Capitula du Supplément d'Alcuin au Sacramentaire Grégorien", *Scriptorium* VII, 1953, 177ff.

Deanesy, Margaret: *A History of Early Medieval Europe, 476 to 911,* 1956.

——: *The pre-Conquest Church in England,* 1961.

Ellard, Gerald, S. J.: *Master Alcuin, Liturgist,* 1956.

Fichtenau, Heinrich: *Das karolingische Imperium,* 1949; trans. Peter Munz, 1957.

Freeman, Ann: "Theodulf of Orleans and the *Libri Carolini,*" *Speculum* XXXII, 1957, 663ff.

Laistner, M. L. W.: *Thought and Letters in Western Europe A.D.* 500–900, ed 2, 1957.

Raby, F. J. E.: *A History of Christian-Latin Poetry,* ed 2, 1953 (*CLP*).

——: *A History of Secular Latin Poetry in the Middle Ages* I, ed. 2, 1957 (*SLP*).

Smalley, Beryl: *The Study of the Bible in the Middle Ages,* 1952.

Wallach, Luitpold: "Alcuin's Epitaph of Hadrian I. A Study in Carolingian Epigraphy", *American Journal of Philology* LXXII, 1951, 128ff.

——: "Charlemagne's *De Litteris Colendis* and Alcuin. A Diplomatic-Historical Study", *Speculum* XXVI, 1951, 288ff.

——: "Charlemagne and Alcuin. Diplomatic Studies in Carolingian Epistolography", *Traditio* IX, 1953, 127ff.

——: "Alcuin on Sophistry," *Classical Philology* L, 1955, 259ff.

——: "Alcuin on Virtures and Vices, "*Harvard Theological Review* XLVIII, 1955, 175ff.

——: "The Epitaph of Alcuin. A Model of Carolingian Epigraphy," *Speculum* XXX, 1955, 367ff.

——: *Alcuin and Charlemagne: Studies in Carolingian History and Art,* Cornell Studies in Classical Philology XXXII, 1959.

Wattenbach-Levison-Löwe: *Deutschlands Geschichtsquellen in Mittelalter* II, 1953, 225ff.

Winston, Richard: *Charlemagne, from the Hammer to the Cross,* 1954.

INDEX